EIBE RIEDEL (ED.)
JAU-HWA CHEN (ED.)

Human Rights Standards Between Recognition, Confirmation, Affirmation and Change

Schriften zum öffentlichen, europäischen und internationalen Recht

Band 31

Human Rights Standards Between Recognition, Confirmation, Affirmation and Change

Edited by Professor Dr. JAU-HWA CHEN,
Soochow University and

Professor (em.) Dr. EIBE RIEDEL,
University of Mannheim

Assistant Editor Assessor iur. LUKAS ROMBERG,
University of Mannheim

BOORBERG

Bibliografische Information der Deutschen Nationalbibliothek | Die Deutsche Nationalbibliothek verzeichnet diese Publikation in der Deutschen Nationalbibliografie; detaillierte bibliografische Daten sind im Internet über www.dnb.de abrufbar.

ISBN 978-3-415-07858-1

Anfragen gemäß EU-Verordnung über die allgemeine Produktsicherheit (EU) 2023/988 (General Product Safety Regulation - GPSR) richten Sie bitte an: Richard Boorberg Verlag GmbH & Co KG, Produktsicherheit, Scharrstraße 2, 70563 Stuttgart; E-Mail: produktsicherheit@boorberg.de

Titelfoto: © Sven Hoppe - Fotolia | Satz: abavo GmbH, Nebelhornstraße 8, 86807 Buchloe | Druck und Bindung: Laupp & Göbel GmbH, Robert-Bosch-Straße 42, 72810 Gomaringen

Richard Boorberg Verlag GmbH & Co KG | Scharrstraße 2 | 70563 Stuttgart
Stuttgart | München | Hannover | Berlin | Weimar | Dresden
www.boorberg.de

Table of content

ACKNOWLEDGEMENTS

The editors wish to thank Richard Boorberg Verlag, and in particular Dr. Arnd-Christian Kulow for accepting this publication in its series *Schriften zum öffentlichen, europäischen und internationalen Recht*. The editors further gratefully acknowledge the assistance of Marcus Preu, Rechtsanwalt and Head of Lectorate at Richard Boorberg Verlag; Dean Professor Dr. Friedemann Kainer; and Kristina Biebricher, M.A., Faculty of Laws and Economics, University of Mannheim as well as the Faculty of Laws and Economics for a generous publication contribution. Last but not least, the editors would like to cordially thank Lukas Romberg, who capably acted as Assistant Editor throughout the publication process.

Introduction

This book was inspired by an event held at Chang Fo-chuan Center for the Study of Human Rights (hereafter as "the Center") at Soochow University in Taipei. Professor Riedel's message moved the parents and children of LGBT+ families,[1] who were invited to talk and share also their update struggles in Taiwan.[2] In his speech, Professor Riedel outlined the long and difficult consultation process that UN experts went through to protect and promote LGBT+ human rights. In Taiwan, many parents and children of same-sex families felt alienated and helpless while battling for their right to family life, as well as miserable fighting against a bureaucratic system that refused to reform. However, this event let them realize that the international advancement of LGBT+ rights is the consequence of the unwavering effort of international human rights professionals over time. In truth, they are not alone; their struggle is part of the global human rights activism, and it is aided by the recent creation of international LGBT+ human rights norms.

Following the event, the contributors to this book understood that organizing the process of writing and debating at the international level will enable marginalized groups in Taiwan and around the world to see that international standards are on their side, diminishing their sense of isolation. Although Taiwan has made significant progress in legalizing same-sex marriage (Nadia Magdalena and Apriani A. Amenes, 2021, 137–48) and mobilizing human rights monitoring mechanisms (Wen-chen Chang, 2009; Yu-Jie Chen, 2023)[3], marginalized groups in Taiwan continue to feel disconnected from global activism, owing to how standards are developed, the types of opposition they face, the realities of implementation in various countries, and the recognition of best practices, which leads to a united front with the international community. This gap is widely believed to be caused by a variety of factors, including differences in legal frameworks, political will, and the ability to implement these standards, such as deficiencies in domestic laws and systems, a lack of political will, conflicts with domestic cultural norms and social practices, or insufficient capacity (Thomas Ham-

1 Please see: *Fighting for Rights Connects Us to the World*: https://vocus.cc/article/653dedc8fd89780001f616c7

2 Their story is documented in the following documentary film, tilted 風雨同舟/ *Together, Stronger in the Rain*: https://www.youtube.com/watch?v=uQecxwmZ3sc

3 https://papers.ssrn.com/sol3/papers.cfm?abstract_id=3536921

marberg, 2009). Although this can explain local governments' formal challenges in adopting international human rights standards, it does not account for the lack of cognition and action that most local oppressed people suffer when confronted with such a gap.[4]

The preceding cases demonstrate that: 1. International human rights standards, particularly those established for marginalized groups in society, will inevitably face various challenges and backlashes during the process of developing international standards because they touch on taboos of religion, culture, and social practice in various countries; 2. The arguments for and against the drafted standards are usually evenly matched, making it difficult to determine the winner. The final version may be the result of bargaining; 3. Such international standards are the result of the perseverance of human rights activists and international experts from all sides, not the prestige of powerful nations; 4. If the local struggles of marginalized groups in defending human rights can be reflected in the process of creating international norms, it will give local minority groups' struggles a salient perspective and make them a global issue, which will support the call for the state to take responsibility.

Due to a misinterpretation of UN General Assembly Resolution 2758 (XXVI)[5], Taiwan has been excluded from the UN human rights apparatus since 1971, which contributes to its estrangement from the international community. Consequently, there are limited opportunities for Taiwan's civil society, particularly underrepresented groups, to engage in the advancement of contemporary international human rights institutions. Despite having an independent assessment process for national human rights reports since 2009 and becoming the first country in Asia to legalize same-sex marriage in 2019, Taiwan's civil society and UN human rights authorities do not have institutional communication channels. Therefore, local research on the creation of international human rights standards is somewhat limited because it is excluded and does not have direct communication with UN human rights bodies. Although there are documents outlining the creation and application of these international human rights standards, Taiwan rarely knows or acknowledges the specific steps involved in their design and adop-

4 Most researches highlighted the inclusive and participatory dialogue, but not the equal participation of the most oppressed groups.

5 Please compare with European Parliament resolution of 24 October 2024 on the misinterpretation of UN resolution 2758 by the People's Republic of China and its continuous military provocations around Taiwan (2024/2891(RSP)). https://www.europarl.europa.eu/doceo/document/TA-10-2024-0030_EN.html

tion. In international development, this partially explains why marginalized populations experience feelings of isolation and abandonment.

Through the unique convention national report review mechanism created in 2009, Taiwan's marginalized groups since then have more opportunities than other nations to interact with experts at the UN Review Mechanism. However, the main focus of these public discussions is whether the nation's policies carry out the human rights Covenants provisions. Both learning from other civil society organizations on shared challenges and comparative observation cases of other national report assessments are lacking. International human rights standards are often viewed as a static, minimum bottom line that countries must meet, rather than a dynamic goal that must be constantly improved through international action networks, and through international connections, non-discrimination and improved human rights protection for marginalized groups can be achieved. At a time when the marginalized groups are struggling for the right to speak out on national policy, if everyone can overcome the misunderstandings mentioned above, they will be more conscious of the critical link between their own local practices and global action networks.

In addition to the inspiration and critical reflections sparked by the aforementioned events, another outstanding human rights advocate, Mary Robinson, visited Taiwan during her Tang Prize winning period and delivered a speech at the Master's Forum for the Rule of Law Award,[6] which was co-organized by the Center, the School of Liberal Arts and Social Sciences, and the Tang Prize Committee. In order to demonstrate that the development of international human rights standards actually originates from the struggles of vulnerable and marginalized groups in many regions, Ms. Robinson used her own personal growth experience as a woman, starting as a lawyer for vulnerable groups in Ireland, taking on individual cases in the Irish courts, the Strasbourg European Court of Human Rights, and the Luxemburg European Court of Justice, and eventually becoming the President of Ireland, the United Nations High Commissioner for Human Rights, and the head of significant international human rights organizations. Only by gathering these experiences on a common discourse platform and reflecting them as part of a global action network will international human rights standards developed for marginalized groups reveal the universality of human rights and their genuine momentum.

---

6 Mary Robinson (2024) Contemporary Challenges on Human Rights and Global Justice. https://www.youtube.com/watch?v=uD-A840Ok_s

How to apply gender equality consequently to family, adoption, artificial reproduction, and other rights after marriage rights are comparatively similarly protected in 2019 is a major concern for Taiwan's LGBT+ population. However, local and international human rights development has been impacted by more pressing humanitarian and human rights challenges since the COVID-19 epidemic at the end of 2019.

In her Laureate Speech for the Tang Prize at Soochow University, Ms. Robinson specifically mentioned that we should safeguard the international rule of law and recognize the need for transparency and accountability in long-term agreements as one of the contemporary challenges of human rights and global justice. This is highlighting the regression of global democracy (autocratization) in 2024, namely, the shrinking of space for free speech, the serious erosion of freedom of assembly and association (V-Dem, 2025: Democracy Report). Despite Taiwan is relatively unaffected by the global trends, and has a stable democracy, which ranks among the best after Japan in East Asia, the worldwide human rights and gender justice crises has also hampered the implementation of gender equality and non-discrimination for excluded groups. The primary source of public and social concern is shifted to the defense of democracy. The Russian invasion of Ukraine in 2022 horrified not only Europe, but also Taiwan's civic society and nationals, which are under assault from Chinese arms forces since the first direct president election in 1996. The question of how to protect Taiwan's democracy from the backsliding of global democracy, as well as how to unite with countries with consolidated democracy and enhance the country's defense force to deter China's invasion, has become more critical.

The contributors of this book believe that Taiwan's democracy's resilience does not clash with the gradual implementation of international human rights norms within the system. On the contrary, only until the most marginalized groups are completely protected by human rights, and free speech and citizen involvement in politics are extended to marginalized groups, can there be so-called democratic resilience. In contrast to Hungary's democratic regression, where the values of democracy and human rights have been severely eroded by "illiberal" and "anti-Western" political orchestration, Taiwan's ability to uphold the value of democracy is precisely due to its voluntary compliance with international human rights norms and the establishment of a unique convention national report review mechanism, covering CEDAW, ICCPR, ICESCR, CRC, CRPD, and ICERD, which enhances the rights of marginalized.

As a result, in addition to focusing on the development of LGBT+ human rights in Taiwan, this book also focuses on the sexual and reproductive rights of women with disabilities, the rights of Taiwan's Atayal indigenous people with disabilities, those who have been denied the right to residency due to forced evictions, the human rights of victims of previous authoritarian systems, and the unfinished business of transitional justice in Taiwan. Since the first CEDAW national report assessment in 2009, Taiwan has gained more than 15 years of experience implementing international human rights rules, necessitating closer examination to understand its strengths and weaknesses. Furthermore, this book examines the specific process of Hungary's democratic regression as a comparison and warning to avoid democratic regression before it occurs.

After hearing Prof. Riedel's address, members of LGBT+ families realized that the restriction of their marriage and family rights was not a minor incident in the private domain, but rather a momentous event in the country and around the world. This motivated us to edit this book. These minor things that are thought to be distributed over the world are tied to the issues of global human rights and justice, which is precisely where Eleanor Roosevelt believed human rights should begin. This is identical to Ms. Robinson's gender-focused analysis of her experience growing up as an Irish woman. Those little, easily neglected areas are where human rights begin and must begin.

Jau-hwa Chen

References:

Chang, Wen-chen (2009). An Isolated Nation with Global-minded Citizen: Bottom-up Transnational Constitutionalism in Taiwan. In *National Taiwan University Law Review*. Vol. 4:3. 203–235.

Chen, Yu-jie (2023). Human Rights Treaty Monitoring 2.0: Taiwan's Local Innovation and Implication for Global Practice. https://papers.ssrn.com/sol3/papers.cfm?abstract_id=3536921

European Parliament resolution of 24 October 2024, on the misinterpretation of UN resolution 2758 by the People's Republic of China and its continuous military provocations around Taiwan (2024/2891(RSP)) https://www.europarl.europa.eu/doceo/document/TA-10-2024-0030_EN.html

Hammarberg, Thomas (2009). Recommendation on Systematic Work for Implementing Human Rights at National Level. Council of Europe Commissioner. For Human Rights. Strasbourg.

Magdalena, Nadia and Amenes, Apriani A. (2021). The Implications of Legalizing Same-sex Marriage in Taiwan. In *Papua Journal of Diplomacy and International Relation*. Vol. 1, Issue 2. 137–148.

Robinson, Mary (2024). Contemporary Challenges on Human Rights and Global Justice. https://www.youtube.com/watch?v=uD-A840Ok_s

V-Dem (2025): Democracy Report: 25 Years of Autocratization-Democracy Trumped?. https://www.v-dem.net/documents/61/v-dem-dr__2025_lowres_v2.pdf

琦琦 (2023). *Fighting for Rights Connects Us to the World*: https://vocus.cc/article/653dedc8fd89780001f616c7

風雨同簷 (2023). *Together, Stronger in the Rain*: https://www.youtube.com/watch?v=uQecxwmZ3sc

A. Contemporary Challenges on Human Rights and Global Justice[1]

Mary Robinson[2]

I. Gender Matters: Personal is Political

I have been asked to speak on a number of contemporary challenges on human rights and global justice, and I will begin with gender equality. I had to think about gender equality very early in my life, because I was the only girl wedged between four brothers, two older than me and two younger than me. So of course I had to think about gender equality, human rights, even using my elbows! My parents were medical doctors and they assured me that I had exactly the same rights and exactly the same opportunities as my four brothers. But Irish society at the time was not telling me that. The woman's place was in the home; it was in our constitution. And there was no sense of equality in Ireland at the time.

I think that's what brought me to want to study law. I wanted to study law as an instrument for social justice. And after four years in Trinity, in the honors course in legal science, I was lucky enough to get a fellowship to the Harvard Law School. I remember very vividly that year – 1967 to 68 – and the class of 1968. It was a particular year as American law student contemporaries were worried about an immoral war, as they saw it, the war in Vietnam. Some of them were actually trying to dodge the draft; and in April Martin Luther King was assassinated; and just after I graduated, Robert Kennedy was assassinated. At the time, those were two horrendous and notable assassinations. It wasn't, I think, like today, when we have so much violence, that issues like that don't have the same resonance.

What I recalled from that year in Harvard was that my young friends and other students were taking leadership. They were actually trying to make a difference. They were going into the civil rights program or the poverty

1 Transcript of speech delivered by Mary Robinson during the 2024 Tang Prize Master's Forum on the Rule of Law, held at Soochow University on 30 September 2024. The speech is based on the outline that was read in the Forum

2 Mary Robinson is an Irish politician who served as the president of Ireland from December 1990 to September 1997. Following her time as president, Robinson became the United Nations High Commissioner for Human Rights from 1997 to 2002.

program in the southern part of the United States. And that was so different from the Ireland that I was growing up in. Because in Ireland you waited, and you waited your turn, and you waited. And if you were a woman, you didn't have much turn to wait for.

When I came back to Ireland and started to practice law in 1968, there was an election in early 1969 of the two houses of our parliament, and in our Senate, which has 60 members and there are six university seats. Traditionally, and inevitably, it was elderly male professors who would get those six seats. And because of my experience in Harvard, and what my husband Nick, or my husband-to-be Nick, called my Harvard humility – he meant the opposite, not humility, but somehow a kind of willingness to take on and change things – I challenged the system and got the support to be elected to the Senate at the age of 25.

The reason I recount that is because it opened up further opportunities for me. I had also in 1969 become the Reid professor of constitutional and criminal law in Trinity College. It's a trust that established the professorship for a practicing young lawyer. You had the title of professor and a very poor salary; it wasn't a real professorship in every sense, but it was nonetheless a professorship. That meant I was teaching law as a professor; I was practicing law as an advocate, as a lawyer, as a barrister; and I was helping to make some law in the Senate. I was trying to use all three to further gender equality, human rights, and open up Irish society.

1. In the Irish Senate

I want, in particular, just to take a moment or two to talk about the gender equality part of that. In 1971, I introduced a bill into the parliament, into the Senate, to legalize family planning in Ireland. The law at the time was that married women could only avail of the contraceptive pill if they had written permission from their doctor that they had cycle regulation problems. And I remember we used to joke as women that it must have been the Irish weather that so many women had cycle regulation problems! It was also against the law to buy or sell a condom – it was not against the law to use it – just to buy or sell.

There was a lot of discussion among young people, but Ireland was a very conservative country. When I introduced this bill on family planning, I suddenly changed from being a somewhat popular figure – because I had been elected to the Senate at a young age – to a very, very unpopular figure. I got hate mail, hate letters. It was the time obviously before social media. But those hate letters were very painful. I was being called a witch from hell, and I was told that I was undermining all the morals in Ireland, and that this is a terrible thing to do. They were very rough letters, tough letters. I had been very affected by those letters, so my husband decided to burn them. Or we decided together. Actually, we regretted it afterwards, because we are natural archivists, and we now regret the loss of that indication of the views and the opinion at that time, about reproductive health and rights and family planning.

The members of the Senate didn't want to give approval to the bill being published. It is the only example so far in Irish legislative history that a measure put forward by a senator, with the help of two male senators, did not get published as a document of the Senate. You have to have three senators to support a bill. Of course, everybody knew what was in it. It was in all the newspapers. It was written up. It was criticized. It was approved by some, but it was not official. In fact, one senator came in with white gloves, he would not even touch the order paper – you cannot even know how strong the adverse opinion was in this very Catholic Ireland of the time. But we persisted. In 1973, we had switched the subject to health. In 1973 we moved it from a criminal law bill to being a health family planning bill; and that actually got printed and got a second reading. We then withdrew it, because the government of the day said they would bring in legislation on family planning. And when they did, half the cabinet voted against it and that bill didn't succeed. It took another seven years for a different government to actually change the law. So, nine years, more than nine years in all it took to get that law changed.

I also recall working with some other senators on other measures like removing the status of illegitimacy for children. Under our law, children born outside marriage were regarded as illegitimate. We felt this was a wrong word entirely for a human being. Again, when we put forward the bill, we withdrew it in favor of a government bill. We should have come in much more quickly.

And there were many other examples of discriminations. I remember a time when a very good friend of mine, a poet called Eavan Boland, a very good Irish poet and close friend who sadly died a year or two ago came to me for advice. She was a member of the women's liberation movement and I was their lawyer. And she came to me and she said, "I'm going to a meeting, can you give me seven laws that discriminate against women?" And I said, "Eavan, why only seven? I can give you more." And she replied, "Well, no, seven's a good number, that's all I could remember." But that again gives you an idea that we were not short of laws.

2. Cases in Court

One of the court cases I was involved in which I will come back to, was about women not being able to serve on juries. Women had to retire from the civil service when they became married. There were a whole lot of legislative discriminations. But it was important to be able to raise these issues and try to bring in legislation that would change the law. But perhaps some of the cases that I was involved in, in the courts, were more impactful in the sense that it was possible to have more success, let me put it that way. It was possible to win more cases. And I recall in particular the cases that made the difference, not just for the individual applicant, but for a whole range of people. And they're the ones that I just want to spend a little bit of time talking about.

A case that I particularly enjoyed working on started without me. It started with the client herself. Josie Airey was a poor woman from a city in the south of Ireland called Cork. Her husband was beating her. There was no divorce in Ireland. She had already got an order from the lowest court to stop the beating. But it didn't stop. So, she wanted to get a separation. No divorce, just a separation. But to do that, she would have to go into the High Court. And the High Court was complex. She went to lawyers, but no lawyer would take her because she was very poor. She couldn't afford to pay. So she wrote a letter to a body she had heard of in the newspapers called the European Commission on Human Rights. The letter was full of irrelevance, but there was something in that letter, and the lawyers in the Commission on Human Rights decided to send this to the Irish government and see what they say. So, they sent the letter to the government and the government of course said, there is no barrier to a woman going in as an individual plaintiff; she can go into court.

The lawyers of the Commission were not entirely satisfied. They felt anybody can walk into the rich hotel, but can they afford to …? It's one thing to say, it's accessible, but what if it's complicated and procedural and difficult? Which, of course, the High Court was. So, the Commission on Human Rights provided legal aid to Josie Airey, and that's where I became involved as a barrister.

It was an extraordinary pleasure in many ways to plead her case and to show that this was contrary to article eight of the European Convention – protection of family life. The reason why I was so excited about it was, it was clear to me that the outcome would mean that Ireland would have to bring in civil legal aid. There had been a lot of efforts of various sorts, but it was that case that required the Irish government to bring in civil legal aid. And actually, because it was a case of a European court, it meant that other European countries should also consider bringing in civil legal aid.

Another case I worked on involved two women who had been accused of a minor crime that allowed a jury trial. But they did not want a trial with only men, and women were barred from the jury. As we were researching and arguing the case, we were aware that in the United States exactly the same issue was being argued before the Federal Supreme Court there. Just before this case called DeBurke and Anderson against Ireland came for hearing before the Supreme Court, it was decided favorably in the United States. The United States Federal Supreme Court decided that women could not be discriminated against and refused to be able to serve on juries. When we came to the Supreme Court to plead our case, the chief justice of the United States sat in the court. He was visiting Ireland and he was very intrigued to know about the same. They just invited him to sit in for the morning, which was very unusual. It's just a memory of how sometimes jurisdictions can help each other, very different jurisdictions. And we did succeed in the Supreme Court in Ireland.

I just want to mention the last case that I pleaded in court, because it was a very impactful case for poor women in Ireland. Our social welfare code was based on the husband, the man, and everything flowed from that. When married women got unemployment benefit, it was less than a man would get and for a shorter period. So, two women, Ms Carter and Ms McDermott, wanted to litigate that. When we went to the High Court, the president of the Court at the time felt that there was some merit in our case, but because of European legislation he said, "I'm not going to decide that myself, I'm going to refer it to the court in Luxembourg for a definitive ruling on whether the directive on equal pay and equal opportunity of the European Union was directly applicable in Ireland", and allowed Ms Carter and Ms McDermott to have the standing to plead it.

So, the president of the High Court referred the case to the European court. And I argued that case before the European court and the European court gave a very strong ruling in our favor. It went back to the High Court for decision. The High Court president understood the implications of giving it the full implementation that Ms Carter and Ms McDermott had been discriminated against in their social welfare benefit, unemployment benefit. He kind of gave a partial judgment that, as of the future, this would apply. But he was not prepared to consider, in their case, the back payment of what they had lost, in not getting the unemployment benefit. He was aware there were hundreds, if not thousands of similar married women who had been discriminated against over the years and, therefore, he made a ruling that it would only apply as of the future.

We were not happy with that because the court ruling of the European Court had been much broader than that and hadn't implied only for the future. So, we appealed to the Irish Supreme Court and the Irish Supreme Court decided to go back to Europe. Meanwhile, I was nominated to be a candidate for the presidency, so I had stopped practicing law. But then this case came up for hearing in October of 1990 and the election was in November.

I said that I have to do it. It's so complicated, nobody else can come in now and take this forward. I need to go for my clients. And I remember, you know, thinking, do you want to win, or do you want to go back to law? I mean, make up your mind. And I thought just let me do this one case.

So I went back to the court of the European Union in Luxembourg and made the case that their ruling, their initial ruling, had clearly implied that it should be retrospective, that the women should be able to get their money. The court reserved their judgment and mentioned when the advocate general would give a ruling, which is what happens in the court in Luxembourg, as I'm sure some of you would know. The lead justice in the court said, "this may or may not be of interest to you, Ms Robinson", meaning either you will be president, or you will still be doing law. And actually, by the time the ruling came, I was elected president, so I didn't go back. I heard the final verdict and was pleased, but I wasn't in court. That cost the Irish exchequer some £300 million at the time. So, it was a very significant case for gender equality for women. I was trying to use it as an illustration. It's lovely when you can take a case for individual clients that will affect a whole sector, that will affect someone in a broader sense.

3. Participation in Public Life

The third way in which I tried to support gender equality was through my participation in public life. I always promoted the importance of gender balance and gender equality in speeches that I made, including going forward for election a number of times over those 20 years.

I had an incident, which did annoy me, because it was discrimination outside Ireland in something I was involved in and surprised me. It happened in Belgium in Brussels. In 1971, I was invited as the only woman to serve on the Vedel Committee on enlargement of the European Parliament. This committee had members of the six original European Union members – European community members, as it was then – and then the four applicant members: the United Kingdom, Ireland, Denmark, and Norway. Norway eventually voted against joining, so you had three new members. But we were looking at what impact this would have on the European institutions. This was a serious piece of work, and it was recognized that we would have to go back and forth to Brussels.

They decided that in order to give us our expenses of travel and our per diem, because there was no salary involved, that we could open a bank account. When they came to me they said, "oh, but you're a married woman". And I said, "Yes". They said, "Oh, you need the written permission of your husband in Belgium to open a back account". I said "What?" Because this did not apply in Ireland. Of course, my wicked husband was only delighted to hear this sentence! But anyway, I became Ms Robinson for once and blurred the idea that I was married and all was well. But I think that what I want to illustrate is that there were so many forms of discrimination, it wasn't that surprising that another country would require the written permission.

By the time I was going forward as the candidate of the Labour Party, but running as an independent in 1990 for election, I was very much part of a broader women's movement in Ireland. That women's movement was significant. When I started, I was very much an outsider, a hundred-to-one outsider, because it was assumed that the party that had always had the presidency would have it. The deputy prime minister was running. He was a shoe-in, as we would say in Ireland; he was a certainty. But gradually, because I had more time, I made the case and the case became more popular, and I was aware that I was gaining ground. It was the women's movement that made all the difference. Not just the women's movement in that progressive sense, but a lot of women who are quite conservative, maybe didn't have careers outside their home, quietly decided to vote differently from their husband or father for the first time. And I heard so many stories. I heard a story of a young woman some years later. The way she put it, summed it all up. She said, "I want to shake your hand." She said to me, "You are my first vote. And when I told my father, how I voted for you, he nearly killed me!"

So, when I was accepting the nomination, the night I was elected not the inauguration, I thanked Mná na hÉireann, which means women of Ireland in a pejorative way. Up to then, there was a way of describing women who weren't active in life, who weren't part of the progressive women's movement, who were housewives, who stayed at home. But I was valuing what they had done. And they understood that perfectly. And it kind of helped me as president to broaden the whole sense of gender equality, just by lifting Mná na hÉireann. I thanked Mná na hÉireann, who instead of rocking the cradle, rocked the system.

It kind of made it easier to have a broader, more integrated sense of gender equality. It wasn't just women who were lawyers or journalists or trade unionists or had careers as business women. It was all women in Ireland who felt part of this gender equality. And I made it very clear that I was determined, as president, to feel that I would do a better job precisely because I was a woman. I was absolutely determined to convey that at all stages. And that was because I felt I had been fortunate enough to get the confidence of women that had helped me to get elected. Of course, it was a universal election. So, men also elected me I'm glad to say, but women changing their vote from the traditional voting was the significant part.

II. Human Rights Protection

Now I come to human rights protection in that sense. I'd like to just reflect on when, after the seven years as president of Ireland, on the 12th of September of 1997, I became the UN High Commissioner for Human Rights, I found that my horizon had to broaden really significantly. Up to then, it was Ireland and Europe. And Europe was very helpful to Ireland: the European Court of Human Rights and the European Union Court were helping Ireland to open up and make progress. Now, I could be asked questions at press conferences about countries or cities or human rights problems somewhere in the world that I hardly even knew about. That was kind of a strange burden of knowing that you were responsible for human rights throughout the world.

1. 1997 Reform Package of Kofi Annan: The Holistic Nature of Human Rights

And even more significantly, I think, before I became UN High Commissioner, Kofi Annan, who had become Secretary General in January of that year, had his 1997 reform package. The UN is always reforming itself or should be. Anyway, this 1997 reform package made the office, the new office of High Commissioner for Human Rights. The only one to be part of the four executive committees of the UN: the Executive Committee on Peace, on Development, on Humanitarian issues, and on Economic and Social Issues. It was a way of affirming the holistic notion of human rights that they were economic and social rights, civil and political rights; and also not western, eastern, northern or southern, they were universal.

We had a small office that was tasked with somehow implementing this. And I remember having a conversation with Kofi Annan earlier enough on, and I said, "I do understand the significance of you making my office part of this, what had you in mind?" He smiled and he said, "No, Mary, that's for you to figure out."

So, it was a case of really trying to work with the way in which the UN worked, the treaty bodies, the work of the rapporteurs, all of them were underfunded, all of them were complaining at the time. One of the things I had to do was try to raise extra budgetary funds to help the office. But I saw the need to embed human rights in the culture of countries. And I strongly supported the emerging national human rights commissions with the Paris principles that you've just heard from our wonderful moderator. You have, and I in my speech on rule of law, referred to the fact that Taiwan had established its own national human rights commission. I didn't know it took 20 years, but I'm very pleased that it is one of the national human rights commissions and that it abides by the Paris Principles.

2. Embedding Human Rights Within Local Culture

I attended quite a number of the regional meetings of national human rights commissions, and I felt that this was an important way of really embedding in the culture of countries.

Obviously, governments do have the main responsibility to protect human rights, but it's also extremely important to have vibrant civil society organizations and individual champions. And I must say, like many of you, I would say, I'm very worried about the shrinking of civil society space in so many countries. We keep hearing this, great complaints from human rights defenders. It's much tougher now, and I'm sure we will want to talk about this a bit. Anyone who protests suddenly finds themselves characterized as a terrorist; the awful problem of the overuse of the word terrorism since the terrible attacks in the United States of 9/11.

3. The Global Compact on Business and Human Rights

I want to speak a bit about business in human rights, because I had a very interesting evolution in my own thinking on business and human rights, as there was a small unit in the Office of High Commission for Human Rights dealing with business. The way in which the office, the unit, dealt with business was that business was, by definition, bad. Business was violating and abusing human rights. I felt, I'm sure, and I know, yes, there are many cases where that is true – mining companies, not respecting land or water rights, lots of other things – but that seems a bit narrow. I was part of the support for the Global Compact on Business and Human Rights, which Kofi Annan announced in 1999. I was very pleased that human rights were the first two principles of the Global Compact, then labor rights and environmental rights. It allowed a recognition that business can also be on the right side of issues of human rights. I became the founding chair of the Institute for Human Rights and Business, and I know that the institute has worked here in Taiwan on human rights issues. I mentioned that in my laureate address.

I'm also linked to another very good large website and human rights activists in the Business and Human Rights Resource Center. They are competitive friends, I would say; they both do very good work on human rights. The Business and Human Rights Resource Center inaugurated a Mary Robinson speaker series 15 years ago. We had our 15th speaker series just before the UN general assembly. In the last few years, since COVID, it has been done virtually, which means you can reach a much larger audience. What they do is they bring human rights activists from ground level, but also business leaders on the right side of the thing. So, it's a very good way of showing the different ways in which business is supportive, or may not be supportive, of human rights, and the importance of the guidelines on business and human rights, etc.

III. Global Justice and Local Context

I turn now to global justice and local content, which is the next section I was invited to speak about. This is where I very much want to emphasize the importance of a climate justice approach to the climate and nature crisis. I say that with some humility, because actually I came very late to the climate change crisis. During my seven years as president of Ireland, I spoke about the environment, but I didn't mention climate change because we weren't aware. Yes, I'm sure there were Irish scientists, climate scientists who probably were writing theses about it, but the general population and their president, we were not aware of what was happening elsewhere. Then I became UN High Commissioner for Human Rights and I became aware of the importance of climate change, but there was another part the UN dealing with it, and I didn't connect it to my large portfolio in the UN of human rights, gender equality, rights of indigenous peoples, rights of people with disabilities. I didn't make the connection.

1. Global Warming: Climate Justice Approach

It was immediately afterwards, in 2002, 2003, 2004, I had already established a small NGO called Realizing Rights, working in African countries, mainly on economic and social rights. And it was so clear at that time, 2003 in particular and 2004 and on, the impact was palpable. Women would say to me, is "God punishing us? What is happening? We don't understand, the rainy seasons don't come. We have long periods of drought and then flash flooding that's destroyed the school. This is outside our experience. What is happening?" Complete, not knowing, but knowing that this was not what the village law knew over 200 years. When they say outside our experience, that's what they mean. Grandparent to grandchild, you know, it would be at least 200 years. Something was happening. I remember sitting at a hearing with Bishop Tutu as Elders for Oxfam, just before the conference in Copenhagen in 2009, we sat and listened to five African farmers, four of them were women. And each of them had a devastating story to tell.

So, the impacts were so much worse and that's part of climate justice. I identify layers of climate justice. The worst thing is that the climate and nature impacts affect the poorest countries, the poorest communities, the Small Island Developing States and the indigenous peoples much earlier and much more severely than more developed parts of the world. Secondly, within that women suffer much more, much more devastatingly, because they are the farmers, because they have to go and get the water and if there's drought, etc. And if there's a heavy typhoon flooding or whatever, they have long skirts, they hold their babies and they die. And we know from figures much more women and children die in climate disasters than men. So, from so many points of view women are building resilience on the ground, but they don't get the climate funding; the climate funding doesn't reach the grassroots level.

2. Geopolitical Segregation: Challenges to the Values of Human Rights

I believe that it will be better for our sense of the urgency of climate if we make it more people-centered in dealing with it. This is more difficult now because of the geopolitical divides and the emergence of a multi-polar world, which is posing challenges to the fundamental values of human rights as set out in the Universal Declaration of Human Rights. Autocratic governments and populism pose threats, as does the overuse of branding protesters, including now even climate protesters, as terrorists, since the terror attacks in the United States of 9/11.

Those divides have affected the work of the United Nations, as we know. In fact, there was an illustration of that, that during the Summits of the Future, which I attended just before coming here. For the first time ever, there was a summit of heads of state where there was actually voting. Usually, when it's a summit of heads of state, it's all agreed beforehand. They come as heads of state to speak, but the work is done. That's the way the UN always worked. This time, there could not be final agreement; Russia, objected, and four or five countries supported Russia in objecting. The UN in these summits, in resolutions on the summit, it's by consensus. So, consensus shouldn't mean everybody, but actually it does. You cannot have, certainly a large country like Russia objecting, you cannot have agreement.

How to resolve this? Fortunately, Uganda was prompted to put forward a procedural motion not to allow the Russian resolution to go to a vote. The procedural motion could be voted on by majority. So, a majority, a large majority, all except about seven, voted in favor of the procedural motion that the Russian resolution should not be put. You could feel the tension in the room when the president of the General Assembly said, "And I now put the resolution to adopt the pact of the future." Bang! He put the gavel down so fast, because nobody objected. This is new. This is an indication of how significant the shifts are and how difficult it is going to be to get consensus.

3. Domination of Social Media

I think I should say a brief word about the way in which we live in a world dominated by social media, which again has power for good, but also a very dark side. I think the impact on young people of social media is something we need to think about very seriously, because I think we're allowing too much bullying and mental health problems of young people because we haven't got proper constraints on what can be used. And we face attacks on truth. We face denial, for example, of results of elections and misinformation at a serious level. These are all aggravated by the impact of generative AI. So, that's another issue. And I should have mentioned when I was talking about business and human rights, because I'm sure we'll want to discuss it, the back sliding now on ESG – economic, social and governance issues – which corporations had been adopting, and good corporations are still adopting, but the push back is very heavy, especially in the United States. There are states in the United States now, which are forbidding corporations to promote economic, social and environmental factors in their business. And then also the diversity and inclusion are under threat.

IV. Concluding Remarks

So let me close my remarks and we'll get to the panel discussion by referring to what The Elders are trying to do in this difficult and fractured world since I'm now currently Chair of The Elders. We have been promoting, and I said this in my laureate speech, long-view leadership. What I wanted to say here in this master's forum, that we've actually amended a way of talking about the long-view leadership. As a result of an intergenerational meeting, which we held in New York during the UN General Assembly week, we had young leaders discussing with us the existential threats that The Elders focus on. We have three major existential threats. The climate and nature crisis, the nuclear weapons crisis and the pandemic crisis because we still haven't learned the lessons of COVID, we're still not ready for the next global pandemic. Then across all those, there is the potential, either for good or for bad, of artificial intelligence, generative artificial intelligence.

So, we have been putting forward our ideas. We have said think beyond short-term political cycles and deliver solutions for both current and future generations:

- Recognize that enduring answers require compromise and collaboration for the good of the whole world.
- Show compassion for all people, designing sustainable policies which respect that everyone is born free and equal in dignity and rights.
- Uphold the international rule of law and accept that durable agreements require transparency and accountability.

- And finally, in our long view, as we were putting it forward, commit to a vision of hope in humanity's shared future, not play to its divided past.

So, this was the way we were messaging our long view. But we heard such strong messaging from the younger generation of leaders that we needed to understand that young people now want to be involved in decision-making. They want to be at the table, they want to participate, they want to be involved in what they called co-creation. So, we have decided, as Elders, that we will now message, that we should commit to long-view leadership and, as well as that, co-creation between generations in coming to consensus on, especially on, global issues.

This was one of the very positive elements that came out of the pact for the future. It has, for the first time, really recognized that young people need to be involved in decision-making. And there are lots of hooks in the pact for the future that reflect this. I must say, because The Elders have been involved in intergenerational discussions a lot in recent years, we were open to the idea of co-creation. We were open to, building this into our messaging. It reminds me in a way of a saying of Kofi Annan, which I heard him use when we were together on his last mission in 2018. In July of 2018, we went together to Zimbabwe to promote a peaceful election there; to help, try to help promote it. And Kofi, again, would repeat a message that he would use a lot: "You are never too young to lead, and you are never too old to learn." So, what we were illustrating as Elders, we were not too old to modify our long-view leadership and bring in the co-creation of younger generations.

B. Witnessing an Era of the Gender Equality in Taiwan

Mei-Nu Yu (Dagmar Yu)[1]

Abstract:

This article is a transcript of a discussion given by Attorney Mei-Nu Yu (also known as Dagmar Yu) at the Mary Robinson Tang Prize Master's Forum, which witnessed the evolution, strategy, thinking, speech, and action of Taiwan's gender equality movement during the last four decades. Although women and LGBT+ groups have made numerous individual efforts and sacrifices along the road, many individuals and groups continue to persist and pave the way for Taiwan to attain gender equality. The essay discusses the inherent link between women and gender movements, as well as how women's organizations use gender mainstreaming tactics to shape Taiwan's gender equality legislation. Simultaneously, Taiwan became the first Asian country to legalize same-sex marriage in 2019. However, the passed statute has several flaws, and there is still plenty of space for development in transnational marriage and family adoption rights for same-sex couples.

Keywords:

Annette Lu, Yuanzhen Li, Awakening Foundation, Wanru Pen, Women's Awareness, Sun Yat-sen Memorial Hall Incident, Gender Equality Work Act, Sexual Assault Prevention Act, Sexual Harassment Prevention Act, CEDAW, Legalization of Same-sex Marriage, Adoption of Children of LGBTI Family

I. Introduction

Mrs. Robinson was raised in an era of male superiority and female inferiority, and even as a member of the European Parliament she needed her husband's permission to create an account. Coincidentally, ten years later and thousands of kilometers away in Taiwan, we were witnessing an era of gender inequality, with marriage and pregnancy requiring compulsory

1 Mei-nu Yu is a practicing lawyer who has been involved in women's and gender movements for more than 40 years, dating back to Taiwan's martial law period. Lawyer Yu is a former legislator who played a key role in passing Taiwan's same-sex marriage bill.

resignation, several national examinations exclusive to men, and all property after marriage going to the husband.

I have been fortunate to be a part of the women's movement since the martial law period in 1982,[2] from the awakening of gender consciousness to the revision of laws from the bottom up; to the reform of the system, allowing women to participate in policy decisions; and to the international integration and domestication of the CEDAW Convention. The past 50 years have been a lifelong journey of learning, progress, and breakthroughs that have continually encountered and solved obstacles.

II. The evolution of the women's movement in Taiwan: Awakening of women's awareness

Women's awareness in Taiwan first emerged during the martial law period in the 1970s. Former Vice President Annette Lu revived Taiwan's women's movement. In 1976, she established the "Pioneer Publishing House" to publish feminist-related materials and the "Protect You" hotline to assist women who have been assaulted. Later, in 1979, the Formosa Incident occurred, Annette Lu was arrested and imprisoned, and the fledgling women's rights movement experienced a period of disruption.[3]

In 1982, Yuanzhen Li, who co-founded the "Protect You Hotline" with Annette Lu,[4] founded the "Awakening Publishing House" to investigate the impact of China's 5,000-year-old culture on women and how to remove the dross while retaining the essence so that the women's rights movement could move forward.[5]

On Women's Day 1984, the magazine released a survey titled "How Much Do You Know About Sexual Harassment?"[6] This was the first time the poll and the term "Sexual Harassment" were introduced from abroad. The

2 Please check the Women's Movement Record of Awakening Foundation to see Mei-nu Yu's Articles for Women's awareness of gender equality. In 1982, there are 9 articles about women's discrimination in laws. https://awakening.lib.tku.edu.tw/Default2_result.aspx.

3 The full name of Annette Lu is Lu, Hsiu-Lian. About her works and activities, please check Lee, Pei-jung. 1997. "The Modern Women's Movement in Taiwan: The Changing Role of Taiwanese Women in a Conscious and Collective Struggle Toward Equality". Halifax NS: Saint Mary's University. 67–75 https://www.collectionscanada.gc.ca/obj/s4/f2/dsk2/ftp04/mq22801.pdf.

4 Comparing with the other activities and publication: https://www.taiwanwomencenter.org.tw/en-global/News/special-exhibitions/Content/4/exhibition_2008.

5 https://www.awakening.org.tw/english.

6 https://www.awakening.org.tw/content/34.

poll results revealed that up to 84% of women had been sexually harassed, which was shocking. The media covered it as headline news, and it became a national event. This inspired the Awakening Foundation to utilize the annual Women's Day to raise issues, generate societal shock, and prompt reflection. Since then, every Women's Day has been "Women's Work Year," which investigates why women must sign a vow to enter the job and immediately resign when they marry or become pregnant. Why are so many national examinations for public service limited to men? "Housewife Year" investigates the whereabouts of housewives' property. "Women's Participation Year," investigates the constitutional provisions during the time when the number of women's political participation was 1/10, which was initially the lowest threshold, but why it ended up being the highest threshold? Those issues fermented strongly in society.

III. Revision of laws from the private to the public sphere

The Sun Yat-sen Memorial Hall incident occurred in 1987 (Chang 2009, 13).[7] The Sun Yat-sen Memorial Hall declared that female employees must automatically resign when they marry, become pregnant, or reach the age of 30, but male employees were not subject to this restriction. In 1987, 57 female employees who were asked to resign owing to their age expressed dissatisfaction and requested that their lawyers produce a letter of evidence. According to the Sun Yat-sen Memorial Hall, female personnel must be "dignified" in order to greet foreign visitors and showcase the beauty of Chinese cultural relics. Women were "old and ugly" after they turned 30, according to the suggestion. As a result, the women's movement, which was still an underground organization at the time, marched to protest. The Sun Yat-sen Memorial Hall argued that no one coerced them to sign the agreement, and that the female employees violated it in accordance with the concept of contract freedom. So, the case was escalated to the Ministry of Education. Following an investigation, it was discovered that this faulty rule applied to all cultural institutions under the Ministry of Education, and the Ministry of Education ordered its abolition. However, the Sun Yat-sen Memorial Hall amended it to a one-year contract, and the female employees who turned 30 were still required to leave the next year.

7 https://www.ios.sinica.edu.tw/people/personal/ccf/台灣女性史入門_勞動篇.pdf.

The original plan was to settle the dispute through litigation, however after reviewing the legal provisions, no basis for the claim could be established (Yu 2015). This sparked the feminist movement and the legislative process, and a draft of the "*Equality Act for Men and Women in Employment*" was drafted. A thorough examination of why women are treated unequally in the workplace reveals that it is primarily because they must give birth to children. So, who is responsible for raising children? Is it the responsibility of women, or of the state and society? Children are the country's future labor force, contributes to the enterprise's production. Having, rearing, and cultivating children increases the production of the firm. How can a business owner not be socially responsible? Women can only compete with men in the job if they are relieved of the burden of raising children. As a result, in addition to regulating equal rights, the "*Equality Act for Men and Women in Employment*" governs menstrual leave, maternity leave, paternity leave, parental leave, and family care leave.

These measures undoubtedly increased the costs for businesses, and business owners protested and submitted a petition to the president, claiming that this was one of the 10 terrible laws that led companies to leave Taiwan. As a result, the draft of the "Equality Act for Men and Women in Employment" remained stuck in the Legislative Yuan until the 2000 presidential election, when political parties shifted. It took until 2002 to finalize the legislation, which is now known as the "*Gender Equality in Employment Act*"[8].

Nonetheless, the significance of this Act stems from the fact that women began to transition from marriage and family to the public realm, learning to participate in national policies through legislation. It also spurred other social groups to pursue their own legislative agendas. So far, in Taiwan, all human rights Acts affecting women, children, and the underprivileged have been developed by non-governmental organizations (NGOs) and submitted to the Legislative Yuan for lobbying. Taiwan lifted the martial law in 1987. Following the lifting of martial law in Taiwan, non-governmental organizations (NGOs) thrived and became the most reliable support for Taiwan's democratization.

8 Please compare with the Amendment to the three Gender Equality Laws in Taiwan: https://english.ey.gov.tw/News3/9E5540D592A5FECD/cd9925f8-8664-49ff-99ac-fa3f-1d0a07d6.

IV. Peng Wanru's Case: Transforming women's movement to national system

Peng Wanru's tragic case took place in November 1996. Peng Wanru[9] was the secretary-general of Awakening Foundation before becoming the director of the Women's division at the Democratic Progressive Party. At the time, women had only a one-tenth guaranteed quota to engage in politics. Peng Wanru worked hard to persuade party colleagues to change the party constitution so that at least one-quarter of women were nominated in various elections. On November 30, 1996, Peng Wanru had a dinner with party members and actively sought support. After the dinner, she took a taxi back to her hotel and disappeared the next day. Two days later, she was found naked and stabbed 35 times in the grass near a factory in Kaohsiung's countryside. So far, the case remains unsolved.

Following the murder, women's groups were outraged and demanded that the Executive Yuan form a Women's Rights Promotion Committee, pass the "*Sexual Assault Prevention Act*" and the "*Domestic Violence Prevention Act*", create a Children's Bureau, and establish a Gender Equality Education Committee in the Ministry of Education. The Executive Yuan welcomed them all, making the representatives feel incredible.

Since then, Taiwan's women's movement has evolved from howling at trains to taking part in policy decision. The Women's Rights Promotion Committee was founded by the Executive Yuan, with the premier serving as its convener.[10] Women's groups, professionals and intellectuals, and ministers from several ministries jointly debated women's policies. The feminist movement infiltrated the national system, and new laws pertaining to gender equality were adopted.

V. Signing CEDAW to align with international standards

In 2004, the National Alliance of Taiwan Women's Association, the Awakening Foundation, and other women's organizations formed a civil society alliance to promote Taiwan's implementation of CEDAW.[11] They asked the

9 About her activities and works, please check: Pen, Wanru (1997). Wanru like a Firefly I&II (婉如火金姑上、下). Feme Book.

10 History of the Committee: https://gec.ey.gov.tw/en/8FB10983A3908085.

11 https://nhrc.cy.gov.tw/en-US/cp.aspx?n=8697.

government to sign the "Convention on the Elimination of All Forms of Discrimination Against Women" (CEDAW) and make it local legislation. Because Taiwan is not a member of the United Nations, the conventions signed cannot be deposited, and the national reports prepared cannot be submitted to the United Nations CEDAW Committee for review. After the CEDAW's proposed suggestion was accepted in the Taskforce on the Promotion of Human Rights Protection convened by the Premier of the Executive Yuan,[12] Taiwan established a unique review system, inviting independent UN experts to Taiwan to review national reports, not only through mutual communication with government organizations, but also with local civil society organizations in formal and informal sessions. The first CEDAW national report review meeting established a new model and served as a template for the review of other international treaties in Taiwan. The first female vice president was elected in 2000, followed by the first female president in 2016, and Taiwan became an Asian model for gender equality. An initiative based on its long-standing struggle for women's and gender equality.

VI. The long road to the same sex marriage

In 2016, the Democratic Progressive Party won the majority in both the executive and legislative branches, citing freedom, democracy, the rule of law, and human rights as important ideals. It was Taiwan's first meaningful party rotation. Furthermore, Taiwan elected Tsai Ing-wen, the first female president to endorse same-sex marriage, and nominated nearly half of the liberal justices. Since 2016, Taiwan has gone through four stages of legislation: constitutional interpretation, referendum, and legislation. On May 24, 2019, same-sex marriage was becoming legal. Taiwan was the first country in Asia to legalize same-sex marriage (Chen 2023).

However, due to the strong boycott of anti-homosexuality parties, same-sex marriage can only be passed as a special law, and it excludes joint adoption, artificial reproduction, and international marriage. Gay organizations continue to fight through various cases (Chi 2019).[13] he Ministry of the Interior issued an administrative decree in January 2023 approving transnational same-sex marriage for marriage registration. In May, the Leg-

12 The Taskforce's protocol of the 10th meeting: https://www.humanrights.moj.gov.tw/media/13433/59815532664.pdf?mediaDL=true.

13 https://english.cw.com.tw/article/article.action?id=2410.

islative Yuan eased the limitations on joint adoption of children, allowing same-sex married couples to adopt children together. Furthermore, the controversial cross-strait same-sex marriage was accepted for registration by the Mainland Affairs Council in September 2024.

VII. Current challenges

With the advancement of technology, cyberbullying incidents are becoming more common, private sexual footages are being maliciously spread online, misogynistic and anti-women speech is intensifying, flesh searches that violate privacy rights are rampant, malicious attacks with a mix of true and fake information are being retained forever, and issues such as how to have the right to be forgotten and remove them are on the rise. They all put our wisdom and intelligence to the test by causing serious, quick, and far-reaching devastation.

References:

The Articles of Mei-nu Yu about women's discrimination in laws, collected in: The Women's Movement Record of Awakening Foundation. https://awakening.lib.tku.edu.tw/Default2_result.aspx

Lee, Pei-jung. 1997. *The Modern Women's Movement in Taiwan: The Changing Role of Taiwanese Women in a Conscious and Collective Struggle Toward Equality.* Halifax NS: Saint Mary's University. 67–75.

Taiwan Women's Center. 2008. *Taiwan Women's Cultural Landmarks Exhibition.* https://www.taiwanwomencenter.org.tw/en-global/News/special-exhibitions/Content/4/exhibition_2008

The Awakening Foundation. https://www.awakening.org.tw/english

Timeline of the Awakening Foundation. https://www.awakening.org.tw/content/34

Chang, Chin-feng. 2009. 台灣女性史入門-勞動篇 (Introduction to Taiwan Women's History – Labor) https://www.ios.sinica.edu.tw/people/personal/ccf/台灣女性史入門_勞動篇.pdf

Yu, Mei-nu. 2015. "The Path of the Gender Equality Movement in My Nation: Creeping Forward Through Litigation and Legislation". In *Sex Equality Controversies: Formosa Lecture, 2013.* By Catharine A. MacKinnon. 138–151.

The Amendment to the three Gender Equality Laws in Taiwan. https://english.ey.gov.tw/News3/9E5540D592A5FECD/cd9925f8-8664-49ff-99ac-fa3f1d0a07d6

Pen, Wanru. 1997. *Wanru like a Firefly* I&II (婉如火金姑上、下). Feme Book.

The History of the Women's Rights Promotion Committee. https://gec.ey.gov.tw/en/8FB10983A3908085

The Civil Society Alliance to Promote Taiwan's Implementation of CEDAW. https://nhrc.cy.gov.tw/en-US/cp.aspx?n=8697

The Protocol of the Taskforce on the Promotion of Human Rights Protection, the 10th meeting. https://www.humanrights.moj.gov.tw/media/13433/59815532664.pdf?mediaDL=true

Chen, Chao-ju. 2023.. First in Asia: *The Story of Mei-nu Yu and Taiwan's Same Sex Marriage Act.* (亞洲第一:尤美女和臺灣同婚法案的故事). Taipei: Spring Hill Publishing.

Chi, Chia-wei (2019). Behind Taiwan's Same-Sex Marriage Law: The 30-Years Crusade. https://english.cw.com.tw/article/article.action?id=2410

C. Dignity, Non-discrimination, and Rights of LGBTIQ+ – Challenges of Same-Sex Family Relations

Eibe Riedel[1]

Abstract:

This contribution[2] addresses one of the most contested human rights problems: human dignity and non-discrimination challenges facing LGBTIQ+[3] people and their family relations. It addresses aspects of fundamental human rights that are complex, developing fast, and in the process of further change in many countries. A brief look at the historical development of LGBTIQ+ rights (henceforth in short LGBT) at the universal level, starting with the notions of dignity and human rights and international law aspects within the United Nations (UN) system is followed by looking at the "Universal Bill of Rights" (i.e. The Universal Declaration of Human Rights (UDHR) 1948, the International Covenant on Economic, Social and Cultural Rights (ICESCR) and International Covenant on Civil and Political Rights (ICCPR) 1966/76), with the focus here on non-discrimination and the specific problems of sexual orientation and gender identity (SOGI). A short look at LGBT issues at the national and European level will follow, illustrating the situation in Germany, Europe, and Taiwan. A few remarks on transgender rights will complete this overview.

Keywords:

Human Dignity, non-discrimination, LGBTIQ+, family relations of non-binary couples, Universal Bill of Rights, ESC and CP rights, sexual orientation and gender identity (SOGI), LGBT law in Germany, Europe and Taiwan, transgender and human rights protection.

---

1 Prof (em.) Dr Eibe Riedel, Chair of German and Comparative Public Law, European and International Law, University of Mannheim; 1997–2012 Member and Vice-Chairperson UN Committee on Economic, Social and Cultural Rights, Geneva, former Swiss Chair of Human Rights, 2009–2012 and Visiting Professor Geneva Academy of International Humanitarian Law and Human Rights, until 2017 Visiting Professor Geneva Graduate Institute (IHEID); Hon. Member German Institute of Human Rights, Berlin. riedel@uni-mannheim.de.

2 This contribution is based on a lecture with participation of a same-sex family held at Soochow University in conjunction with the Taiwan National Human Rights Commission on 26 October 2023. I wish to very much thank Senior Research Assistant and Doctorand Lukas Romberg and Student Assistant Louis Berthoux for their editorial assistance to this article and the whole book.

3 For glossary of terms see De Groot 2022, 1–12.

I. International Approaches to Human Dignity, Non-Discrimination and LGBTIQ+ Rights

Since the 1990s, international NGOs have increased their focus on human rights issues connected with LGBT.

1. The Historical Setting of LGBTIQ+ Rights

After the ravages of two world wars in one century with over 65 million deaths during World War II alone, and unbelievable horrors committed by the Nazi-dictatorship and other Fascist or authoritarian régimes, world leaders got together to pave the way for a new approach to international law, by setting up the UN. The notion of human dignity was one of the answers that emerged for structuring the future of the new world order. Clear definitions and fields of practical application of dignity were not outlined by those who saw human dignity as a foundational principle for national constitutions, but also for international organizations. While the Charter of the UN failed to lay down precise norms about dignity, and did not contain a Bill of Rights, the world leaders agreed, however, that this task should be fulfilled subsequently by the newly set-up Human Rights Commission (1945) which was eventually transformed into the Human Rights Council (HRC) in 2006. That "Bill of Rights" project was adopted as a Declaration of the UN General Assembly in 1948 under the title "Universal Declaration of Human Rights" (UDHR) of 1948.[4] While the UDHR was frequently still regarded as legally non-binding in the 1960s to 1980s by many States, despite having signed and ratified the UN-Covenants, that legal position changed almost dramatically after the demise of the Soviet Union in 1990 and particularly since the Vienna World Conference on Human Rights of 1993. By that time, the UDHR had been accepted by most States either as part of customary rules of international law (with few exceptions, such as the right to property and the law of aliens), or even as general principles of law or international law.[5] Moreover, in 1966/76 the two UN Covenants on Economic, Social and Cultural Rights (ICESCR) and the one on Civil and Political Rights (ICCPR) were adopted and entered into force and, in fact, spelled out the UDHR promises in more detail and legally binding form. By 2025, of the 193 member States of the UN 174 States have ratified the ICCPR and 173 the ICESCR.

---

4 See Riedel, 2020a, 231–57, 235 f.

5 See Riedel, 2020a 241–43.

Looking briefly at the norms that shaped and structured modern interpretations of LGBT rights, one notices that the UDHR preamble starts with a clear formulation of purpose and aims: "*Whereas recognition of the inherent dignity and of the equal and inalienable rights of all members of the human family is the foundation of freedom, justice and peace in the world ...*", the preamble finishes with the proclamation that the UDHR is to be regarded as "*a common standard of achievement for all peoples and all nations.*" Human dignity then is mentioned in Art. 1 UDHR: *"All human beings are born free and equal in dignity and rights. They are endowed with reason and conscience and should act towards one another in a spirit of brotherhood".*

Human dignity had been accepted as the primary foundation for all states and human beings after 1945. It asserted that each person is gifted with intrinsic worth and the capacity for reason, famously elaborated by *Immanuel Kant* in his *Metaphysik der Sitten* in 1785. Each person is endowed with autonomy, equality and freedom, based on the *categorical imperative* ("Act in such a way that the maxim of your will can always serve as the basis of general legislation" "*Handle nur nach derjenigen Maxime, durch die du zugleich wollen kannst, dass sie ein allgemeines Gesetz werde*")[6] and deserves respect and acceptance, despite physical or other differences of appearance. Dignity affirms the moral, legal, political and philosophical foundation of rights, and concentrates on the inherent worth of everyone.[7]

The principle of non-discrimination complements human dignity, at a slightly lower level of abstraction, by ensuring equal treatment regardless of race, gender, religion, political views or other status,[8] and provides the legal criteria for guaranteeing and enforcing the human rights, outlawing prohibited grounds of discrimination, by providing protection assurances against unjustified unequal treatment: Dignity affirms the foundation of rights, either as legally directly binding norm or as a foundational value, while non-discrimination provides the specific criteria for guaranteeing and enforcing the human rights, forbidding specific forms of discrimination.

The UDHR of 1948 initially was not legally binding, but by 1993 had been accepted with few exceptions by most States, either as part of customary

6 Kant, 1902–1968 AA IV 420–421.

7 On dignity see Riedel 1999, 25–52, 37–47; Waldron 2020. 28–37; see also Muders 2020. 75, 84–103; Finck 2016. 26–53, 27–31; Lorz 1992. 373–76, emphasizing dignity and freedom, and "it is every person's autonomous decision how to use the scope given for its exercise", at 373; see generally on this notion of Kantian freedom in relation to women's rights, Chen 2025 manuscript. Kant as a Human Rights Defender and Educator, 6 and 8–9; Etinson 2020, 353–81.

8 See Riedel 2020a, 231–257, 235 f.

international law or as *general principles of international law* or general principles of law.[9]

In 1966/76 the two UN Covenants on Economic, Social and Cultural Rights and Civil and Political Rights were adopted and later ratified, containing nearly all human rights promises of the UDHR of 1948, but spelled out in more detail and with legally binding provisions. Since the Vienna World Conference on Human Rights of 1993 the community of States has accepted that the UDHR and the two UN Covenants on Human Rights can be seen as the combination of previously only desired, but by then operationalized "Universal Bill of Rights" that the founders of the UN had had in mind in 1945.

The *Universal Bill of Rights* by now can be regarded as binding law, as customary international law for most of its provisions, or as general principles, or even as *ius cogens*; yet the two UN Covenants do not mention specific rights to SOGI. Almost two decades of discussion at all levels in international diplomacy, State Reporting, and many conferences primarily dealt with the overarching question whether all rights spelled out in the UDHR, and in more detail in the two Human Rights Covenants, were fully binding or merely statements of norms *de lege ferenda*. This changed during the 1980s and in the 1990s after the demise of the Soviet Union, and certainly after the Vienna World Conference on Human Rights in 1993.[10] Within a very short time, many States that previously had kept silent now declared to agree with the outcome of the Vienna Declaration of 1993, that all human rights, be they civil and political, or economic, social or cultural, form the two pillars of international human rights law stressing the universality, indivisibility, inter-dependence, and inter-relatedness of all human rights.[11] The Vienna Conference concluded that "the international community must treat human rights globally in a fair and equal manner, on the same footing, and with the same emphasis".[12]

2. Sexual Orientation and Gender Identity

Climbing down the level of abstraction, the issues of SOGI soon became a much-discussed issue of human rights activists. The realization that LGBT issues affect the core area of integrity of individuals became obvious, and it

9 Riedel, Giacca, and Golay 2014, 3–48, 4–8; see also Riedel 2020b, 63, 369–417, 381–88; Riedel 2015, 79–91.

10 UN World Conference on Human Rights, Vienna 1993, Part I, para. 5.

11 Nowak 2005.

12 A/CONF/157/23, Part I, para 5; see also Riedel, Giacca, and Golay 2014, chap. 1, 7 et seq.

soon emerged that the human rights dimension of their position met the most essential criterion of rights violations: human rights become necessary whenever the affected persons find no other remedy or redress for elementary experiences of injustice and fundamental violations of their dignity and equality.

To begin with, no-one really knew the precise ramifications concerning questions of SOGI. But within the last 40 years of international practice, the drive to include LGBT issues in the legally recognized non-discrimination and equality areas has increased tremendously. And LGBT NGOs were particularly active in regarding the LGBT issues as components of non-discrimination. International NGOs and academics did not restrict their analyses to the *"acquis des droits de l'homme"* (now *"humain"*) reached in the early 1990s. Instead, the issues relating to sexual orientation and gender identity, and specifically to LGBT rights, were prominently addressed in increasing detail and with very convincing arguments in many NGO representations at the universal and national levels. The basic assumption of all these studies and positions was: *"All human beings are born free and equal in dignity and rights"* (UDHR, Art.1).

3. Yogyakarta Principles

Sexual orientation and gender identity now were considered as integral to every person's dignity and humanity and should not be the basis for discrimination or abuse. In the early 2000s the International Commission of Jurists and the International Service for Human Rights, on behalf of a coalition of human rights organizations, started a project to develop a set of international legal principles relating to human rights violations based on SOGI, and to emphasize with greater clarity the human rights obligations of States.[13] In 2006, a group of 29 distinguished human rights experts from all over the world had met at Yogyakarta in Indonesia, and had unanimously adopted 29 "*Yogyakarta Principles*", later supplemented by 10 further principles in 2017, and specific recommendations to States on how their human rights law obligations affect issues of sexual orientation and gender identity (Yogyakarta Principles 2007, introduction). The introduction forcefully summarizes the existing obligations resting on States: "The experts agree that the Yogyakarta principles reflect the existing state of international human rights law in relation to issues of sexual orienta-

13 See Balzaretti 2016, 9 et seq.

tion and gender identity. They also recognize that States may incur additional obligations as human rights law continues to evolve".

The principles adopted cover almost all rights of the Universal Declaration of Human Rights, ranging from universal enjoyment of human rights (principle 1), equality and non-discrimination (2), life (4), security of the person (5), privacy (6), arbitrary deprivation of liberty (7), treatment with humanity while in detention (9), and a whole list of ESC-rights, such as in relation to SOGI in work, social security, an adequate standard of living, housing, education, health, and protection from medical abuses (12–18), to specific CPR-rights like freedom of opinion, thought, conscience and religion, asylum-seeking and the right to found a family (19–24). The final principles addressed questions of remedies, redress of grievances, and accountability (28–29). The overall approach was neatly summarized in the last paragraphs of the Introduction to the Yogyakarta Principles: "The *experts agree that the Yogyakarta principles reflect the existing state of international human rights law in relation to issues of sexual orientation and gender identity …".* These principles were spread world-wide and, in fact, quite a few States subsequently changed their legal positions in national statute law, and UN bodies generally began to address SOGI questions more frequently, unlike before 2000.[14]

The Yogyakarta Principles were also widely discussed in academia, international and national civil society organizations, in the UN treaty bodies, in the Human Rights Council (HRC), and even in the UN General Assembly.[15]

However, some water must be added to the wine of SOGI human rights as *Vitit Muntarbhorn*, the then UN Independent Expert on Sexual Orientation and Gender Identity of the Human Rights Council (HRC), pointed out clearly in 2016.[16] However, in a much-quoted passage in his first report he strongly argued for a comprehensive approach, maintaining: Sexual Orientation and Gender Identity are based on existing international human rights law and its interrelationship with gender identity: "there is no advocacy of new rights for particular groups" (ibid., para. 17). An optimistic and broad interpretation of the Universal Bill of Rights guarantees unfortunately is not shared by a large group of States in the UN General Assembly, namely African States – with very few exceptions –, Middle Eastern States, India, China, and many Latin-American States, as well as the USA and most other larger European

14 See Moeckli, Shah, and Sivakumaran 2014, 310 ff.; Wintemute and Andenæs 2001 generally on this topic.

15 See only HRC 2017 A/HRC/RES/32/2 with further references.

16 Human Rights Council 2017, A/HRC/35/36.

States. In addition, more than 70 States still criminalize same-sex relationships, and Uganda introduced a new and strong anti-LGBT law in May 2023. Under that statute even the death penalty can be decreed. In Brunei, moreover, the death penalty can be carried out by stoning.[17]

Amongst the opponents of including LGBT persons in the existing human rights framework, the most outspoken critics are Russia, China, and the USA under the Bush Junior and Trump administrations. The Organization of the Islamic Conference is the most critical, accusing the countries supporting the General Assembly resolution of:

> *"Attempting to undermine the international legal framework in trying to normalize pedophilia, among other acts" (Syrian Representative in UNGA 8 December 2008).*

Later, a group of Western and Caribbean States meeting in an LGBT Core Group supported the HRC's position in the matter of LGBT rights, but the vote in the Council was close: 23 for, 18 against. The Council position called for close assessment and awareness raising of global discrimination based on SOGI. The HRC further called for institutional methods to address anti-discrimination policies, and particularly implored States, NGOs, and UN agencies to address issues of anti-LGBT violence.[18]

The NGO International Lesbian, Gay, Bisexual, Trans and Intersex Association (ILGA) publishes Annual Reviews of the status of LGBT rights worldwide. The 2022/23 European Report is followed by a country-by-country analysis which shows that many countries have their own national laws, and that national courts have gradually taken up some of the Yogyakarta Principles. Without going into details, it can be said that despite fierce opposition from the mentioned groups of States, LGBT rights have gradually been accepted by an increasing number of States and by other stakeholders and have been regarded as part of existing binding human rights law. The ILGA EUROPE Annual Report 2025 summarizes the state of affairs in its Rainbow Map as follows: (1) No protection at all exists in 6 European countries; (2) full coverage protection in Belgium, Bosnia & Herzegovina, Denmark, Finland, Greece, Iceland, Montenegro, Serbia, Spain; (3) marriage equality for same

17 Uganda, Anti-Homosexuality Act 26 May 2023; Brunei, Anti-Homosexuality Law under Sharia Law 22 April 2014, but after strong international criticisms the Government introduced a moratorium.

18 On the role of the HRC see, for example, HRC Resolution *Protection against violence and discrimination based on sexual orientation and gender identity*, 30 June 2016, A/HRC/RES/32/2, and its predecessor resolutions A/HRC/RES/17/19, A/HRC/RES/27/32.

sex couples is only available in 22 countries; (4) in 18 countries no legal protection for same-sex partners exist; (5) trans parenthood is only recognized in 8 countries; (6) Only Germany, Greece, Iceland, Malta, Portugal and Spain prohibit unnecessary surgical or medical interventions on intersex children; (7) 11 countries have no legal procedure for gender recognition; (8) only in 12 countries can trans people have legal gender recognition based on self-determination and (9) in at least 4 countries the freedom of assembly and association is restricted.[19]

4. Non-Discrimination and Specific Human Rights Relating to LGBT and the Practice of UN Bodies

Against this background, a closer look at the Universal Bill of Rights and the scope and extent of non-discrimination is called for. The wording of the UDHR in Art. 2 (1) is unmistakably clear:

> *"Everyone is entitled to all the rights and freedoms set forth in this Declaration, without distinction of any kind, such as race, colour, sex, language, religion, political or other opinion, national or social origin, property, birth or other status".*

This wording on non-discrimination was taken over in both Human Rights Covenants (Arts. 2(2), and 3 ICESCR, 2(1), 26 ICCPR).

While the actual wording of the Covenants differs, that difference no longer plays a big role. Western States originally wanted ESC-rights to merely contain programmatic statements, whose realization rests entirely in the hands of States Parties, while CP-rights imposed direct legal obligations, or only needed implementation steps at the national level, before becoming fully operative. The Committee on ESC-Rights (CESCR) has maintained that while there are undoubtedly some aspects of the individual rights enshrined in the Social Covenant (in Part III) which realistically cannot be fully realized in a short period of time, thus leaving room for governmental discretion, every single Covenant right, does contain elements also lending themselves to immediate implementation, such as in relation to the right to food and the freedom from hunger. This notion has been maintained by CESCR in constant practice since 1990, when the Committee adopted General Comment (GC) 3 on the nature of States Parties' obligations (Art. 2(1) of the ICESCR). Since 2013, the Optional Protocol to the ICESCR has been in

19 See ILGA Europe Annual Review 2025, Rainbow Map.

force, rendering the procedural distinction between ICCPR- and ICESCR-rights largely redundant.

The most important example for this position is the principle of non-discrimination under Art. 2(2) ICESCR and Art. 2(1) ICCPR. From the beginning the CESCR – like the HRCee, CEDAW and CRC committees – took the view that every specific right of Parts III of the Covenants (Arts. 6–15 ICESCR, Arts. 6–27 ICCPR) follows the chapeau of Art. 2(2) ICESCR or Art. 2(1) ICCPR on non-discrimination as a fully binding norm of customary international law, or even as a general principle of law under Art. 38(1) c ICJ – Statute. The argument is strengthened by the fact that each State Party of the Covenants can fulfil that obligation without further ado, because it is not essentially resource-dependent, but requires States making policy choices, in line with internationally agreed obligations. Any failure by a State to guarantee the prerequisites for leading an adequate and dignified life, ensuring a "survival kit" as a minimum, clearly breaches the Covenant obligations.[20]

Unless, of course, the State can show that it was practically impossible to guarantee even those minimum rights, due to resource scarcity, armed conflict, earthquakes, tsunamis or other natural disasters. But the State retains the burden of proof that it was unable to fulfil even the core minimum basic requirements of survival rights.[21] In its General Comment No. 20 (2009), the CESCR has dealt with those issues extensively, and maintains that the Covenant provisions are cross-cutting and overarching principles that are to be applied read in conjunction with each specific right, depending on the problems at hand.[22]

Most of LGBT issues are raised in the Human Rights Committee (HRCee), CEDAW and CRC, but non-discrimination, as shown above, is a key concern of all treaty bodies.[23] The ICESCR legally opens the same patterns of argumentation for LGBT issues as under the ICCPR, CEDAW or CRC. CESCR clearly pointed this out when interpreting the non-discrimination example of "*other status*":

> "'**other status**' *as recognized in article 2, paragraph 2, includes sexual orientation. States parties should ensure that a person's sexual orienta-*

20 Riedel, 2015, 79–91, 85 and 90–91.

21 See CESCR Statement 2007, paras. 5, 6, 8, 11; see also Riedel, Giacca, Golay 2014. 14; Riedel 2020c. 107–23.

22 Committee on Economic, Social and Cultural Rights 2009, paras. 13–14; Riedel 2020a. 237–239.

23 For overview see Walker 2001, 743–57; and Riedel 2013.1289 et seq.

tion is not a barrier to realizing Covenant rights, for example, in accessing survivors' pension rights. In addition, gender identity is recognized as among the prohibited grounds of discrimination. For example, persons who are transgender, transsexual or intersex often face serious human rights violations, such as harassment in schools or in the workplace."[24]

The CESCR has consistently confirmed its view on this matter in subsequent years, but several of its members do not share this opinion in public sessions. They will prefer concentrating on the more general scope of non-discrimination avoiding that specific LGBT examples are taken up in concluding observations. Thus, the question of LGBT treatment in treaty bodies, unfortunately, is not a full success story. Persistent opposition to homosexuality and massive violations of personal integrity, and access to pensions or healthcare, to the workplace, or in education, remain, and are serious impediments for LGBT persons in many countries even today.

As the Annual Reports of ILGA show on the worldwide, regional or national level, questions relating to LGBT increasingly are being raised as serious matters of concern, and the NGO community is closely addressing the relevant problems. States parties to the key human rights treaties still are reticent or even tabooing LGBT problems, decision-makers feeling uncomfortable to discuss the issues involved because of strong religious or conservative opposition to liberalizing and equalizing the treatment of opposite-sex or same-sex people.[25]

For example, while I served on the CESCR between 1997 and 2012, LGBT questions were hardly addressed. The reasons for this lack of attention are many: the composition of the CESCR comprises 18 members from many different legal and political cultures, standing in the way of consensus; discussion under the general part of the Covenant usually concentrated on other pressing issues, like equal treatment of men and women, or children, older persons, or people with disabilities; and the time available for all relevant rights is extremely short, now only 3 to 6 hours per country in open sessions. Even if issues were raised in the dialogue with the State under review, often no concluding observation would follow, as the CESCR – like all other treaty bodies – when sitting in private session to draft their concluding observations, only accept them, if agreed by consensus, meaning

24 CESCR 2009, para. 3, *emphasis added.*

25 Bell 2001, 653–76; and Halley 2001, 97–112; for details see Riedel/Giacca/Golay 2014. 14; CESCR Statement No.16; see particularly Limburg Principles No. 25, referring to the obligation to 'guarantee respect for the minimum rights of survival for all', independent of available resources; see also ILGA Europe 2025, covering January to December 2024.

adopted unanimously. That also explains why such observations, when accepted by the Committee, sometimes contain formula compromises, or remain abstract and general. Only very rarely will decisions be taken by majority vote.

The advantages of bringing in such theoretically imperfect draft observations, however, are evident: Vague and general formulations will usually be taken up by academia, and civil society at the universal, regional or domestic law level; and government departments will look at the issues again, sometimes even changing their position. This procedure essentially applies to all treaty bodies and slows down quick development of new human rights interpretations.

But sometimes positions rapidly do change: Before 2000, when the CESCR advocated a human right to water – although not specifically mentioned in Art. 11 of the Covenant – no agreement could be mustered on this question, but since GC 15 on the right to water (2002) the world has generally accepted access to water as a human right, like access to food, housing, health and education.[26]

A lot more needed to be said about the large array of reports, statements and declarations offered at the global level, that in sum tend to advance awareness of the seriousness of LGBT violations of rights, and slowly but surely are seeping into the practice of State authorities and of decision-makers, improving the LGBT situation step-by-step. But of course, whenever there are changes of government, the situation can also deteriorate drastically and quickly, such as happened in the USA under the first Trump administration and reappears in the second term with even greater intensity.

5. National and Regional European Level: Challenges Posed for Same-Sex Families

So, if the legally binding status of LGBT rights remains in part disputed and not fully accepted by a large group of States, NGOs, and foremost amongst them ILGA, Amnesty International and Human Rights Watch, decided to focus attention on LGBT rights at the national and regional levels, utilizing a "bottom-up" approach, showing how LGBT rights progress in particular areas could be used as *best practices* at the higher regional or international levels. The "top-down" avenue can enhance the rights' situation of affected

26 Riedel 2005, 585–606, 595 et seq.; but see Chirwa 2020, 55–69, 68: "... the right to water is still in the process of evolution and in search of full formal legal recognition".

individuals (for example in the *communications procedure* of the Optional Protocol to the ICESCR (OP ICESCR)). If that does not produce measurable results, then NGOs and academia will employ the "bottom–up" approach, starting at the national level and bringing domestic experiences up at the regional and international levels. I will illustrate this by merely looking briefly at some issues,[27] concentrating on the legal situations in Germany, Europe and Taiwan.

a) Germany

In Germany, discussion of LGBT rights did not start early, even though *Magnus Hirschfeld* and others had tried unsuccessfully since 1897 to get the ban of homosexuality in paragraph 175 of the Criminal Code abolished. During the Weimar Republic *Gustav Radbruch* tried to restrict the application of paragraph 175 to adult homosexuals, but also without success. A recommendation of the Parliamentary Committee on Criminal Law which was narrowly adopted had asked for the total abolition of the Criminal Code provision, but that attempt again failed in the plenary of parliament. It was not until after the "Third Reich", and much later still, that criminalization of homosexuals amongst adults above 21 years old ended in 1968 in East Germany and 1969 in West Germany. Registered same-sex partnerships were available to same-sex couples since 2001, and in 2017 parliament passed a bill to compensate homosexuals that had been sentenced after 1945.[28] That same year, parliament allowed same-sex marriage across the board.[29]

This late recognition of same-sex marriage did not solve all problems relating to family matters: The right to mutual adoption of children and stepchild adoption was recognized only late. In 2013 the Federal Constitutional Court (FCC) had established that to forbid second adoption in a same-sex partnership unlike in opposite-sex relations was a breach of Article 3 Basic Law (GG) on non-discrimination and equality, and full equal treatment of opposite-sex and same-sex marriage was not reached until October 2017.

The same applies to guardianship for children, which for a long time had marked a clear difference between opposite-sex and same-sex partnerships/marriage.

27 For a full display of the issues involved, see Wintemute and Andenaes 2001; Whisnant, 2013; FRA Handbook 2018.18 f, 20–23, 28–38, 155 et seq. ('protected grounds'), 224–228 ('other status'); Riedel 2020c. 414–416.

28 *"Gesetz zur strafrechtlichen Rehabilitierung der nach dem 8. Mai 1945 wegen einvernehmlicher homosexueller Handlungen verurteilten Personen vom 17. Juli 2017." (BGBl. I S. 2443)*

29 *"Gesetz zur Einführung des Rechts auf Eheschließung für Personen gleichen Geschlechts", BGBl. I 2017, S. 2787, in force since 1 October 2017.*

In labour law, particularly in employment contracts, the fight for non-discrimination lasted longest. The General Equality Law 2006 ultimately brought full equalization of marriage rules in labour law, and in the whole civil law of the Civil Code *"Bürgerliches Gesetzbuch" (BGB)*.

As could be expected, this change of law was not readily accepted by *inter alia,* the Roman Catholic Church, and other religious groups, while the Protestant churches were in favour of the new law. The opposing religious institutions sought to maintain their own rules of anti-homosexuality, but up to now without success, following European Union Law, and dicta of the European Court of Human Rights (ECHR).[30]

b) European Court of Human Rights (ECtHR)

It was remarkable that once Germany had taken a progressive stand on same-sex issues, the Strasbourg Human Rights Court still maintained a reserved position. Instead of ensuring a common European stand on new issues, the Court tended to pay lip-service to alleged national cultural differences of approach, justifying the denial of a breach of the European Convention on Human Rights. That approach can be explained by the fact that the Court always seeks to steer a balanced course: On the one hand to be progressive and enhancing human rights positions, on the other hand showing respect for local and cultural differences amongst then 47 member States.[31]

The leading case on same-sex couples originated in Austria, where the European Convention has direct constitutional effect. In the case of Karner v. Austria in 2003 the ECtHR had to deal with a situation where the male partner had died of AIDS in 1994, and the landlord tried to evict Mr. Karner from his tenancy, as a legally not related person of the deceased. The Court held that this situation offended against non-discrimination (Art. 14 ECtHR) and respect for his home (Art. 8). The Court established a new principle that same-sex couples must be granted all the rights and duties of unmarried opposite sex couples.[32]

10 years later, in X. and others v. Austria (2013) the ECtHR went even further: Austria now must allow same-sex couples to adopt each other's chil-

30 See Wintemute, in Wintemute and Andenaes 2001, 4 and there further references in footnote 12; see also Moeckli 2018, 48–74.

31 See Wintemute 2001, 717, 727, 728–729: arguing that initially national legislations and court decisions will shape the ECtHR judgments; only gradually will a "European consensus" evolve with social changes facilitating a change of views. The United Kingdom since left the EU; see also Mikovski, 166 et seq.

32 See *Karner v. Austria*, Appl. No. 40016/98, July 24, 2003.

dren, through a second-parent adoption, provided that would be in the best interest of the child.[33]

The *Karner* principle should also apply to access to donor insemination for Lesbian couples. The overarching question of whether same-sex couples could base their civil and labour law claims on the European Convention on Human Rights has not been fully responded to by the ECtHR, but by 2016, 30 out of then 47 States of the Council of Europe had changed their laws accordingly. But problems remain in relation to artificial insemination, or second parent adoption of a partner's child, or the joint adoption of an unrelated child, where States may still hold different views.

c) European Union Law

Just a few remarks on the LGBT rights situation in the European Union (EU) follow. A fuller discussion would exceed the format of this contribution. As can be expected, no unanimity on the whole spectrum of family rights and recognition of same-sex relationships can be found in the Member States of the EU. The legal framework of discrimination on grounds of sexual orientation and gender identity is to be found in a few EU primary law provisions: Article 10 of the Treaty on the Functioning of the EU (TFEU) and Articles 2 and 3 of the Treaty on the European Union (TEU) form the basis for discussion. In addition, Article 21(1) of the Charter of Fundamental Rights of the EU (FRCh) supplements the primary sources.[34] The FRCh clearly states and prohibits discrimination on the grounds of "sexual orientation". But that position was achieved only gradually and fastened by Art. 13 of the TEU by the Amsterdam Treaty 1997.

In addition, in EU secondary law several landmark anti-discrimination directives were adopted based on article 13 TEU in 2000: the Race Equality Directive implemented the principle of equal treatment for all, irrespective of racial or ethnic origin; the Employment Equality Directive forbids discrimination on the grounds of religion or belief, age, disability or sexual orientation.[35] The Race Equality Directive has relatively broad application, while the Employment Equality Directive merely affects one area of LGBT discrimination, namely employment, occupational and vocational training.

33 See *X. and others v. Austria*, Grand Chamber, Appl. No. 19010/07, February 19, 2013, with 10 international NGOs admitted as Third-Party Interventions.

34 For a succinct overview on Council of Europe and EU non-discrimination issues, see European Union Agency for Fundamental Rights and Council of Europe [FRA] 2018, 15–23; see also Mickovski 2020, 166 et seq.

35 Employment Equality Directive 2000; Racial Equality Directive 2000; Gender Goods and Services Directive 2006; Directive on the Right to Family Reunification 2003; cf. Mickovski, 2020, 52 et seq.

While these directives gave at least some indication on how to treat non-discrimination in the context of ensuring the common market of the Union, the family relations issues of LGBT persons were not addressed sufficiently.[36]

The European Commission submitted a draft proposal for a new and comprehensive directive, covering the areas of religion or belief, disability, age or sexual orientation beyond the restricted area of employment. The European Parliament (EP) adopted that draft directive in April 2009 under its consultation procedure. Since the Lisbon Treaty 2007 the issue falls under Article 19 TFEU and requires consent of Parliament plus unanimity in the European Council. Since such unanimity has not been reached for decades, the draft directive remains blocked. Several other EU programmes and strategies have been tried by EU institutions, but little progress has been made. Recital 22 of the Employment Directive does not affect existing national laws on marital status and benefits reserved for married couples. The proposal for a new anti-discrimination directive leaves the recognition of marriage or family status, adoption and reproductive rights to national law, reflecting the "diverse national traditions and policy choices."[37]

As can be expected, substantial differences of views between the 27 Member States on same-sex marriage and adoption continue to exist, despite slow changes of public awareness and perception. The hindrances of new approaches are increased by the fact that Member States show considerable varieties of regulations. Some of the newer ones, such as Bulgaria, Croatia, Hungary, Latvia, Lithuania, Poland and Slovakia, even have constitutional provisions against same-sex marriage (De Groot 2022, 6).[38]

The European Court of Justice (CJEU) rarely dealt with questions of LGBT rights and generally has taken a more restrictive view on EU treaty interpretation around marriage and adoption rights. It does not look likely that the more conservative approach of the Court will change radically soon, but it remains a viable alternative, much like the alternative solution of European soft law developments. *David de Groot* convincingly argues that according to CJEU case law "same-sex partners [...] should not be treated [...] in a way that is arbitrarily different from their treatment if marriage was open to them."[39]

---

36 Cf. De Groot 2022, 4–7.

37 European Commission 2008, 6; see also FRA 2018, 155 et seq., 162–181.

38 See also the instructive lists of all Member States on marriage, adoption and non-discrimination generally, and on public opinion reflected in European Commission 2025; see also FRA 2018,155 et seq. (protected grounds), 'other status' 224–228.

39 De Groot 2022, 7; and see the cases *Maruko* (C-267/06), *Römer* (C-147/08), *Hay* (C-267/12), *Oliari and Others v. Italy* (2015, ECtHR, App. Nos. 18766/11 and 36030/11), and *Fedorova and Others v. Russia* (ECtHR, App. Nos. 40792/10, 30538/14, and 43439/14).

This glimpse on the EU legal framework leads to the conclusion that so far, the European Union does not stand at the forefront of recognition of same-sex marriage and adoption rights of LGBT persons.[40] However, some national and regional jurisprudence and soft law attempts to change the existing framework, as well as academic writing and NGO advocacy may bring about the desired changes for LGBT persons. LGBT related issues at least are increasingly discussed all over Europe, and a slow trend towards accepting LGBT positions is discernible. As illustrated, much depends on the economic, social, cultural and political climate prevailing in a particular country. And there are, it must be conceded, also signs of deteriorating equal status situations in countries where right-wing, extremist or populistic notions are forcefully debated, as presently occurs in Hungary, Poland, and other European countries[41]: Western States' pro-LGBT diplomacy has been criticized by queer scholars pointing to the hypocrisy of many states' international stances. Criticisms have focused on the imperfect legal and social conditions for LGBT communities in Global North States and the "homocolonialist" implications of framing new standards of "civilization" and "modernity" by which to judge their former colonies and other societies in the global South.[42]

d) Taiwan

Briefly looking at Taiwan, the assessment of *Hsiaowei Kuan* of 2019 deserves full support, when she said that the world was impressed by the decision of the Taiwanese Constitutional Court Interpretation No. 748 regarding the constitutionality of the legal ban on same-sex marriages. It was the first Asian country that openly changed its views regarding homosexuality.[43] Opinion polls had always seen a large majority arguing against LGBT rights, allegedly due to cultural, religious or political reasons.[44] The de-stigmatization of same-sex sexual relations would probably not have occurred, if it had not been for the extremely active and organized civil society awareness-raising and insistence on human rights improvements, while violations of LGBT rights still could be seen in society at all levels.[45]

40 Cf. Waaldijk 2001, 638–651, at 641 et seq.

41 See Conway and Edenborg, 2025, 1065–86, particularly 1070.

42 Rahman 2014, 274–289; see also Delatolla 2020, 148–152.

43 Kuan 2019a, 593; 2019b, 1–44; see also Lau 2020.

44 See Lo 2024, 446–461.

45 For a good overview of the Confucius heritage and human rights see Lee 2016, No. 7, 978–992, 979 et seq., and generally Lin 2020; critically on the whole process Kao 2024.27.1/2,

While the Constitutional Court maintained the actual legal position that existed prior to the landmark decision of 2017, it developed the method of prospective overruling, by saying that if the State authorities would fail to implement its decision to allow same-sex couples to marry within two years, then the same-sex persons would be allowed to have their marriage registration effectuated, by submitting a written document signed by two or more witnesses, as is provided by the marriage chapter for legally recognized couples. But that left untouched other issues of the same-sex parents and their children: Thus adoption, artificial reproduction and surrogacy were not specifically dealt with, and thus still demand the adoption of new legislation.[46]

The Constitutional Court really took a very bold step in favour of non-discrimination under the human rights provisions in Taiwan. The Court also invited six legal experts as *amici curiae* to provide opinions during the oral hearings.[47]

That the decision was revolutionary can be gauged by looking at the prevailing political situation in the country. In a Referendum in 2018 the questions put asked voters: 1. "*Do you agree that marriage defined in the Civil Code should be restricted to the union between one man and one woman?*" 2. "*Do you agree to protect the rights of two people of the same sex to live together permanently through a form other than the marriage provisions in the Civil Code?*" And 72.5 % of voters agreed and only 27.5 % disagreed. On May 24, 2019, the *Act for Implementation of Judicial Yuan Interpretation No.748 (Same-Sex Marriage in Taiwan)* was enacted, and soon after in 2019 the first same-sex marriage under changed law took place.[48]

As regards adoption rights: while adoption of same-sex families since 2023 is legally possible, the role of step-parents, artificial reproduction and surrogacy remain to be regulated.[49] Against this background, discriminatory treatment of same-sex couples to my knowledge still is widely accepted. But it seems that Taiwan will eventually follow the path paved by European and American States, and pressure from NGOs, hopefully in the not-too-distant future.

---

147 et seq.

46 On the development in this area see Chien 2012, 187–201; also, Su 2022.

47 On the analysis of development in this area see Chien 2012, 187–201; see also Su 2022, 1–34.; Cf. Lin 2025, 7.

48 Details of the three proposals Definition of Marriage, Special Law Referendum, and Referendum to Ban the Implementation of LGBT Education, see Lin 2025, 10 f.; for a critical view on the whole process see Hsu 2022.

49 See Lo 2024, 453 f.

The Yogyakarta Principles spelled out clearly in 2006 and 2017: what is now needed is larger-scale academic and civil society awareness-raising, in schools, on television, in the mass media, films and cultural activities, as detailed in Principles 25–27[50]. Moreover, the focus should be on remedies, redress of grievances and accountability of all public authorities and other decision makers. The Government of the day and departments of ministries have a key role to play in this. Teacher training on LGBT issues, regular special training for judges, the police, military staff, teachers at schools and universities, parents and parents' associations should regularly inform on LGBT issues, so that the general anti-atmosphere still existing in society at large may bring about change. Moreover, children ought to be informed of their basic rights, including LGBT rights, in easy-to-understand language, and it seems a worthwhile task for the National Human Rights Commission (NHRC) to undertake, as happened in its German counterpart in Berlin (German Institute for Human Rights).[51] I am convinced that Taiwan will benefit much by unceasing academic and excellent national and international civil society efforts to protect LGBT persons to finally bring the whole spectrum of non-discrimination and ESC- as well as CP-rights to light, eventually ensuring full equal treatment of opposite-sex (binary) and (non-binary) same-sex couples.

II. The Legal Position of Transgender People

Another unresolved and much debated problem concerns the right of transgender persons to change their legal gender identity. This aspect of LGBT rights has raised many discussions and the anti-trans movements muster much support, often negatively influencing the general LGBT opinions prevailing in society.

Transgender activism in Taiwan did not emerge until the year 2000, when the Taiwan Transgender Butterfly Garden ("TG Garden") was established. TG Garden is Taiwan's first transgender support group, established in 2000 and provides information, support, advocacy and resources for transgender persons and their families.[52] Discrimination of transgender persons happened in a society, still quite hostile to all transgender persons, like in most other countries of the world. The change of legal gender depended since

50 Yogyakarta Principles 2006, particularly principles 1–9 and 24–29.

51 See for example Annual Report/Jahresbericht 2023/24 of the German Institute for Human Rights, published July 2024, with a special focus on protection from discrimination and use of force in relation to Sexual Orientation and Gender Identity.

52 Details in Kuan 2019a, 603–604.

1988 on a medical diagnosis of primary transsexualism, signed by two psychologists, and medical proof that sex reassignment surgery had been carried out, removing sexual organs and reconstructing the genitals[53].

As a result of "TG Garden" and other LGBT groups' efforts, the Ministry of the Interior decreed a new directive in 2018, whereby three conditions had to be fulfilled before a change of legal gender could be brought about:

(1) for male-to-female and female-to-male applicants: medical opinions on a diagnosis of primary transsexualism, signed by two psychologists;

(2) for female-to-male applicants: medical proof confirming the removal of female sex organs, including breasts, uterus and ovaries;

(3) for male-to-female applicants: medical proof confirming removal of male sex organs, including penis and testicles.

In addition, transsexuality still was/is seen as a mental disease, despite contrary views of most medical associations, the WHO, CEDAW and despite the Conclusions of the Taiwan Second Report of the International Review Committee on the Implementation of CEDAW that had stressed that transsexuality is not a disease.[54]

In other countries, transgender issues are also treated with great reserve. In Germany, for example, the legal position of transgender persons was based on the "Law Concerning the Change of First Name and Determination of Gender Identity in Special Cases" (the "*Transsexuellengesetz" (TSG)* of 1980): to change either name or gender, two medical experts had to be appointed by the family court; these medical experts had to evaluate whether the person does not identify with the birth-assigned sex or gender, but with the other one; and the person feels compelled to live according to his/her ideas for at least three years; furthermore it was to be assumed with high probability that the feeling of belonging to the other sex/gender was not going to change.

Under the TSG 1980, one could either obtain a change of name alone or together with a change of gender, in a single legal procedure. A name change then was registered in the "resident registration" ("*Melderegister*"). To change legal gender before 1980, two strict requirements had to be met:

(a) the applicant was permanently infertile; and

(b) has had surgery whereby the outer sexual characteristics were changed to a "significant approximation" to the appearance of their preferred biological sex.

---

53 See Chao, 2024, 1885–97.

54 See Kuan 2019a, 604.

The TSG was found to be unconstitutional on several counts: In 1982 the candidate age of 25 was declared unconstitutional; in 2006 the TSG was also held to apply to non-Germans with residency status in Germany; in 2008 the proviso that the candidate was unmarried was declared unconstitutional, offending against equality and non-discrimination under Article 3 *GG*, and finally, in 2011, the FCC declared unconstitutional the criteria for gender change that required gender-affirming surgery and sterilization or infertility.[55]

The new Law of 1st November 2024 on *Self-Identification ("Gesetz über die Selbstbestimmung in Bezug auf den Geschlechtseintrag" (SBGG)* BGBl. 2024, Nr. 206 21.6.2024) was passed by a vote of 374 for and 251 against in the *Bundestag* introducing the following new provisions:

- Self-identification for adults to change the gender marker and first name/s in the civil registry;
- The same applies for 14–17-year-olds with the consent of their parents or guardians;
- Changes are recorded by the Civil Registration Office ("*Standesamt*") – no longer by the Family Court and take effect after only a three-month waiting period ("*Karenzzeit*");
- After a change has taken place, the gender and name cannot be changed for one year.

The text is written in typical legalistic mode, because many existing legal provisions all over the civil law and civil code (*BGB*) need to be changed, but the law now covers most open questions. One political reason for the unwieldiness of the text may be that it was hotly debated in the relevant parliamentary committees that often leads to compromise formulations. Anti-transgender and pro-transgender LGBT positions clashed, and so the compromise drafting was difficult.

In Taiwan, positions on transgender issues differ as much as in most other countries.[56] The *International Review Committee of Taiwan (IRC)* in its *Concluding Observations to the Third Government Report* in 2022 (published in 2023) dealt extensively with non-discrimination and equality.[57] The Committee stressed that LGBT persons do enjoy some protection, but that anti-discrimination clauses are still scattered in several Acts and can

55 See the detailed analysis of Engle 2013.

56 Cf. Sun, Karmilah, Ong 2025, 1–21.

57 Third IRC – Report 2023, paras. 26–29.

easily be overlooked. The Committee further highlighted that there still is no comprehensive anti-discrimination legislation covering all grounds of discrimination in all contexts (para. 28).

It is up to civil society at all levels, especially at university, in NGOs, and particularly in the National Human Rights Commission (NHRC), but also up to the relevant government departments, to utilize the civil society influence on government to bring about the needed changes in approach and law for the benefit of all LGBT people.

III. Conclusion

The contribution looks at the historical setting of LGBT rights at the universal level, placing particular emphasis on the *Yogyakarta Principles* drafted by eminent international law specialists in 2006 and 2017, where 29 areas of serious discrimination against LGBT persons are analyzed meticulously. The Principles declare that many of those discriminations already clearly violate existing human rights guarantees, but also pre-cast future developments. State practice in the last 20 years shows that the Yogyakarta Principles, although as such not fully not legally binding, have strongly influenced positions taken by many States. Then follows a short description of the right to non-discrimination at the universal and regional levels, highlighting the challenges posed for same-sex families. By way of example, LGBT family relations laws at the national level in Germany and Taiwan are then briefly assessed. A picture of mixed success and failure emerges, and as ILGA, Amnesty International, Human Rights Watch and other civil society organizations are closely examining, persistent attempts at improving the legal situation of LGBT families can be recorded, but counter-positions of large UN Member States like Russia, China, the USA and many other States render persistent attempts at improving family rights of LGBT persons a time-consuming, and often frustrating endeavour. Yet it is remarkable how civil society organizations, academia, National Human Rights Institutions, mass media programmes and individuals continue their attempts at improving the plight of LGBT persons, despite strong opposition from States and their institutions.

In sum, non-discrimination in all its ramifications proves to be the key to new interpretations of the Human Rights Covenants, the jurisprudence of regional and international institutions, amongst them the ECtHR and ECJ, as well as the European Fundamental Rights Charter (FRCh), plus primary and secondary EU-Law with LGBT relevance. Moreover, national legislative and administrative new approaches to previously challenged positions can be found in some States, such as in Germany or Taiwan, whose example can serve as "good" or even "best practices" for reticent other States. The tableau of existing human rights claimed against violations of LGBT persons is further strengthened by recourse to human dignity as an over-arching principle and *raison d'être* of all human rights.

References

Balzaretti, Sofia. 2016. La protection internationale des personnes LGBT au sein de l'Organisation des Nations Unies. Master's thesis, University of Lausanne.

Bell, Mark. 2001. "Sexual Orientation Discrimination in Employment: An Evolving Role for the European Union." In *Legal Recognition of Same-Sex Partnerships*, edited by Robert Wintemute and Mads Andenaes, 653–76. Oxford: Hart Publishing.

CESCR Statement No.16: An evaluation of the obligation to take steps to the 'maximum of available resources' under an optional protocol to the Covenant (38th sess.), E/C.12/2007/1 of 21 September 2007.

Chao, Kuo-Yu, et al., 2024. Gender Self-Identification: Opinions About Transgender Women from a National Online Survey in Taiwan, in Archives of Sexual Behaviour 53: 1885–1897, doi.org./10.1007/s10508-024-02819-3.

Chen, Jau-hwa. 2025. Kant as a Human Rights Defender and Educator, Manuscript, 1–11.

Chien, Chih-Chieh. 2012. "From 'Same Sex Marriage' to 'Pluralistic Family Arrangements': The Legislative Movement for Democratic Intimate Relationship." *Taiwan Human Rights Journal* 1, no. 3 (December): 187–201.

Chirwa, Danwood M. 2020. "Access to Water as a New Right in International, Regional and Comparative Constitutional Law." In *International Human Rights Law and Access to Water*, edited by Jorge E. Viñuales, 55–69.

Committee on Economic, Social and Cultural Rights. 2007. *An Evaluation of the Obligation to Take Steps to the "Maximum of Available Resources" under an Optional Protocol to the Covenant.* UN Doc. E/C.12/2007/1.

Committee on Economic, Social and Cultural Rights. 2009. *General Comment No. 20: Non-discrimination in Economic, Social and Cultural Rights (Art. 2, Para. 2 of the International Covenant on Economic, Social and Cultural Rights).* UN Doc. E/C.12/GC/20 (2 July 2009).

Concluding Observations on the Implementation of the International Human Rights Covenants, Third Report of Concluding Observations and

Recommendations adopted by the International Review Committee (IRC) Taipei, 13 May 2022.

Conway, Daniel and Emil Edenborg. 2025. Rainbow diplomacy: LGBTQ+ rights and everyday diplomatic practice at Pride, in International Affairs, 3, 1065–1086.

Council of the European Union. 2000a. *Council Directive 2000/43/EC of 29 June 2000 Implementing the Principle of Equal Treatment Between Persons Irrespective of Racial or Ethnic Origin.* Official Journal L180, 19.7.2000, 22–26.

Council of the European Union. 2000b. *Council Directive 2000/78/EC of 27 November 2000 Establishing a General Framework for Equal Treatment in Employment and Occupation.* Official Journal L303, 2.12.2000, 16–22.

Council of the European Union. 2003. *Council Directive 2003/86/EC of 22 September 2003 on the Right to Family Reunification.* Official Journal L251, 3.10.2003, 12–18.

De Groot, David. 2022. *The Rights of LGBTI People in the European Union.* European Parliamentary Research Service PE 729.426, 1–12.

Delatolla, Andrew. 2020. "Sexuality as a Standard of Civilization: Historicizing (Homo)colonial Intersections of Race, Gender and Class." *International Studies Quarterly* 64, no. 1: 148–52.

Engle, Eric. 2013. Transsexuality and Heteronormativity: Post-Categorical Law Before the German Constitutional Court, https:// dx.doi.org/10.2139/ssrn.2239203, accessed 30.7.2025.

Etinson, Adam. 2020. What's So Special About Human Dignity? Philosophy and Public Affairs 48, issue 4, 353–81.

European Commission. 2023. *Eurobarometer on Discrimination 2023: The Social Acceptance of LGBT People in the EU.* https://europa.eu/eurobarometer/surveys/detail/2972. Retrieved 17 June 2025.

European Parliament and Council. 2006. *Directive 2006/54/EC of 5 July 2006 on the Implementation of the Principle of Equal Opportunities and Equal Treatment of Men and Women in Matters of Employment and Occupation (Recast).* Official Journal L204, 26.7.2006, 23–36.

European Union Agency for Fundamental Rights and Council of Europe (FRA). 2018. *Handbook on European Non-Discrimination Law* edited by Roderick Liddel and Michael O'Flaherty, Luxembourg: Publications Office of the European Union.

European Union. 1997. *Treaty Amending the Treaty on European Union, the Treaties Establishing the European Communities and Certain Related Acts* (Amsterdam Treaty). Official Journal C 340, November 10, 1997.

European Union. 2000a. *Council Directive 2000/43/EC of 29 June 2000 implementing the principle of equal treatment between persons irrespective of racial or ethnic origin*. Official Journal of the European Communities L 180 (19 July): 22–26.

European Union. 2000b. *Council Directive 2000/78/EC of 27 November 2000 establishing a general framework for equal treatment in employment and occupation*. Official Journal of the European Communities L 303 (2 December): 16–22.

European Union. 2003. *Council Directive 2003/86/EC of 22 September 2003 on the right to family reunification*. Official Journal of the European Union L 251 (3 October): 12–18.

European Union. 2006. *Directive 2006/54/EC of the European Parliament and of the Council of 5 July 2006 on the implementation of the principle of equal opportunities and equal treatment of men and women in matters of employment and occupation (recast)*. Official Journal of the European Union L 204 (26 July): 23–36.

European Union. 2007. *Treaty of Lisbon Amending the Treaty on European Union and the Treaty Establishing the European Community*. Official Journal C 306, 13 December 2007.

Finck, Michèle. 2016. "The Role of Human Dignity in Gay Rights Adjudication and Legislation: A Comparative Perspective." *International Journal of Constitutional Law* 14 (1): 26–53.

FRA Handbook on European non-discrimination law, edited by Roderick Liddel and Michael O'Flaherty, 2018.

Halley, Janet. 2001. "Recognition, Rights, Regulation, Normalization: Rhetorics of Justification in the Same-Sex Marriage Debate." In *Legal Recognition of Same-Sex Partnerships*, edited by Robert Wintemute and Mads Andenaes, 97–112. Oxford: Hart Publishing.

Hsu, Han-Yu. 2022. "'I Agree with LGBT Rights, but…': Authoritarianism and Social Dominance Orientation Underlying Hypocritical Attitudes of Taiwan Society." *Frontiers in Psychology* Brief Research Report. https://doi.org/10.3389/fpsyg.2022.10

ILGA-Europe. 2025. *Annual Review of the Human Rights Situation of LGBTI People in Europe and Central Asia 2025: Rainbow Map*. Brussels: ILGA-Europe.

Kant, Immanuel. 1902–1968. *Metaphysik der Sitten*. Akademie-Ausgabe, Band IV. Berlin: Walter de Gruyter.

Kao, Ying-Chao, 2024.The coloniality of queer theory: The effects of "homonormativity" on transnational Taiwan's path to equality. 27.1/2, 136–53.

Kuan, Hsiao-Wei. 2019a. "LGBT Rights in Taiwan – The Interaction Between Movements and the Law." In *Taiwan and International Human Rights, Economics, Law, and Institutions in Asia Pacific*, edited by J. A. Cohen et al., 593–607. https://doi.org/10.1007/978-981-13-0_33.

Kuan, Hsiao-Wei. 2019b. "Marriage Equality and Legal Mobilization: The Litigation and Legislative Actions before Judicial Yuan Interpretation No. 748." *Taiwan Foundation for Democracy* 16, no. 1: 1–44.

Lau, Holning. 2020. Courts, the Law, and LGBT Rights in Asia, in Oxford ResearchEncyclopediaofPolitics,atdoi:10.1093/acrefore9780190228637.013.ORE_POL-01230.RI, accessed 30.7.2025.

Lorz, Ralph Alexander. 1992. Modernes Grund- und Menschenrechtsverständnis und die Philosophie der Freiheit Kants. Eine staatstheoretische Untersuchung an Maßstäben des Grundgesetzes für die Bundesrepublik Deutschland. Dissertation Marburg.

Lee, Po-Han. 2016. "LGBT Rights versus Asian Values: de/reconstructing the universality of human rights." *The International Journal of Human Rights* 20, no. 7: 978–992, 979 et seq.

Limburg Principles on the Implementation of the International Covenant on Economic, Social and Cultural Rights, UN doc. E/CN.4/1987/17, Annex.

Lin, Pei-Chun. 2025. "The Quest for Equality: Changes in the Taiwanese Legal Landscape for LGBTQ+ Rights." In *Riedel and Chen (eds.), in this volume.*

Lo, Iris Po Yee. 2024. "LGBTQ+ Families, Welfare, and Same-Sex Marriage Legalization in Taiwan: A Social Policy Perspective." *Social Policy & Society* 23, no. 2: 446–461. Cambridge.

Mickovski, Kiril. 2020. LGBT Rights: How Politization of LGBT Issues Leads to Violence Against Sexual Minorities. Master Thesis University of Venezia.

Moeckli, Daniel, Sangeeta Shah, and Sandesh Sivakumaran, eds. 2014. *International Human Rights Law.* 2nd ed. Oxford: Oxford University Press.

Moeckli, Daniel. 2018. "Interpretation of the ICESCR: Between Morality and State Consent." In *The Human Rights Covenants at 50: Their Past, Present and Future*, edited by Daniel Moeckli and Helen Keller, 48–74. Oxford: Oxford University Press.

Muders, Sebastian. 2020. "Human Dignity." *Rivista di estetica* 75: 84–103.

Nowak, Manfred. 2005. *UN Covenant on Civil and Political Rights: CCPR Commentary.* 2nd rev. ed. Kehl: N.P. Engel Verlag.

Rahman, Momin. 2014. "Queer Rights and the Triangulation of Western Exceptionalism." *Journal of Human Rights* 13, no. 3: 274–89.

Riedel, Eibe, Gilles Giacca, and Christophe Golay, eds. 2014. *Economic, Social and Cultural Rights in International Law: Contemporary Issues and Challenges*. Oxford: Oxford University Press.

Riedel, Eibe. 1999. "Universality of Human Rights and Cultural Pluralism." In *Constitutionalism, Universalism and Democracy: A Comparative Analysis*, edited by Christian Starck. Baden-Baden: Nomos.

Riedel, Eibe. 2005. "The Human Right to Water." In *Weltinnenrecht. Liber amicorum Delbrück*, edited by Klaus Dicke et al., 585–606. Berlin: Duncker & Humblot.

Riedel, Eibe. 2011. "New Bearings in Social Rights? The Communications Procedure under the ICESCR." In *Essays in Honour of Judge Bruno Simma*, edited by Ulrich Fastenrath et al., 574–89. Oxford: Oxford University Press.

Riedel, Eibe. 2013. "Global Human Rights Protection at the Crossroads: Strengthening or Reforming the System" in W. Breuer et al. (eds.) Der Staat im Recht, Festschrift für Eckart Klein, Duncker & Humblot, Berlin, 289–306.

Riedel, Eibe. 2015. "Core Obligations in Social Rights and Human Dignity." In *Von der Kultur der Verfassung: Festschrift für Friedhelm Hufen*, edited by Max Emanuel Geis et al., Munich: C. H. Beck, 79 – 91.

Riedel, Eibe. 2020a. "Human Rights Protection as a Principle". In *Oxford Handbook on the Friendly Relations Declaration*, edited by Jorge E. Viñuales. Oxford: Oxford University Press, 231–57.

Riedel, Eibe. 2020b. "Standards as Sources." *German Yearbook of International Law* 63: 369–417.

Riedel, Eibe. 2020c. "The Right to Health under the ICESCR – Existing Scope, New Challenges, and How to Deal with It." In *Cambridge Handbook on New Human Rights – Recognition, Novelty, Rhetoric*, edited by Andreas von Arnauld, Kerstin von der Decken, and Mart Susi, 107–23. Cambridge: Cambridge University Press.

Su, Tung-Chieh. 2022. "Tension and Negotiation among Judicial Review, Referendum, and Legislation: The Course of Legalizing Same-Sex Marriage in Taiwan." *Public Administration & Policy*, no. 74: 1–34.

Sun, Wenxiao, Abdullah Karmilah, and Sharon Ong Yong Yee. 2025. "Queer Identities and Marginalization in East and Southeast Asia: Promoting SDG5 Gender Equality and LGBTQ+ Rights". *SDGs Review* 5 (e03112): 1–21. Florida, USA.

United Nations Committee on Economic, Social and Cultural Rights (CESCR). 1990. *General Comment No. 3: The Nature of States Parties' Obligations (Art. 2, Para. 1 of the Covenant)*. E/1991/23, 14 December.

United Nations General Assembly. 1948. *Universal Declaration of Human Rights*. Resolution 217 A (III), December 10.

Waaldijk, Kees. 2001. "Towards the Recognition of Same-Sex Partners in European Union Law: Expectations Based on Trends in National Law." In *Legal Recognition of Same-Sex Partnerships*, edited by Robert Wintemute and Mads Andenaes, 638–651, at 641 et seq.

Waldron, Jeremy. 2020. "Human Dignity." In *The Oxford Handbook of Comparative Environmental Law*, edited by Jorge E. Viñuales and Emma Lees. Oxford: Oxford University Press, 23–37.

Walker, Kristen L. 2001. "United Nations Human Rights Law and Same-Sex Relationships: Where to from Here?" In *Legal Recognition of Same-Sex Partnerships*, edited by Robert Wintemute and Mads Andenaes. Oxford: Hart Publishing, 743–57.

Whisnant, Clayton. 2013. Male Homosexuality in West Germany: Between Persecution and Freedom 1945–69, New York Palgrave Macmillan.

Wintemute, Robert. 2001. "Strasbourg to the Rescue? Same-Sex Partners and Parents under the European Convention." In *Legal Recognition of Same-Sex Partnerships*, edited by Robert Wintemute and Mads Andenaes, Oxford: Oxford University Press, 713–29.

Yogyakarta Principles. 2007. *Yogyakarta Principles on the Application of International Human Rights Law in Relation to Sexual Orientation and Gender Identity*. Accessed July 30, 2025. https://www.yogyakartaprinciples.org.

D. The quest for equality: Changes in the Taiwanese legal landscape for LGBTQ+ rights

Pei-Chun Lin[1]

Abstract:

In 2019, Taiwan became the first country in Asia to legalize same-sex marriage, following the Constitutional Court's ruling in Judicial Yuan Interpretation No. 748 and the enactment of a special law. Although Interpretation No. 748 provided the judiciary with a framework to re-conceptualize discrimination, recent employment-related court cases continue to expose the persistence of hostile work environments and the enduring presence of a "separate but equal" mindset within Taiwanese society. At the same time, the judicial expansion of the concept of "gender discrimination" to include gender identity signals a growing recognition by Taiwanese courts that transgender individuals have the right to determine how they live – particularly in terms of their appearance and identity. Nevertheless, a more comprehensive understanding of what substantive equality means for LGBTQ+ individuals remains largely underdeveloped in both judicial reasoning and public discourse.

Keywords:

same-sex marriage, LBGTQ+ rights, Taiwan same-sex marriage, workplace discrimination

I. Introduction

In 2019, Taiwan became the first country in Asia to legalize same-sex marriage, as a new law came into effect[2] following the Constitutional Court's

---

1 Dr. Pei-Chun Lin is an Associate Professor in the MA Program in Human Rights at Soochow University, Taiwan. She holds a Ph.D. in Law from National Chengchi University, Taiwan. Her research focuses on international human rights law, children's rights, and the principles of equality and non-discrimination. The author wishes to express particular thanks to attorney Victoria Hsu for her insightful comments and valuable feedback on an earlier draft of this article.

2 In February 2019, the Executive Yuan, in accordance with the intent of SHIZI NO. 748 JIESHI (釋字第748號解釋) [Judicial Yuan Interpretation No. 748] (2017) made by the Constitutional Court, proposed the "Act for Implementation of Judicial Yuan Interpretation No. 748". The law took effect on 24 May 2019. See the news report: *Marriage Equality Comes to Taiwan in a Historic First in Asia*, The Time Magazine (May 23, 2019), https://time.com/5594339/

ruling in Interpretation No. 748. The Constitutional Court declared that the Civil Code, which had previously prohibited two people of the same sex from forming a permanent and exclusive union for the purpose of living together[3], violated the constitutional principles that guarantee the freedom of marriage and equality for all citizens[4]. It is important to note that one of the petitioners for Interpretation No. 748, Chi Chia-Wei (祁家威), had submitted Taiwan's first same-sex marriage application to the court back in 1986[5]. For Chi Chia-Wei, Interpretation No. 748 represents a 30-year journey in the pursuit of equality.

While a groundbreaking moment for local LGBTQ+[6] activism, the new law did not grant same-sex couples the same rights as heterosexual couples. Since then, supporters of same-sex marriage legalization have continued their efforts to challenge discriminatory policies and practices in various areas, including around adoption, transnational marriages and transgender discrimination.

To explore the development of LGBTQ+ equality in the law in Taiwan, this chapter first provides an overview of the background and content of Interpretation No. 748. It then examines major court cases that followed the interpretation and provides an analysis of the legal landscape and the evolving understanding of equality in terms of LGBTQ+ rights.

II. Legalization of same-sex marriage

1. The quest for same-sex marriage legislation

In 1986, when Taiwan was still under martial law, the country witnessed its first public demand for same-sex marriage. At the age of 28, Chi Chia-Wei held a press conference to come out as a gay man and declare his commitment to promoting HIV prevention and advocating for same-sex marriage, making him the first openly gay man in Taiwan. In the same year, Chi Chia-Wei submitted a petition to the Legislative Yuan, requesting the prompt le-

taiwan-gay-rights/. The official English translation of the Judicial Yuan Interpretation No. 748 is available at https://cons.judicial.gov.tw/en/docdata.aspx?fid=100&id=310929 (hereinafter J.Y. Interpretation No. 748).

3 Section 1 of the Marriage Chapter of the Civil Code, Article 972, stipulated: "An agreement to marry shall be made by the male and the female parties in their own [con]cord."

4 The violations specifically related to Article 7 and Article 22 of the Taiwanese Constitution, which guarantee equality for all citizens and the freedom of marriage, respectively.

5 Details of their application are discussed below.

6 Lesbian, gay, bisexual, transgender, and queer (LGBTQ+).

galization of same-sex marriage. This petition for "prompt legislative actions to legalize same-sex marriages" was met with the response that homosexuals are a minority perversion, merely seeking to satisfy their sexual desires, and that "same-sex marriage is incompatible with the provisions of our nation's Civil Code, which provides for one-man-and-one-woman marriage. It is not only in conflict with good morals of the society, but also incompatible with our national conditions and traditional culture"[7]. This individual effort to legalize same-sex marriage did not gain widespread attention, and it wasn't until a decade later, when renowned writer Xu You-Sheng and his foreign partner held Taiwan's first publicly recognized same-sex wedding, that the issue sparked widespread social attention and discussion (Chien 2012).

At the same time, Taiwan's LGBTQ+ movement started to emerge in the 1990s when the first lesbian group, Between Us, was established. It is worth noting that same-sex activity or relationships have never been criminalized, nor have they been punished or prohibited, by law in Taiwan. With the proliferation of LGBT groups in 1995 and 1996 (Chien 2012, 189), however, such issues came to the forefront. For example, women's groups sought an amendment to the Civil Code to include "same-sex sexual relations or violent behaviors" as one of the grounds for filing for divorce in the Civil Code amendment. Ultimately, though, backlash from society and a series of controversial events[8] put a halt to these initial quests for same-sex marriage by LGBTQ+ groups. It was not until 2006, when legislator Bi-khim Hsiao (蕭美琴) proposed the "Same-Sex Marriage Bill", that LBGTQ+ and women's groups united to put same-sex marriage and partnership rights on their combined agenda and advocated for the draft "Partnership Act".

Chih-chieh Chien, looking back at the collaborative efforts of women and LGBTQ+ groups during this period, observed that while the aim of the proposed Partnership Act aimed to challenge the definition of intimate relationships at that time to include broader forms, including cohabiting couples who were not married, it was nonetheless "an empty concept, with expectations from various parties but no substantial content in the context of the discussion at that time" (Chien 2012, 193).

7 See J.Y. Interpretation No. 748.

8 For example, the "Changde Street Incident" in 1997, where police conducted large-scale raids on LGBTQ+ individuals near a park where gay people typically gathered. On 30 July 1997, six or seven armed police officers surrounded around 40 to 50 LGBTQ+ individuals on the street, forcing them to hand over their IDs and pushing them onto police vehicles. They were then wrongfully registered and photographed at the police station.

Subsequent efforts by various groups to advance same-sex marriage legislation through the Legislative Yuan–including the draft proposed by legislator Mei-Nu Yu (尤美女) and other members of the Democratic Progressive Party, as well as the bill drafted by the Taiwan Alliance to Promote Civil Partnership Rights (TAPCPR) around 2012–ultimately failed. In light of enduring legislative barriers, the imperative to pursue a parallel path to legal recognition through the judiciary became increasingly apparent (Tsu 2019).

2. The concept of equality for LGBTQ+ people in the Constitutional Court

In 2015, nearly 30 years after Chi Chia-Wei first publicly demanded same-sex marriage, his petition for constitutional interpretation on the issue was considered by the Constitutional Court[9]. Chi Chia-Wei's petition was backed by the TAPCPR's team of lawyers. During the press conference, an emotional Chi Chia-Wei tearfully expressed that he was no longer fighting alone, "now that so many lawyers are willing to stand up and help me realize this goal". He knelt to thank the legal team, creating an emotional moment that was widely covered by the media (PTS Plus n.d.). As Taiwan's first openly gay man and an inspiration to many social activists involved in the LGBTQ+ rights movement, it is believed that Chi Chia-Wei's collaboration with LGBTQ+ organizations to file for constitutional interpretation held historic significance (Kuan 2019, 21–22).

Scholar Hsiao-Wei Kuan has traced the constitutional interpretation process in detail and noted that the Marriage Equality Coalition, through their "One Person, One Story, Write to the Constitutional Court" initiative, collected a total of 57 real-life stories from the LGBTQ+ community, highlighting inequalities in labor rights, social welfare, and taxation. The coalition also gathered 14 amicus curiae briefs from a wide range of contributors, including legal scholars, lawyers, gender studies institutes at three Taiwanese universities, and pastors. These amicus curiae briefs were submitted to the Judicial Yuan, marking the first time in Taiwan's democratic history that "informal amicus curiae briefs" were presented to it (Kuan 2019, 23–24).

9 In 2013, Chi Chia-Wei's application for marriage registration was rejected by the local household registration office. He subsequently initiated administrative litigation, which was ultimately dismissed by the Supreme Administrative Court in September 2014. Following this, in August 2015, he filed a petition for constitutional interpretation with the Constitutional Court.

Interpretation No. 748 was issued by the Constitutional Court on 24 May 2017, acknowledging that the freedom to marry is crucial for personal development and the preservation of human dignity. The interpretation stated that provisions in Chapter 2 of Title 4 of the Civil Code[10], which regulate marriage, do not allow two individuals of the same gender to form a permanent, intimate, and exclusive union for the purpose of living together. This contradiction undermines the intent of Article 22 of the Constitution, which protects the freedom to marry, and Article 7, which guarantees equality before the law for all citizens[11].

One of the most contentious issues[12] involved whether individuals with same-sex sexual orientation have the freedom to choose their marriage partners and whether they are entitled to the same equal protection of marriage freedom as those with opposite-sex sexual orientation. For example, the Taipei City Government, as one of the petitioners, argued that the Civil Code's differential treatment between "same-sex partners" and "heterosexual partners" prevents same-sex unions from enjoying the same marriage protections as those of heterosexual couples. This sends a message to the world that LGBTQ+ individuals are treated as second-class citizens, rather than as equal members of the nation (Taipei City Government 2017, 42–44).

The Constitutional Court invited six legal experts to provide their opinions during the oral arguments[13]. While the experts had differing views on

10 The provisions of Chapter 2 include Article 972, *supra* note 3, and Section 2 of the same chapter outlines the substantive and formal requirements for marriage.

11 Articles 7 and 22, 23 of the Constitution provide the following.
Article 7: "All citizens of the Republic of China, irrespective of sex, religion, race, class, or party affiliation, shall be equal before the law."
Article 22: "All other freedoms and rights of the people that are not detrimental to social order or public welfare shall be guaranteed under the Constitution."

12 The major issues of this constitutional interpretation are: 1. Does Chapter 2, Title on Marriage, in Part 4 of the Civil Code allow two people of the same gender to marry? 2. If the answer to the first question is negative, does it violate the Constitution's guarantee of marriage freedom under Article 22? 3. If the answer to the first question is negative, does it violate the Constitution's guarantee of equality under Article 7? 4. If the legislature creates an alternative system to marriage (such as civil unions for same-sex couples), does it align with the constitutional guarantees of equality under Article 7 and marriage freedom under Article 22?.

13 Article 13(1) of the Constitutional Court Procedure Act (previously known as Judicial Yuan Justices Procedure Act) allows for oral arguments or investigations for controversial matters, either at the request of the petitioner or as required by the Court, in order for the Justices to gain further clarification on important points of dispute, receive professional opinions, and enhance the credibility of the proceedings. Chi Chia-Wei applied for oral arguments in accordance with this provision. The Court not only granted its permission but also allowed, for the first time in Taiwanese constitutional history, for the hearing to be publicly broadcast via live-streaming.

whether the current Civil Code is unconstitutional[14], they all shared the same perspective that the Constitution ought to provide some form of protection to same-sex couples. In the end, the Constitutional Court affirmed the right of same-sex couples to marry, arguing that, like opposite-sex couples, same-sex partners also seek marriage as a means to maintain social order. This rests on the concept that similar cases must be treated alike, drawing a comparison between LGBTQ+ individuals and heterosexuals. The Court also reaffirmed that recognizing marriage equality for same-sex couples would not harm social order. Therefore, restricting the marriage freedom of same-sex couples cannot be justified as "reasonable differential treatment" under the equality test. Scholar Chen criticizes the Court's conclusion for completely disregarding the inequalities within heterosexual marriages and the inequality faced by unmarried individuals, "as if simply entering into marriage would automatically grant equality" (Chen 2021, 2).

Interpretation No. 748 is not the first time that the Constitutional Court has touched upon the issue of "marriage" in Taiwanese laws. In previous interpretations, the Constitutional Court had emphasized that marriage should be a permanent union between one man and one woman for the purpose of living together. This permanent union, arising from marriage, not only allows the spouses to support and rely on each other spiritually and materially, but also extends to serve as the foundation for family and society[15].

The Constitutional Court, however, refrained from ruling on the specific form through which equal protection of marriage freedom should be achieved, leaving this thorny issue to the legislature. The Court only went to the extent of requiring the relevant authorities to amend or enact the necessary laws within two years from the publication of its interpretation. By pointing to the legislative freedom in forming laws, the Constitutional Court effectively avoided one of the most hotly debated issues: namely, "whether to amend the Civil Code or enact a special law to achieve marriage equality for LGBTQ+ individuals" (Huang 2018, 32). In the ensuing debate between whether to pursue the "Civil Code approach" or the "Special Law approach", the legislature ultimately chose the latter, but also

---

14 For example, on the issue regarding whether or not it is a violation of the right to equality if the Civil Code does not allow same-sex marriage at least two of the six legal experts were of the opinion that it is not a violation of the Constitution, one of the reasons being that traditionally, heterosexual marriage is a naturally formed institution, not one intentionally created by law to impose restrictions on specific groups. Therefore, if same-sex couples are provided with full legal protections but are not given the title of marriage, it would not create institutional discrimination.

15 For example, Interpretations No. 242, 362, and 552, which dealt with bigamous marriages, as well as Interpretation No. 554, which ruled on the criminality of the act of adultery.

adopted an unprecedented approach in naming the special law it enacted after the Constitutional Court's interpretation number (Su 2022, 19–20)[16].

On 17 May 2019, just before the deadline set by Interpretation No. 748[17], the Legislative Yuan enacted the "Act for Implementation of Judicial Yuan Interpretation No. 748" (the 748 Implementation Act), a special law to enable same-sex marriage. This special law allows same-sex couples to register their marriage and grants them rights and obligations similar to, but not exactly the same as, those of parties to a marriage under the Civil Code. However, as argued, by avoiding making a decision in the debate between amending the law and enacting a special law, the Constitutional Court effectively allowed the option of "enacting a special law" – a legislative choice that inherently creates a "'separate but equal' phenomenon", which raises significant constitutional concerns (Huang 2018, 34–35). Legal scholars have questioned this conclusion by asking whether the "separate but equal" situation created by the "enactment of a special law" model can still be considered a form of equality? (Huang 2018, 38). In other words, if the law chooses to isolate LGBTQ+ individuals from the general marriage system, legally categorizing them as special and drawing a distinction between "us" and "others" outside of society, can equality be considered achieved for LGBTQ+ individuals?[18]

It is worth noting that the outcome of the Constitutional Court prompted opponents of the legalization of same-sex marriage to intensify their efforts toward initiating a referendum. In early 2018, they launched a referendum comprising three proposals: the Referendum on the Definition of Marriage,

---

16 The difficulty was that, if the special law proposed by the Executive Yuan was titled "marriage", it may provoke strong backlash from anti-same-sex marriage groups. However, if the special law was not titled "marriage", but used other terms like "partnership", it may have been argued that it was not consistent with Interpretation No. 748.

17 During the two-year period left by the Constitutional Court, a referendum was held and the two questions put forward: 1. "Do you agree that the Civil Code's marriage provisions should be limited to a union between one man and one woman?"; 2. "Do you agree to protect the rights of two people of the same sex to live together permanently through a form other than the marriage provisions in the Civil Code?" For more information on the referendum, see Su, T.-C., *id*, at 12–17.

18 A leading LGBTQ group in Taiwan describes the special law approach as follows: "By separating same-sex couples, they cannot directly apply the existing Civil Code marriage provisions, but instead a separate set of laws (or special chapters, or specialized clauses) must be created for same-sex couples. The 'special law' in this round of discussions can take the form of 'same-sex partner law,' 'same-sex marriage law,' 'special chapter in the Civil Code for same-sex partners,' 'same-sex partner rights protection law,' or 'same-sex marriage agreement'... Regardless of the name, the goal is the same: to create a distinction between heterosexual and homosexual relationships, and the purpose of this distinction is to allow heterosexuals to continue enjoying a legitimate status, while homosexuals can only be seen as a special category." TAPCPR, https://tapcpr.org/main-topics/marriage-equality/subject-speciallaw.

the Special Law Referendum, and the Referendum to Ban the Implementation of LGBT Education[19] – (commonly known as the "Protect the Family Referendum"). The purpose of this referendum was to urge the government to enact legislation protecting same-sex couples outside the scope of marriage as defined in the Civil Code (Su 2022, 15). The vote was held in November 2018, and all three proposals were passed by a substantial margin, effectively leaving the enactment of a special law to protect same-sex marriage as the only viable option under the constraint of complying with Interpretation No. 748 (Su 2022, 16).

Furthermore, to avoid sentiments from anti-LGBTQ+ groups, the term "same-sex marriage" is not used in the Act. Instead, "Article 2 relationship"[20] is adopted to refer to the partners in a same-sex marriage relationship. While the rights and obligations of same-sex marriage largely mirror those for heterosexual marriage outlined in the Civil Code, and the legal rights and obligations typically associated with spouses in marriage can be directly applied to same-sex couples, issues remain in areas such as adoption and the recognition of international marriages.

III. The ongoing journey from same-sex marriage to LBGTQ+ rights

1. "Forced coming out" and the problem of a comparator

The breakthrough in same-sex marriage paved the way for the LGBTQ+ rights movement in Taiwan to combat prejudice and discrimination. Since Interpretation No. 748, LGBTQ+ individuals have begun challenging discriminatory practices through the courts – something that was not seen before the legalization of same-sex marriage. These cases have primarily involved issues such as transgender individuals' use of dormitories, workplace discrimination, and access to gender affirming surgery.

19 The three referendum questions were: (1) Do you agree that the Civil Code should define marriage as the union between one man and one woman?; (2) Do you agree that the rights of two persons of the same sex living together in a permanent, committed relationship should be protected through means other than the Civil Code's provisions on marriage?; and (3) Do you agree that during the national education stage (elementary and junior high school), the Ministry of Education and schools at all levels should not implement LGBT education as stipulated in the Enforcement Rules of the Gender Equity Education Act?, respectively.

20 Article 2 of the 748 Implementation Act states: "Two persons of the same sex may form a permanent union of intimate and exclusive nature for the purpose of living a common life".

In June 2019, a highly publicized case became the first in Taiwan's judicial history where an intersex person won a civil lawsuit for workplace discrimination, with an intersex employee successfully challenging workplace discrimination in the Taipei District Court (Taiwan Taipei District Court 2020). The case confirmed that "forced coming out" constitutes hostile work environment and sexual harassment under the relevant laws[21], violating the individual's right to personality and requiring compensation for emotional distress[22].

The court, ruling in favor of the plaintiff who had been dismissed by the company on the ground that they had falsified their personnel form by marking "female", which did not match the sex category listed on their ID card, stated that the company not only failed to provide a friendly workplace environment but violated the relevant employment laws by forcing the plaintiff to resign[23]. The court took the view that although the plaintiff's gender was male on the ID card, their gender identity was female. This being the case, it was neither false nor misleading when the plaintiff selected their own gender identity when filling out the personnel form upon employment.

In another case[24], a transgender lesbian informed a company during a job interview that, due to their gender identity, they needed to use the women's restroom. The company did not object at the time of the interview, but subsequently made an inquiry to its female employees asking, "Would you mind sharing a restroom with someone who appears female but is biologically

21 Relying on the Sexual Harassment Prevention Act and the Gender Equality in Employment Act, the court elucidated in its judgment (at p. 8) that: "In the workplace, regardless of rank or gender, mutual respect should be maintained. Any words or actions that are sexually suggestive or discriminatory based on sex or gender, which create a hostile, coercive, or offensive work environment and improperly affect work, constitute sexual harassment. Such behavior infringes upon the legal rights to workplace freedom and personal dignity". See Taipei District Court, 2020 Nian Du Lao Su Zi No. 78 (109年度勞訴字第78號) (hereinafter Taipei District Court, 2020).

22 When the plaintiff applied for the front-desk position at the defendant company, they filled out their personal information and, due to their intersex characteristics and the discrepancy between their gender identity and the gender listed on their ID card, asked a supervisor how to fill out the gender field. The supervisor did not provide a clear answer, so the plaintiff selected female based on their gender identity. Later, two supervisors (the defendants in this case) asked the plaintiff to disclose their intersex characteristics to colleagues and stated that if any colleagues could not accept this, the plaintiff would have to leave the job. The plaintiff was then subjected to teasing about their gender identity during staff meetings.

23 The Court took the view that "gender can be distinguished into different aspects, including biological sex, gender expression, and gender identity. Biological sex refers to an individual's inherent physical condition, while gender identity, regardless of biological sex, represents an individual's personal sense of gender" (Taiwan Taipei District Court 2020).

24 See Taipei High Administrative Court, Su Zi Di No. 1077 (2020) (臺北高等行政法院判決109年度訴字第1077號) (hereinafter Taipei High Administrative Court, 2020).

male?". Concerns were raised by female workers[25] and the company suggested to the transgender jobseeker that, if hired, an accessible restroom on the first floor would be available for their use instead (Taipei High Administrative Court 2020). Feeling discriminated against, the transgender jobseeker filed a complaint against the company, after the company failed to respond to the jobseeker's inquiry about the interview results.

Relying on relevant provisions of the Gender Equality in Employment Act[26], which prohibits discrimination on the ground of gender or sexual orientation in the workplace, as well as Interpretation No. 748, the Taipei Administrative High Court's reasoning emphasizes the marginalization that transgender individuals face in Taiwanese society:

In Taiwan, individuals with same-sex sexual orientation have long been marginalized due to societal traditions and customs, resulting in their confinement to the "closet" and subjecting them to various forms of practical or legal exclusion or discrimination. Additionally, due to demographic factors, individuals with same-sex sexual orientation constitute a small, isolated minority in society. They have long been politically weak and have struggled to reverse their disadvantaged legal status through ordinary democratic procedures. Therefore, any differential treatment based on sexual orientation should be subject to a stricter standard of review to assess its constitutionality (referencing the interpretation of Constitutional Court Interpretation No. 748) (Taipei High Administrative Court 2020, Paragraph 7(1)).

The Court also acknowledged that the general concept of gender equality still revolved around "the binary distinction between male and female, which may lead individuals with gender dysphoria or same-sex sexual orientation to face discrimination due to their gender characteristics or identities that differ from mainstream societal norms and stereotypes" (Taipei High Administrative Court 2020, Paragraph 7(1)). The right to live according to one's gender identity is inseparable from personal dignity

25 Among the responses, there were indications that female employees "would wait for the transgender lesbian to finish using the restroom before using it themselves".

26 Most importantly, articles 7 and 31, which provide:
Article 7: "Employers shall not discriminate against applicants or employees because of their gender or sexual orientation in the course of recruitment, screening test, hiring, placement, assignment, evaluation and promotion. However, if the nature of work is only suitable to a specific gender, the above-mentioned restriction shall not apply."
Article 31: "After employees or applicants make prima facie statements of the discriminatory treatment, the employers shall shoulder the burden to prove the non-sexual or non-sexual-orientation factor of the discriminatory treatment, or the specific sexual factor necessary for the employees or the applicants to perform the job."

and individual autonomy, which are fundamental human rights protected under the Constitution.

In the court proceedings, the company argued that the concept of "discrimination" inherently entails a "factual comparison". Specifically, it asserted that a claim of discrimination may be substantiated "if it can be shown that the individual in question and a comparator share the same professional qualifications but are treated unequally due to a factor unrelated to job performance—or conversely, that they differ in qualifications but are treated the same due to such a factor" (Paragraph 3(2)). On this basis, the company contended that there are several homosexual employees within the organization and that no evidence of discriminatory conduct toward them had been presented.

The transgender jobseeker appeared in court dressed in female clothing, making a powerful statement: "If I don't speak up today, countless other transgender people may continue to suffer similar treatment in silence and without support. And who knows how many more years it would take before another transgender person—someone with the opportunity, the strength, and the courage to speak without fear—can stand up in court as I do now" (TAPCPR 2021a).

Upon considering the evidence, the Court found the company did not solely consider the jobseeker's ability to perform the job. The issue regarding the jobseeker's gender identity, which led to the restroom usage disagreement, clearly resulted in differential treatment, constituting "indirect adverse treatment" based on gender identity in the hiring process (Taipei High Administrative Court 2020, Paragraph 7(2)(3)). Moreover, addressing the company's proposed compromise – that the transgender jobseeker use the accessible restroom on the first floor, despite their office being located on the seventh floor, as an alternative to a gender-inclusive restroom – the court held that, although this may appear neutral, it in fact constituted an overreach by the employer. By disclosing the jobseeker's gender identity to third parties and soliciting other employees' opinions on their restroom use, the employer effectively forced the individual to conform to binary gender norms. Ruling in favor of the employee, the court found that these actions risked reinforcing stigma and invalidating the individual's gender identity (Taipei High Administrative Court 2020, Paragraph 7(2)(3)).

2. Evolving conceptions of gender equality and the need for an Equality Act

Both of the above cases were represented *pro bono* by the legal team at TAPCPR, the NGO that also represented Chi Chia-Wei in securing Interpretation No. 748. While there is a growing trend of LGBTQ+ discrimination litigation in Taiwan (TAPCPR 2021b), such cases remain relatively rare. The lack of incentives for victims of discrimination to seek redress in court is evident in the amount of civil damages awarded in the intersex case[27]. Additionally, the risk of encountering unsympathetic courts, judges unfamiliar with the specific challenges faced by LGBTQ+ individuals, and concerns over insufficient privacy protections may further discourage victims from pursuing legal claims.

Moreover, the facts of these cases make it clear that discrimination against LGBTQ+ individuals extends far beyond the issue of marriage equality. Incidents such as being asked to use an accessible restroom on a different floor or enduring a hostile work environment serve as vivid reminders of the long-discredited doctrine of "separate but equal," once used to justify racial segregation. But what does substantive equality entail for LGBTQ+ individuals in Taiwan? In a society shaped by a broader range of religious and cultural traditions than many Western countries, the path toward meaningful equality is not necessarily straightforward. This is evident in the recently proposed draft Non-Discrimination Act, where one of the most contentious issues during public consultations remains whether gender identity should be explicitly listed as a protected characteristic.

Nonetheless, the broader impact of Interpretation No. 748 cannot be overlooked. The above cases establish an expanded judicial interpretation of "gender discrimination", which includes gender identity, and reflects Taiwanese courts' acknowledgment that transgender individuals have the right to decide how to live, in what appearance and form. Taiwanese courts' recognition that LGBTQ+ individuals have the right to determine how they live – particularly with regard to appearance and identity – and their emphasis on the need for greater public dialogue to deepen understanding of gender, mark important steps toward advancing gender equality and inclusion. This evolving concept of discrimination places less emphasis on

27 In the 2019 intersex employment case, the plaintiff claimed approximately NT$536,676 (approximately US$18,889), but was awarded NT$200,000 (approximately US$6,666) in damages. In the transgender jobseeker case, the plaintiff did not file a civil lawsuit. Instead, a fine of NT$300,000 (approximately US$10,000) was imposed by the Taipei Administrative High Court.

identifying a direct comparator or rigidly applying the principle of treating like cases alike. Instead, it reflects a more nuanced understanding of inequality, which is actively reshaping the rights of LGBTQ+ individuals. At the same time, Interpretation No. 748 has served – and continues to serve – as a pivotal force in challenging and redefining the traditional binary gender framework.

IV. Conclusion

Although Interpretation No. 748 paved the way for Taiwan to become the first country in Asia to legalize same-sex marriage and provided the courts with a foundation to re-conceptualize discrimination – focusing more on an individual's right to self-identify, rather than being categorized within a binary sex framework – the 748 Implementation Act is a special law that left the broader concept of equality for LGBTQ+ individuals and groups open to interpretation.

Despite the fact that Interpretation No. 748 has been relied upon in subsequent court rulings in favor of LGBTQ+ individuals facing discrimination – particularly in workplace-related cases – the reasoning behind these decisions often lacks a nuanced explanation of how the individuality of LGBTQ+ groups, especially their unique experiences and challenges, should be considered. Parties' arguments inevitably tend to focus on comparing LGBTQ+ individuals to binary gender norms, leaving the deeper meaning of substantive equality for LGBTQ+ individuals largely unexplored.

References

Chen, Chao-ju. "Non-Marriage Jurisprudence: (In)equality Beyond Marriage." *Taiwan Jurists*, no. 3 (2021): 1–18.

Chien, Chih-chieh. "From 'Same Sex Marriage' to 'Pluralistic Family Arrangements': The Legislative Movement for Democratic Intimate Relationship." *Taiwan Human Rights Journal* 1, no. 3 (December 2012): 187–201.

CNN News. *A Glimpse into the Past: Chi Chia-wei, a Pioneer of Taiwan's LGBTQ Rights Movement.* March 8, 2024. https://www.cna.com.tw/news/ahel/202403075003.aspx.

Kuan, Hsiao-Wei. "Marriage Equality and Legal Mobilization: The Litigation and Legislative Actions before Judicial Yuan Interpretation No. 748." *Taiwan Foundation for Democracy* 16, no. 1 (March 2019): 1–44.

Hsu, Victoria. "The Unfinished Journey of Marriage Equality in Taiwan: My Movement Notes" (還沒走完的台灣婚姻平權之路：我的運動筆記) (January 31, 2019) https://www.gender.ey.gov.tw/Multimedia/System/Notes/DealData.aspx?sn=S76QK4jz899u7Khj0vJqDA@@.

Huang, Shih-Ping. "The Ambiguous Freedom of Legislative Formation: Guarantee or Obstacle to the Freedom of Marriage? – A Commentary on Judicial Yuan Interpretation No. 748." *Fu Jen Law Review* 55 (2018): 1–48.

PTS Plus. "How Did Chi Chia-wei Succeed in Promoting Marriage Equality in Taiwan?" *Undated.* https://issues.ptsplus.tv/articles/2610/.

Su, Tung-Chieh. "The Tension and Negotiation among Judicial Review, Referendum, and Legislation: The Course of Legalizing Same-Sex Marriage in Taiwan." *Public Administration & Policy*, no. 74 (2022): 1–34.

Taipei City Government. *Written Opinion on Issues for Oral Argument in Relation to Constitutional Interpretation No. 748.* March 23, 2017.

TAPCPR (Taiwan Alliance to Promote Civil Partnership Rights). *Facebook*, April 26, 2021a. Accessed May 10, 2025. https://www.facebook.com/tapcpr/photos/10158009309395965/.

TAPCPR. "The Kodak Hotel Discrimination Case, with a Judgment Awarding the Plaintiff NT$200,000 in Mental Distress Damages, Has Been Finalized!" January 12, 2021b. Accessed May 10, 2025. https://tapcpr.org/hot-news/press-release/2021/01/12/柯達飯店歧視雙性人案-判賠當事人20萬精神損害賠償判決確定

E. Making "Intersectionality" Through Human Rights Reporting: Sexual and Reproductive Health of Disabled Women

Chong-Min Su[1] and Po-Han Lee[2]

Abstract:

Although Taiwan's domestic laws do not explicitly recognize intersectionality, the concept has gradually informed human rights policymaking through the treaty implementation reviews of CEDAW, CRPD, ICCPR, ICESCR, CRC, and ICERD. This chapter examines how intersectionality and related methodologies have reshaped the discourse on sexual and reproductive health (SRH) for women with disabilities. By systematically reviewing state reports, non-governmental organization submissions, and International Review Committee documents from 2009 to 2022, it traces the shift from single-axis frameworks to more integrated analyses of gender and disability, arguing that treaty reviews have become a crucial site for articulating intersectional concerns, prompting both governmental and non-governmental actors to adopt a multilayered approach to discrimination. The case of SRH rights in Taiwan illustrates how intersectionality can function not only as an analytic tool but also as a political strategy for challenging structural inequality and advancing reproductive justice for women with disabilities.

Keywords:

Anti-Discrimination Act; Concluding Observations and Recommendations; Convention on the Elimination of All Forms of Discrimination Against Women; Convention on the Rights of Persons with Disabilities; documentary research; Feminist Disability Studies; Genetic Health Act; human rights monitoring; International Review Committee; intersectional discrimination; parallel reports; Reproductive Health Act; sexual and reproductive health; shadow reports; women with disabilities

---

1 Chong-Min Su is a PhD student in the Department of Public Health Sciences at Stockholm University. He received academic training in health policy and management, as well as public health, in Taiwan. His research interests encompass sexual and reproductive health, disability studies, human rights, and global health.

2 Po-Han Lee is an Associate Professor at the National Taiwan University Institute of Health Policy and Management. He serves as an editor for *Feminist Review*, *Sociology Compass*, and other academic journals. His publications include co-editing *Towards Gender Equality in Law* (Palgrave 2022), *Plural Feminisms* (Bloomsbury 2023), and *Feeling Taiwan* (Routledge 2026). pohanlee@ntu.edu.tw.

I. Introduction: Legal and policy contexts of reproductive rights

A global rollback in compliance with international human rights norms has increasingly threatened the sexual and reproductive health (SRH) rights of women and girls, particularly those with disabilities. In response to the regressive practices of many states, human rights scholars, advocates, and United Nations (UN) treaty bodies have voiced concern over limited access to elements recognized as central to women's reproductive health, such as essential and adequate services and information (Addlakha, Price, and Heidari 2017; Lee and Jhang 2023; Mofokeng 2021). In a joint statement, the Committee on the Elimination of Discrimination Against Women (CEDAW) and the Committee on the Rights of Persons with Disabilities (CRPD) reaffirm a human rights-based approach to SRH, emphasizing accessibility in legislative and policy processes and service delivery. Women must neither be stigmatized nor penalized for voluntarily terminating a pregnancy nor subjected to forced abortion or sterilization without informed consent – practices that women with disabilities in many societies have historically endured (CEDAW and CRPD 2018).

Under CEDAW, state parties are obligated to ensure equal access to health services, including those related to family planning (Article 12(1)). Denial of or inadequacy in SRH care constitutes gender-based discrimination (Cook and Dickens 2003), a position also reaffirmed by the Committee on Economic, Social, and Cultural Rights (CESCR). The CRPD, in General Comment No. 3 of 2016, further clarifies that states must guarantee disabled individuals equal access to affordable, quality, and gender-sensitive health programs and services, including in the SRH domain (Article 25(a)). Informed reproductive decision-making is now also widely acknowledged as an indicator of both gender equality and the protection of disability rights, especially at their intersection. A particularly underexplored issue in this domain concerns reproductive and healthcare decisions of women with disabilities, especially considering the political and ethical ambiguity surrounding resource allocation regarding (mis)treatment received by women with disabilities in clinical and other health-related settings. This has sparked legal debates worldwide and created tension in human rights discourses (Su and Lee 2025).

In this context, Taiwan provides a case study that reveals how the interplay between ableism and heteropatriarchy shapes reproductive policy and rights discourse. Despite having incorporated most of the major international human rights treaties (six out of the nine core UN treaties) into its domestic legal framework, Taiwan continues to criminalize abortion under the Criminal Code, permitting it only under a limited set of exceptions that reflect a biomedical and paternalistic view of reproductive decision-making (C.-C. Lin 2009). Since the enactment of the Genetic Health Act in 1984, abortion has been allowed in specific circumstances (Article 9(1)(2)), including:

1. She or her spouse acquires a genetic, infectious, or psychiatric disease detrimental to reproductive health.
2. Anyone within the fourth degree of a kin relative of herself or her spouse acquires a genetic disease detrimental to reproductive health.
3. By medical consideration, pregnancy or delivery may cause life-threatening risks or harm to her physical and mental health.
4. By medical consideration, the risk of teratogenesis may be present for the fetus.
5. Pregnancy due to rape, lured into sexual intercourse, or in sexual intercourse with a man prohibited from marrying her lawfully.
6. Pregnancy or childbirth will likely affect her mental health or family life.

The law requires spousal consent for abortion or sterilization if the pregnant person is married (Article 10(1)). In cases where the individual is under guardianship or assigned legal assistance, the decision must also be approved by a legal representative (Articles 9(2) and 10(2)). Physicians are further obligated to advise patients to consider abortion or sterilization, reinforcing a top-down, medicalized approach to reproductive decision-making. Given these constraints, this chapter examines the development of intersectionality within Taiwan's human rights reporting framework, particularly concerning the SRH rights of women with disabilities. By analyzing state reports, non-governmental organizations (NGOs) submissions, and review outcomes from treaty monitoring bodies between 2009 and 2022, we trace how discourse around SRH rights has evolved – specifically, how women with disabilities have been structurally "disabled" from accessing these rights, and how the concept of "intersectionality" has been introduced through human rights reporting and review processes to address these concerns.

The discursive development of reproductive rights for women with disabilities in Taiwan has largely mirrored the global trend of integrating intersectionality into international human rights practice (de Beco 2020; P.P.-C. Lin 2020). Although CEDAW had already recognized the specific vulnerabilities of women with disabilities in its 1991 General Recommendation No. 18, it was not until the early 2000s that intersectionality gained formal traction in treaty interpretations. For instance, CESCR's 2005 General Comment No. 16 noted the structural nature of gender-based discrimination and the ways it intersects with other identities such as disability, class, and ethnicity (para. 5). The Convention on the Rights of Persons with Disabilities (CRPD), adopted in 2006, enshrines intersectional protection throughout its text, while CEDAW's 2010 General Recommendation No. 28 explicitly names intersectionality as essential to understanding states' core obligations (para. 18).

In Taiwan's 2014 review of the implementation of CEDAW, the Concluding Observations and Recommendations specifically urged the government to address intersectional discrimination. Since the CRPD and relevant disability rights norms and standards were incorporated into domestic law in the same year, intersectionality has become a recurring theme in state and civil society submissions across treaty reviews (P.P.-C. Lin 2020). This has led to increasing scrutiny of how reproductive policies affect women with disabilities and has gradually institutionalized intersectionality as a key framework for human rights-based monitoring.

II. Intersectional discrimination against women with disabilities

Under the influence of ableism, previous human rights research and rights advocacy have greatly excluded disabled individuals, subjecting them to societal scrutiny based on normative bodily standards (Alhusen et al. 2021). Since the 19th century, the rise of the biomedical model has framed disability as an individual abnormality, disorder, or deficiency that causes functional limitations – conditions presumed to require correction through medical diagnosis, treatment, or rehabilitation. Rooted in etiology, the biomedical model defines "disease" as a deviation from physiological norms, from which "disability" is subsequently derived. As medicalization intensifies, its reach extends from clinical settings into everyday life, pathologizing and marginalizing the diverse experiences of people with non-normative bodyminds (Garland-Thomson 1997, 2011). This dominance of medical knowledge reinforces disabled individuals' dependence on healthcare institutions, a key critique of the model: its conflation of non-normativity with pathology (Oliver and Barnes 2012).

In the 1970s, the Union of the Physically Impaired Against Segregation (UPIAS) in the UK launched an anti-institutional care movement, marking a turning point in disability rights advocacy. Vic Finkelstein, a central figure in UPIAS, was among the first to interpret disability through a social-structural lens, emphasizing systemic disadvantages over individual impairments. Building on this foundation, Michael Oliver introduced a sociological analysis that led to the development of the social model of disability, which has profoundly shaped the discourse on disability rights and service reform (Oliver and Barnes 2012). While the model acknowledges that impairments can cause functional limitations, it rejects ableist assumptions by locating disability within unjust social arrangements. Rather than attributing responsibility to individuals, it emphasizes institutional and environmental failures as key barriers to inclusion.

Under the dominance of the medical model, disabled people have often been expected to adapt to inaccessible environments or remain confined to segregated institutions. Ableist biases are entrenched in social attitudes, policy frameworks, and public institutions, reinforcing systemic marginalization. The social model challenges this exclusion by advocating for anti-discrimination measures to ensure equal rights, opportunities, and participation for individuals with disabilities (Sun 2019). However, while it effectively critiques structural barriers, it has also been criticized for failing to account for the diverse lived experiences of people with different types of impairments. This limitation has contributed to the emergence of the human rights model of disability (P.P.-C. Lin 2020; Sun 2019). Although the social and human rights models influence each other, they serve different purposes and focus on various subjects. In the human rights context, their roles are better understood as complementary and mutually supportive rather than overlapping or in competition (Lawson and Beckett 2021).

Articulated in the CRPD, the human rights model affirms that all individuals, including disabled people, are entitled to fundamental human rights. It recognizes the diversity within the disabled population and confirms that rights must not be diminished due to impairment, identity, or disability category. Given that individuals require varying levels of support, the model centers on the lived experiences of disabled people, positioning them as rights-holders rather than passive recipients of state welfare. Unlike earlier treaties that portray states as passive duty-bearers, the CRPD demands comprehensive systemic and institutional reforms and positive obligations, including personalized support to ensure that disabled persons can exercise their rights. It also emphasizes the reciprocal nature of rights and responsibilities, envisioning disabled people as active citizens. Substantive and, therefore, transformative equality – especially the recognition that denying reasonable accommodation constitutes discrimination – remains a foundational principle of the CRPD (Quinlivan 2019).

As noted, disabled women have historically been excluded from feminist discourse, in part due to enduring stereotypes that portray them as passive, dependent, or desexualized (Hall 2011). Similarly, early disability rights movements have been critiqued for being male-centered, often neglecting the unique experiences of disabled women. These women experience both patriarchal and ableist oppression, which intersect to create layered and compounding forms of discrimination (Sommo and Chaskes 2013). Intersectionality theory has thus become vital in understanding the complex ways that systems of oppression affect disabled women. Coined by Black feminists in the late 1980s, intersectionality critiques the limitations of the single-axis analysis, which treats forms of marginalization, such as racism or sexism, as independent and mutually exclusive (e.g., Crenshaw 1991). Past feminist approaches often fail to capture the compounded experiences of individuals of multiple marginalized identities. Instead, intersectionality acknowledges that group members are not homogeneous and may experience overlapping, context-dependent forms of discrimination.

While it originated in Black feminist thought, the concept has since been widely applied in disability studies to examine how multiple marginalized identities intersect to shape lived experiences of oppression. Early intersectional studies on disabled women often employed the "double disadvantage" framework, treating different forms of oppression as additive. However, this approach risks oversimplifying complex realities by failing to address the relational and intersubjective aspects of an event of discrimination and the person discriminating vis-à-vis the person being discriminated against (Nicki 2001; Wendell 1989). In response, Black disability feminist scholar Ayesha Vernon proposed a multiple oppression framework, emphasizing that different identity categories become salient depending on specific social and political contexts (Vernon 1999). The increasing recognition of intersectional discrimination has also influenced international human rights discourse. Under the leadership of Mary Robinson, then UN High Commissioner for Human Rights, treaty bodies began incorporating intersectional analyses into their interpretations.

As the first major human rights treaty of the 21st century, the CRPD explicitly acknowledges intersectional and multiple forms of discrimination in its preamble and provisions. Article 6 of the CRPD specifically addresses the compounded forms of discrimination that women with disabilities face. Resonating with intersectional disability research, Rosemarie Garland-Thomson developed Feminist Disability Studies (FDS), a field that bridges feminist and disability studies (Garland-Thomson 2002). FDS examines how historical, cultural, and material forces construct discriminatory value systems that uniquely impact disabled women, who may face both double and multiple marginalizations. Drawing from the social model of disability, FDS rejects the notion that disability is a personal tragedy or defect, instead framing it as a form of bodymind diversity (Nicki 2001). It argues that the functional limitations experienced by disabled individuals often result not from impairment itself but from failures in public policy and social infrastructure to accommodate different bodies.

As previously discussed, the portrayal of disabled women as passive or dependent has led to their exclusion from mainstream feminist movements – and, at times, has placed disability justice in conflict with feminist claims. This is especially evident in debates over reproductive autonomy and motherhood, in which mainstream feminist ideals of independence clash with calls for interdependence from disability perspectives. FDS critiques the abstraction of setting "independence" as a feminist goal, instead advocating for the recognition of "interdependence" as a fundamental aspect of human life (Fonow and Cook 2005). FDS challenges the structures of exclusion that operate at the intersection of gender and disability. It reimagines the knowledge produced through lived experiences of disabled women as central to broader social justice efforts. Garland-Thomson identifies four key research areas in FDS: representation, body image, identity, and activism (Garland-Thomson 2005a).

Representation is the process through which meaning is assigned to the material world, shaped by language, cultural values, discursive framing, metaphors, and knowledge production. Gender and disability identities are constructed through these processes and often reflect historical power imbalances. Cultural norms have long reinforced dominant narratives that marginalize alternative perspectives. For instance, Aristotle's depiction of women as "incomplete men" positioned them as "the Other", subjecting them to exclusion and control. Similarly, ableist ideologies portray disabled individuals as incapable of contributing to or participating in society, thereby justifying their marginalization. Garland-Thomson also contends that FDS, drawing on theoretical and ethical implications of intersectionality as a methodology, seeks to disrupt these dominant representations and reframe the identities and social roles of disabled women from their perspectives (Garland-Thomson 2005b).

Therefore, for this chapter, we define intersectionality as a critical analytical framework for understanding the ways in which multiple and overlapping forms of discrimination – such as those based on gender, race, ethnicity, class, disability, health conditions, sexual orientation, gender identity, and other social categories – interact to shape an individual's lived experiences. In the context of human rights, intersectionality offers a lens through which we can identify the mechanisms that make legal, political, and social structures systematically exclude or disadvantage individuals or groups of people whose identities span multiple marginalized groups (Cho, Crenshaw, and McCall 2013). It underscores the importance of inclusive policy design and legal frameworks that recognize and address the complexity of these interlocking forms of oppression.

III. Presenting "intersectionality" through human rights reporting

Since Taiwan began incorporating core international human rights treaties into its domestic legal framework in 2009, women's and disability rights advocates have repeatedly called for amendments to the Genetic Health Act, including renaming it as the Reproductive Health Act [生育保健法/shēngyù-bǎojiàn-fǎ] and revising discriminatory language related to induced abortion and sterilization. To better protect the reproductive and bodily autonomy of women with disabilities, advocates have also emphasized the need to remove physicians' legal obligation to advise individuals to undergo abortion or sterilization. They have also pushed for the establishment of support systems that enable people under guardianship to participate meaningfully in reproductive decision-making. However, no substantive progress has been achieved despite eight major amendment proposals submitted by the Executive and Legislative Yuan since 2009 (Su 2023). Meanwhile, abortion remains a criminal offense under the Criminal Code.

Against this backdrop, we have employed a systematic documentary research approach to examine the protections afforded to the reproductive health and rights of women with disabilities in Taiwan. Although Taiwan is not a UN member, it has nonetheless incorporated five/six core human rights treaties into domestic law – namely, besides CRPD, the International

Covenant on Civil and Political Rights (ICCPR), the International Covenant on Economic, Social and Cultural Rights (ICESCR), the Convention on the Rights of the Child (CRC), the Convention on the Elimination of All Forms of Discrimination Against Women (CEDAW) (J.-J. Lin and Chang 2023; Sun 2019). Notably, Taiwan, represented by the government of the Republic of China, signed and ratified the International Convention on the Elimination of All Forms of Racial Discrimination (ICERD) in 1965. As such, the treaty has been considered binding upon Taiwan. However, it was not enforced until 2023, when the initial state report was submitted.

Based on the Implementation Acts regarding each human rights treaty, the government regularly convenes International Review Committees composed of independent human rights experts to monitor treaty implementation. However, no Implementation Act has been enacted to explicitly incorporate ICERD's provisions into domestic law, thereby positioning ICERD in a unique place within Taiwan's legal framework (Teng 2019; Liao 2010). These committees review state reports and NGOs' parallel reports, provide a List of Issues (LOI), and hear oral statements and responses from government representatives and civil society (Chang 2019; Teng 2019). Parallel reports are crucial in bringing forward civil society's diverse and sometimes divergent perspectives on issues, highlighting gaps or concerns overlooked or omitted in state reports prepared by agencies under the Executive Yuan (Alford, Hu, and Wharton 2019). Since the National Human Rights Commission (NHRC) was established under the Control Yuan in 2020, the NHRC has also submitted independent investigative reports and opinions on state submissions. Drawing on all available inputs, the International Review Committees produce Concluding Observations and Recommendations (COR), which commend progress and identify areas for improvement.

To examine how "intersectionality" has been introduced and developed within Taiwan's human rights protection framework, we collected all publicly available documents produced as part of the implementation reviews for the ICCPR, ICESCR, CEDAW, and CRPD from 2009 to 2022 (up until March 2023, see Figure 1). Our objective was to trace the emergence of the discourse of intersectionality – particularly its application to the SRH rights of women with disabilities – focusing on the evolving practices through documentation (Lee 2023). This methodology considers the role of human rights reporting as a site of norm diffusion and discursive negotiation (Alford, Hu, and Wharton 2019; P.P.-C. Lin 2020). Since 2012, ICCPR and ICESCR have undergone three joint review cycles, generating 107 documents, including reports from government agencies, NGOs' parallel submissions, responses from the NHRC, and International Review Committees' COR. Of these, 61 documents were analyzed, of which 46 NGO documents were not published online.

Figure 1 Timeline of human rights treaty reviews in Taiwan (with key reviews highlighted).

Moreover, CEDAW and CRPD have undergone four and two reviews, respectively, since 2009 and 2017. Remarkably, the first CEDAW review took place before the treaty's Implementation Act was passed; instead of an international review, the government convened eight thematic consultation meetings with NGOs and individual experts, among whom disabled women were not represented, and their experiences were not considered. Including these meeting records, we reviewed 87 CEDAW-related and 30 CRPD-related documents. With triangulation between the two authors, we examined the frequency and contextual framing of key terms – such as "disabilit*" [障礙/zhàng-ài], "pregnan*" [懷孕/huái-yùn], genetic health [優生保健/yōu-shēng-bǎo-jiàn], and reproductive health [生育保健/sheng-yù-bǎo-jiàn] (see Table 1). Our analysis has attended to intersectional concerns raised regarding those affecting women with disabilities. SRH has been a key entry point through which intersectionality is introduced, voiced, and gradually recognized in Taiwan's human rights monitoring practices.

Convention		Government			NGOs			NHRC		Review Committee	Total
		Reports	Replies to LOI	Replies to previous COR	Parallel reports	Replies to LOI	Replies to previous COR	Opin-ions	Replies to LOI	COR	
ICCPR & ICESCR	1st* (2012)	3	2	0	2	0	0	0	0	1	**8**
	2nd** (2016)	3	2	1	2	1	1	0	0	1	**11**
	3rd*** (2020)	3	4	1	9	22	0	1	1	1	**42**
	Sum	**9**	**8**	**2**	**13**	**23**	**1**	**1**	**1**	**3**	**61**
CEDAW	1st**** (2009)	1	0	0	8	0	0	0	0	1	**10**
	2nd (2014)	3	1	0	24	0	0	0	0	1	**29**
	3rd (2018)	2	1	0	19	1	0	0	0	1	**24**
	4th (2022)	2	1	0	17	1	0	1	1	1	**24**
	Sum	**8**	**3**	**0**	**68**	**2**	**0**	**1**	**1**	**4**	**87**
CRPD	1st (2017)	2	1	0	3	4	0	0	0	1	**11**
	2nd (2021)	3	1	1	4	7	0	1	1	1	**19**
	Sum	**5**	**2**	**1**	**7**	**11**	**0**	**1**	**1**	**2**	**30**

* 15 parallel reports from NGOs were unavailable online.

** 7 parallel reports and 6 replies to LOI from NGOs were unavailable online; 2 parallel reports and 1 reply to LOI from NGOs were undisclosed.

*** 11 parallel reports and 4 replies to the LOI from NGOs were undisclosed.

**** No parallel report from NGOs in the first international review. Instead, 8 meeting records with NGOs and governmental agencies were included.

Table 1: Summary of documentary data collection

1. Before 2014: Disabled women as a "category" of disadvantage

During the initial CEDAW review, both governmental agencies and various stakeholders discussed the prenatal examination and abortion services provided under the Genetic Health Act, whose formal title in Chinese is "優生保健法" [yōu-shēng-bǎo-jiàn-fǎ]. Translated literally as a law for "eugenic health", the title carries discriminatory connotations. Hence, recommendations were made to rename the law as the Reproductive Health Act. Among the services provided under the Act, "fertility regulation for specific groups" includes medical interventions that specifically target women with disabilities. According to the Act, "specific groups" refer to individuals – or their spouses or children – diagnosed with mental illnesses or other conditions deemed detrimental to biogenetic health. These include diseases being specified, such as sexually transmitted infections, genetic disorders, and rare diseases. Eligibility is further determined by holding an official disability certificate or being registered as a low-income household. The prescribed "fertility regulation" measures include intrauterine device (IUD) insertion and sterilization procedures.

Furthermore, in the first state report on the ICESCR in 2012, the government, for the first time, noted that women with disabilities are entitled to more subsidized prenatal examinations than the general population under the Genetic Health Act. However, the report framed women with disabilities through a medicalized, risk-based lens, identifying them as a "high-risk pregnancy group" or as "individuals with medical needs". It is noteworthy that NGOs' shadow reports during the same review process did not address SRH issues among women with disabilities.

Early human rights treaty reviews did not explicitly adopt an intersectional approach, and the discourse surrounding SRH issues for women with disabilities was embedded in the category of "specific groups" under the Genetic Health Act. This framing portrayed women with disabilities as "high-risk populations" or "targets for genetic disease prevention", and the services provided were grounded in a logic of fertility control rather than in supportive care or rights-based protection. While the Genetic Health Act does include maternal and child health measures (e.g., prenatal screenings, genetic testing, and legally permitted exceptions for abortion), it also promotes the improvement of "quality of population", a framing that reflects a eugenic and discriminatory stance toward persons with disabilities and other marginalized groups. This has led to repeated calls for the Act to be renamed and amended.

2. Turning point: The CEDAW and CRPD review in 2014 and 2017

In the second CEDAW review in 2014, the state report continued to justify the existence of the Genetic Health Act, citing the lack of social and political consensus without providing substantive updates. In contrast, the parallel report led by the League for Persons with Disabilities, informed by the norms of the right to health, emphasized that disabled women face numerous physical and social barriers when accessing SRH services, including cervical and breast cancer screenings, prenatal care, and childbirth services. Meanwhile, there were no tailored SRH services available for pregnant persons with disabilities, and the government had failed to implement Article 21 of the People with Disabilities Rights Protection Act, which mandates accessibility of SRH services to persons with disabilities. This review marked the first time a human rights treaty body formally urged the government to examine the environmental and structural factors affecting SRH access for women with disabilities and to move beyond a risk-based or controlling approach toward one that provides supportive care.

In its COR regarding the implementation of CEDAW, the International Review Committee explicitly stated that Taiwan's legal framework failed to address the multiple and intersecting forms of discrimination experienced by women, including those with disabilities. The Committee requested the government assess the specific circumstances of women with disabilities (especially women with intellectual disabilities), emphasizing that health policies must go beyond disease prevention to ensure equitable access to healthcare for marginalized groups to mitigate intersectional discrimination.

During the first CRPD review in 2017, the state report continued to frame SRH issues for women with disabilities within the context of the Genetic Health Act. However, it included more extensive statistical data on "specific groups" receiving prenatal and fertility regulation services. By this time, the Committee reviewing CRPD-related progress had already begun to focus on the intersectional discrimination faced by women with disabilities. In its LOI, the Committee raised several detailed questions, including how proposed amendments to the Genetic Health Act would safeguard the bodily integrity of people with disabilities and what concrete measures were being taken to protect and promote their SRH rights, both at present and in the future. These questions made it difficult for the government to neglect SRH concerns. In response, the government outlined measures such as improving the accessibility of healthcare facilities and providing disability awareness training for health professionals.

Meanwhile, NGOs continued to expand and deepen their focus on intersectional discrimination faced by women with disabilities in accessing SRH services. For example, the League for Persons with Disabilities and its allies emphasized the urgent need for comprehensive and accessible sexuality education, reproductive health services, and parenting support, calling for policies that directly address structural discrimination. In addition, the parallel report led by Covenants Watch urged the government to investigate cases of forced sterilization and abortion. In its COR, the International Review Committee for CRPD implementation criticized the government's lack of concrete policy measures to address the intersectional identities of women with disabilities. It expressed deep concern over continued instances of forced sterilizations and abortions, particularly involving women with intellectual disabilities. The Committee also underscored the state's obligation to ensure access to SRH information and supportive services, safeguarding both the right to health and the right to form a family.

Since 2014, when NGOs first raised concerns about the neglect of SRH rights for women with disabilities in the CEDAW review, the Committee explicitly drew reference to the concept of "intersectional discrimination", and intersectionality has become an increasingly important discursive tool among NGOs and in Taiwan's human rights treaty review processes. This focus was significantly reinforced during the 2017 CRPD review, which initiated a more systematic discussion of these issues. Since then, applying an intersectional framework to the SRH rights of women with disabilities has become a recurring theme in CEDAW and CRPD reviews.

Nevertheless, it is important to note that such intersectional discussions have remained largely confined to these two conventions – CEDAW, which addresses women and gender minorities, and CRPD, which focuses on persons with disabilities. For instance, during the second review of the ICCPR and ICESCR in 2016, the state report under ICESCR reiterated references to the Genetic Health Act without responding to the concerns previously raised during the CEDAW review. Among NGO submissions, only Covenants Watch highlighted the barriers faced by women with disabilities in accessing SRH services and information. These issues were not reflected in the Committees' LOI or COR. By the third review of both Covenants in 2020, SRH-related concerns for women with disabilities remained omitted from the reports of governmental agencies, NGOs, and the Committees altogether.

3. "Intersectionality" being highlighted: The CRPD review in 2021

In the third CEDAW review in 2018, the state report, while reiterating content related to the Genetic Health Act, began to acknowledge how women with disabilities benefit from reproductive policies. It noted plans to conduct gender-based analyses using nationwide surveys on the lives and needs of people with disabilities. Meanwhile, the International Review Committee and NGOs continued to adopt a stance that took into account the intersectionality of people's lived experiences during the review process, even drawing on CRPD principles as a cross-referencing practice to accentuate the interrelatedness of human rights. For example, to consistently monitor the protection of SRH rights for women with disabilities, the denial of reasonable accommodations should be recognized as a form of discrimination. The parallel report led by Covenants Watch placed the experiences of women with disabilities at the center of its analysis. Additionally, more NGOs began to advocate for SRH rights in this context, including the Taiwan Disabled Women's Alliance for Equal Rights, an organization led by women with disabilities established in 2017.

By the time of the second CRPD review in 2021, the content of the state report had undergone significant changes. While the Genetic Health Act remained in play, the government also provided more detailed accounts of protective measures for the SRH rights of women with disabilities. These included, for instance, improvements in access to SRH services and education, parenting support and consultation, and information about assistive devices; a public listing of accessible cancer screening facilities; initiatives to enhance physical accessibility in healthcare environments; gender and disability awareness training and rights campaigns targeting health professionals; and the inclusion of SRH counseling for pregnant women with disabilities as a public health performance indicator. These developments enabled the government to respond more concretely to the Committee's extensive inquiries into SRH-related issues.

Nevertheless, a more comprehensive report does not necessarily equate to the full realization of SRH rights for women with disabilities. Civil society actors continued to express concern over inadequate accessible services and procrastination in amending the Genetic Health Act. Some organizations proposed substantive policy changes. The League for Persons with Disabilities demanded that the government set clear timelines and goals for implementing reproductive counseling services. The Taiwan Association for Disability Rights recommended prioritizing the SRH rights of disabled women in the *Gender Equality Policy Guidelines*. Covenants

Watch further argued that universal design in healthcare must be accompanied by actionable strategies, including supportive assistance or persons for women with disabilities in reproductive decision-making, thus advancing reproductive autonomy. Both the NHRC and the International Review Committee echoed these calls, emphasizing that SRH services must go beyond fertility control to ensure comprehensive and supportive reproductive and parenting care.

These trilateral and detailed discussions continued into the 2022 CEDAW review. While progress on amending the Genetic Health Act and improving physical accessibility remained slow, the availability of statistical data on the SRH of women with disabilities became more robust. Targeted information and resources – such as the *Pregnancy Guidebook for Persons with Disabilities*, developed in collaboration with NGOs – have been produced and disseminated, representing a modest but meaningful step toward greater inclusion.

4. Intersectional concerns voiced through SRH rights monitoring

In summary, eleven key issues concerning the SRH rights of women with disabilities have emerged through Taiwan's human rights treaty review processes (see Table 2). This trajectory illustrates the growing recognition of SRH as a critical site of rights violations, reflecting inequalities at both the infrastructural and policy levels, and the broader institutionalization of intersectionality as an analytical and advocacy tool. The intersectionality of one's subject positions and lived conditions – being both women and persons with disabilities – has prompted human rights actors to engage with the multilayered oppressions experienced by those at the margins. In Taiwan, this intersectional awareness has been clearly expressed through interactions between the CEDAW and CRPD frameworks, particularly during various review cycles, where issues raised under one treaty often reappear or evolve under the other. The significance of this overlap lies in the alignment of gender equality and disability rights, as well as the emergence of a shared language and logic for addressing complex structural injustices.

Crucially, it was through these human rights review mechanisms that intersectionality was first actively introduced into Taiwan's policy discourse, not as an abstract theorization, but as a practical tool for comprehending, articulating, and elaborating on lived inequities. While SRH has served as a vivid and urgent example, given how it intertwines biological sex, gender norms, and bodily autonomy, intersectionality has also shed light on broader systemic exclusions that extend beyond reproductive health. It has offered a framework for identifying how diverse bodyminds are excluded in healthcare, education, employment, legal recognition, family life, and civic participation. The visibility of SRH concerns thus operates as a gateway issue, drawing attention to intersectional injustice and pushing both governmental and non-governmental actors to develop more inclusive, context-sensitive responses.

Through repeated participation in the treaty review cycles, governmental agencies and NGOs have become increasingly adept at navigating the expectations and strategies of the process. On the one hand, governmental agencies, initially passive and reactive, have begun presenting evidence-based responses to each rights concern and realizing limited but meaningful policy changes. On the other hand, NGOs have matured in their engagement, submitting parallel reports that now offer more concrete, intersectionally informed recommendations. This mutual learning process reflects a growing institutional literacy around intersectionality and its practical value in human rights-based public-private dialogue and governance.

Ultimately, the integration of intersectionality into Taiwan's human rights reporting and monitoring mechanism has generated a transformative effect. The structured, cyclical nature of reviewing the implementation progress of CEDAW and CRPD has provided a durable platform for intersectional concerns to gain traction, evolve, and be translated into policy demands. The case of SRH rights for women with disabilities stands as a particularly visible illustration of this shift, but it also signals a broader potential: to use intersectionality as a conceptual bridge across movements, human rights treaties, and social groups, and as a political strategy for advancing substantive equality in Taiwan's legal and policy landscape.

Table 2. Mentions of SRH rights of women with disabilities in Taiwan's human rights reports (2009–2022)

No	**Issues**		**CEDAW**	**ICCPR & ICE-SCR**	**CEDAW**	**ICCPR & ICE-SCR**	**CRPD**	**CEDAW**	**ICCPR & ICE-SCR**	**CRPD**	**CEDAW**	**Men-tions**	**Total**
			1st	1st	2nd	2nd	1st	3rd	3rd	2nd	4th		
			(2009)	(2012)	(2014)	(2016)	(2017)	(2018)	(2020)	(2021)	(2022)		
1	Amending the Genetic Health Act (Based on the protection of the reproductive rights of women with disabilities)	GA	X		X		X	X		X	X	6	**14**
		NGOs					X	X		X	X	4	
		NHRC								X	X	2	
		IRC					X			X		2	
2	Subsidies for reproductive healthcare services (Fertility regulations, obstetric examinations, and abortion)	GA	X	X	X	X	X	X			X	7	**14**
		NGOs			X		X	X		X	X	5	
		NHRC										0	
		IRC			X			X				2	
3	Accessible medical environment and services	GA					X	X	X	X	X	5	**17**
		NGOs			X	X	X	X		X	X	6	
		NHRC							X	X	X	3	
		IRC					X	X			X	3	
4	Accessible, supportive services for SRH and childcare	GA				X	X			X	X	4	**15**
		NGOs			X	X	X	X		X	X	6	
		NHRC								X	X	2	
		IRC					X	X		X		3	

Table 2 (continued). Mentions of SRH rights of women with disabilities in Taiwan's human rights reports (2009–2022)

No	Issues		CEDAW	ICCPR & ICE-SCR	CEDAW	ICCPR & ICE-SCR	CRPD	CEDAW	ICCPR & ICE-SCR	CRPD	CEDAW	Men-tions	Total
			1st	1st	2nd	2nd	1st	3rd	3rd	2nd	4th		
			(2009)	(2012)	(2014)	(2016)	(2017)	(2018)	(2020)	(2021)	(2022)		
5	Statistics and investigation regarding SRH, marital, and childcare	GA						X		X	X	3	**13**
		NGOs			X		X	X		X	X	5	
		NHRC								X	X	2	
		IRC					X	X		X		3	
6	Education in gender equality, marriage, and SRH	GA					X	X		X	X	4	**14**
		NGOs				X	X	X		X	X	5	
		NHRC								X		1	
		IRC					X	X		X	X	4	
7	Accessible information for SRH and childcare	GA							X	X	X	3	**12**
		NGOs				X	X	X		X	X	5	
		NHRC								X	X	2	
		IRC						X			X	2	
8	Personnel training in care skills and disability awareness	GA					X		X	X	X	4	**11**
		NGOs					X	X		X	X	4	
		NHRC								X		1	
		IRC					X				X	2	

Table 2. Mentions of SRH rights of women with disabilities in Taiwan's human rights reports (2009–2022)

No	Issues		CEDAW	ICCPR & ICESCR	CEDAW	ICCPR & ICESCR	CRPD	CEDAW	ICCPR & ICESCR	CRPD	CEDAW	Mentions	Total
			1st	1st	2nd	2nd	1st	3rd	3rd	2nd	4th		
			(2009)	(2012)	(2014)	(2016)	(2017)	(2018)	(2020)	(2021)	(2022)		
9	Assistive devices for women with disabilities during pregnancy and childcare	GA								X	X	2	**5**
		NGOs					X			X	X	3	
		NHRC										0	
		IRC										0	
10	Inventory of accessible resources for SRH	GA									X	1	**4**
		NGOs								X	X	2	
		NHRC									X	1	
		IRC										0	
11	Personal assistants for women with disabilities during pregnancy and childcare	GA										0	**1**
		NGOs								X		1	
		NHRC										0	
		IRC										0	

* GA = Governmental Agencies; IRC = International Review Committees.

IV. Concluding remarks

Although intersectionality is not explicitly codified in Taiwan's domestic legal framework, this chapter has shown how the concept has gradually entered the realm of human rights policymaking through the institutional mechanisms of international treaty reporting. By analyzing official and civil society submissions between 2009 and 2022, we have traced how intersectionality, though initially absent from legal and policy discourse, has come to shape debates and recommendations concerning, for instance, the SRH rights of women with disabilities. Three key moments mark this trajectory: the 2014 CEDAW review, where intersectional concerns were formally acknowledged; the 2017 CRPD review, which initiated more systemic scrutiny of reproductive rights frameworks; and the 2021 CRPD review, which saw intersectionality more fully embedded in both state and non-state responses. These moments represent a discursive shift as well as institutional learning processes, through which the government and NGOs alike have come to recognize the need for integrated approaches to address equality and non-discrimination (de Beco 2017).

As disability rights organizations have long argued, Taiwan's SRH laws, particularly the Genetic Health Act, carry eugenic undertones and reinforce ableist and paternalistic structures. Earlier approaches that treated disability and gender as separate categories have proven insufficient, if not inadequate, in capturing the specific and compounded challenges faced by disabled women. "Intersectionality" offers a powerful alternative by demonstrating how overlapping identities result in distinct forms of structural marginalization. Its application in Taiwan reveals the limitations of both mainstream feminist and disability rights advocacy when pursued in isolation (de Beco 2020; Lee and Torres Celis 2024). In this chapter, we emphasize that disability justice and reproductive autonomy should not be framed as competing or conflicting agendas. Rather, both are situated within broader systems of oppression, where patriarchy and ableism intersect and co-function on both local and global levels to systematically deny disabled women full reproductive citizenship (Hermannsdóttir and Dybbroe 2023; Lupton 2012).

While intersectionality has gained traction in advocacy and policy discourse, its formal incorporation into Taiwan's legal framework remains limited. For example, the concepts of "multiple discrimination" and "intersectional discrimination" are acknowledged and defined in the General Explanation accompanying the first draft of the Anti-Discrimination Act, proposed by the Executive Yuan's Department of Human Rights and

Transitional Justice in May 2024. While the commentary on the definition and types of discrimination draws references from CRPD's General Comment No. 6, which distinguishes between the compounding nature of multiple discrimination and the indivisible interaction of intersectional discrimination, these two concepts, however intriguing, are absent from the draft provisions themselves (Executive Yuan 2024). The omission raises questions about the institutional willingness or technical capacity to codify intersectionality in enforceable legal norms.

Codifying intersectionality presents legal drafting challenges, such as defining thresholds of harm or responsibility across multiple stakeholders, and it is crucial to enable courts and administrative bodies to recognize and redress multifaceted forms of disadvantage. While the General Explanation to the draft Anti-Discrimination Act engages with CRPD's General Comments and acknowledges the layered nature of discrimination, the absence of explicit clauses operationalizing intersectionality reflects a broader reluctance to translate rhetorical commitments into statutory obligations within the domestic legal framework. Without formal codification, intersectionality risks remaining a normative ideal rather than a legally actionable principle (Conaghan 2009). Future iterations of anti-discrimination legislation in Taiwan could benefit from incorporating an explicit recognition of intersectional discrimination, drawing from international best practices. This could include provisions mandating that public institutions consider intersecting identities in policy design, service delivery, and legal redress mechanisms.

However, intersectionality remains a critical framework for bridging these agendas, revealing common ground between relevant rights campaigns, and providing a basis for solidarity and more inclusive policymaking. Importantly, SRH is just one example where sex, gender, and bodymind differences intersect in complicated ways. The institutional recognition of intersectionality, thus, opens up possibilities for applying the concept across other policy areas. As treaty implementation reviews continue, and as governmental and non-governmental actors stay attuned to intersectional analysis, there is potential for broader transformations in how to articulate rights. That is, the growing presence of intersectionality in rights advocacy and treaty monitoring signals a meaningful, though still incomplete, shift toward recognizing and addressing the multilayered realities of discrimination that shape the lives of marginalized groups. For women with disabilities, this shift has been significant, offering new pathways to voice concerns, assert their rights, and demand policies that reflect the full complexity of their lived experiences.

References

Addlakha, Renu, Janet Price, and Shirin Heidari. 2017. "Disability and sexuality: claiming sexual and reproductive rights." *Reproductive Health Matters* 25 (50): 4–9. https://doi.org/10.1080/09688080.2017.1336375.

Alford, William P., Qiongyue Hu, and Charles Wharton. 2019. "People Over Pandas: Taiwan's Engagement of International Human Rights Norms with Respect to Disability." In *Taiwan and International Human Rights: A Story of Transformation*, edited by Jerome A. Cohen, William P. Alford, and Chang-fa Lo, 643-659. Singapore: Springer Singapore.

Alhusen, Jeanne L., Tina Bloom, Kathryn Laughon, Lillian Behan, and Rosemary B. Hughes. 2021. "Perceptions of barriers to effective family planning services among women with disabilities." *Disability and Health Journal* 14 (3): 101055. https://doi.org/https://doi.org/10.1016/j.dhjo.2020.101055.

CEDAW, and CRPD. 2018. *Joint statement on guaranteeing sexual and reproductive health and rights for all women, in particular women with disabilities*. 29 August 2018. https://www.ohchr.org/en/treaty-bodies/crpd/statements-declarations-and-observations.

Chang, Wen-Chen. 2019. "Taiwan's Human Rights Implementation Acts: A Model for Successful Incorporation?" In *Taiwan and International Human Rights: A Story of Transformation*, edited by Jerome A. Cohen, William P. Alford, and Chang-fa Lo, 227–247. Singapore: Springer Singapore.

Cho, Sumi, Kimberlé Williams Crenshaw, and Leslie McCall. 2013. "Toward a Field of Intersectionality Studies: Theory, Applications, and Praxis." *Signs* 38 (4): 785–810. https://doi.org/10.1086/669608.

Conaghan, Joanne. 2009. "Intersectionality and the Feminist Project in Law." In *Intersectionality and Beyond: Law, Power and the Politics of Location*, edited by Emily Grabham, Davina Cooper, Jane Krishnadas, and Didi Herman, 21–48. London: Routledge.

Cook, Rebecca J., and Bernard M. Dickens. 2003. "Human Rights Dynamics of Abortion Law Reform." *Human Rights Quarterly* 25 (1): 1–59. http://www.jstor.org/stable/20069652.

Crenshaw, Kimberle. 1991. "Mapping the Margins: Intersectionality, Identity Politics, and Violence against Women of Color." *Stanford Law Review* 43 (6): 1241–1299. https://doi.org/10.2307/1229039.

de Beco, Gauthier. 2017. "Protecting the Invisible: An Intersectional Approach to International Human Rights Law." *Human Rights Law Review* 17 (4): 633–663. https://doi.org/10.1093/hrlr/ngx029.

de Beco, Gauthier. 2020. "Intersectionality and disability in international human rights law." *The International Journal of Human Rights* 24 (5): 593–614. https://doi.org/10.1080/13642987.2019.1661241.

Executive Yuan. 2024. *Draft Anti-Discrimination Act: General Explanation and Article-by-Article Explanation*. Taipei: Executive Yuan. https://www.ey.gov.tw/File/2498FE176F4CBF86?A=C.

Fonow, Mary Margaret, and Judith A. Cook. 2005. "Feminist Methodology: New Applications in the Academy and Public Policy." *Signs: Journal of Women in Culture and Society* 30 (4): 2211-2236. https://doi.org/10.1086/428417.

Garland-Thomson, Rosemarie. 1997. *Extraordinary Bodies: Figuring Physical Disability In American Culture And Literature*. New York: Columbia University Press.

Garland-Thomson, Rosemarie. 2002. "Integrating Disability, Transforming Feminist Theory." *NWSA Journal* 14 (3): 1–32. http://www.jstor.org/stable/4316922.

Garland-Thomson, Rosemarie. 2005a. "Feminist Disability Studies." *Signs* 30 (2): 1557–1587. https://doi.org/10.1086/423352.

Garland-Thomson, Rosemarie. 2005b. "Disability and Representation." *PMLA/Publications of the Modern Language Association of America* 120 (2): 522–527. https://doi.org/10.1632/S0030812900167835.

Garland-Thomson, Rosemarie. 2011. "Misfits: A Feminist Materialist Disability Concept." *Hypatia* 26 (3): 591–609. http://www.jstor.org/stable/23016570.

Hall, Kim Q. 2011. "Reimagining Disability and Gender through Feminist Disability Studies." In *Feminist Disability Studies*, edited by Kim Q. Hall, 1–10. Bloomington: Indiana University Press.

Hermannsdóttir, Turið, and Betina Dybbroe. 2023. "Components of reproductive citizenship: narratives from a restrictive abortion landscape." *Citizenship Studies* 27 (8): 1022–1037. https://doi.org/10.1080/13621025.2024.2310284.

Lawson, Anna, and Angharad E. Beckett. 2021. "The social and human rights models of disability: Towards a complementarity thesis." *The International Journal of Human Rights* 25 (2): 348–379. https://doi.org/10.1080/13642987.2020.1783533.

Lee, Po-Han. 2023. "Un(ac)countable no-bodies: the politics of ignorance in global health policymaking." *Critical Public Health* 33 (1): 48–59. https://doi.org/10.1080/09581596.2022.2025578.

Lee, Po-Han, and JhuCin Rita Jhang. 2023. "The Stolen Freedoms of Abortion: An International Human Rights Analysis of the Dobbs Case." *Journal of Science & Health Law* 28 (1): 93-146.

Lee, Po-Han, and Stephanie Torres Celis. 2024. "Crip-queer intimacy, alliance and activism: towards holistic sexuality education in Taiwan." *Sex Education* 24 (4): 562–577. https://doi.org/10.1080/14681811.2023.2225159.

Liao, Fort Fu-Te. 2010. "Partly Virtual, Partly Real: Taiwan's Unique Interaction with International Human Rights Instruments." *Asian Yearbook of International Law* 16: 25–64. http://www.jstor.org/stable/10.1163/j.ctv2gjwnxn.5.

Lin, Chih-Chieh. 2009. "Regulating Pregnancy in Taiwan: An Analysis from an Asian Legal Feminist Using Feminist Legal Theories." *University of Baltimore Law Forum* 39 (2): 204–226.

Lin, Jun-Jie, and Heng-Hao Chang. 2023. "Reconsidering disability in Taiwan: a perspective on globalisation and postcolonialism." *Disability & Society*: 1–19. https://doi.org/10.1080/09687599.2023.2205993.

Lin, Peggy Pei-Chun. 2020. "A Preliminary Examination of Intersectional Discrimination in Taiwan: CEDAW, CRC and CRPD." *Taiwan Journal of International Law* 16 (2): 7–23.

Lupton, Deborah. 2012. "'Precious cargo': foetal subjects, risk and reproductive citizenship." *Critical Public Health* 22 (3): 329–340. https://doi.org/10.1080/09581596.2012.657612.

Mofokeng, Tlaleng. 2021. *Report of the Special Rapporteur on the right of everyone to the enjoyment of the highest attainable standard of physical and mental health. Sexual and reproductive health rights: Challenges and opportunities during the COVID-19 pandemic.* 16 July 2021. United Nations General Assembly (Geneva). https://docs.un.org/en/A/76/172.

Nicki, Andrea. 2001. "The Abused Mind: Feminist Theory, Psychiatric Disability, and Trauma." *Hypatia* 16 (4): 80–104. https://doi.org/10.1111/j.1527-2001.2001.tb00754.x.

Oliver, Michael, and Colin Barnes. 2012. *The New Politics of Disablement.* London: Bloomsbury Publishing.

Quinlivan, Shivaun. 2019. "Reasonable Accommodation: An Integral Part of the Right to Education for Persons with Disabilities." In *The Right to Inclusive Education in International Human Rights Law,* edited by Gauthier de Beco, Shivaun Quinlivan and Janet E. Lord, 169–189. Cambridge: Cambridge University Press.

Sommo, Anthony, and Jay Chaskes. 2013. "Intersectionality and the disability: Some conceptual and methodological challenges." In *Disability and Intersecting Statuses,* In Research in Social Science and Disability, 47–59. Emerald Group Publishing Limited.

Su, Chong-Min. 2023. "The Urgency of Amending the Genetic Health Law in Taiwan: From the Perspective of Rights of Persons with Disabilities." *Taiwan Journal of Public Health* 42 (2): 144–147. https://doi.org/10.6288/TJPH.202304_42(2).111110.

Su, Chong-Min, and Po-Han Lee. 2025. "Activist Allyship, Unspoken Dilemma: Deconstructing the Tension between Reproductive Autonomy

and Disability Justice." The International Journal of Human Rights, November, 1–23. doi:10.1080/13642987.2025.2588184.
Sun, Nai-Yi. 2019. "On the Road to Equal Enjoyment of Human Rights for Persons with Disabilities: The Development of Domestic Laws in Taiwan and Their Dialogue with the CRPD." In *Taiwan and International Human Rights: A Story of Transformation*, edited by Jerome A. Cohen, William P. Alford, and Chang-fa Lo, 661–678. Singapore: Springer Singapore.
Teng, Yean-Sen. 2019. "The Problems with the Incorporation of International Human Rights Law in Taiwan." In *Taiwan and International Human Rights: A Story of Transformation*, edited by Jerome A. Cohen, William P. Alford, and Chang-fa Lo, 249–273. Singapore: Springer Singapore.
Vernon, Ayesha. 1999. "The Dialectics of Multiple Identities and the Disabled People's Movement." *Disability & Society* 14 (3): 385–398. https://doi.org/10.1080/09687599926217.
Wendell, Susan. 1989. "Toward a Feminist Theory of Disability." *Hypatia* 4 (2): 104–124. https://doi.org/https://doi.org/10.1111/j.1527-2001.1989.tb00576.x.

F. The Dialogue Between Indigenous Persons with Disabilities in Taiwan and the CRPD: An Investigation of an Atayal Tribe

Yi-Chun Chou[1]

Abstract:

This study explores the relationship between persons with disabilities in Atayal communities in Yilan, Taiwan, and community services, focusing on the applicability of CRPD Article 19 in Indigenous areas. While the CRPD highlights social discrimination and environmental barriers, the main challenges for Atayal persons with disabilities stem from the historical impacts of capitalism and colonialism. These factors create a structural condition of social suffering beyond CRPD-defined social barriers. Through secondary data, fieldwork, and 16 interviews, the study identifies key causes of disability: inadequate medical care, poor transport, poverty, and weak social support—not direct discrimination. Atayal persons value family and tribal support over government services, do not link terms like "handicap" with stigma, and prioritize financial aid over community services. The findings suggest that CRPD's universal social model does not fully fit Indigenous contexts. Disability policies should integrate Indigenous culture and focus on economic and infrastructure improvements to achieve genuine inclusion.

Keywords:

Atayal; CRPD; Article 19; Indigenous disability; social suffering, colonialism; community services

I. Introduction

Since the Renaissance in the 17th century, disability has often been regarded as a divine punishment or a matter of personal destiny. Disabled individuals were labeled as heretics, patients, or unproductive persons, corresponding to the "individual model of disability" and the "medical model of disability," which focused on confinement, correction, and isolation (Chang & Su, 2019). Following World War II, the disability movement gained momen-

1 Professor, department of Sociology, Soochow University Taipei (Taiwan).

tum, and in the 1980s, activists and scholars proposed the "social model of disability," attributing disability to social structures (Liao, 2017). Building on this model, the United Nations adopted the *Convention on the Rights of Persons with Disabilities* (CRPD) in 2006, which came into effect in 2008, explicitly making the elimination of social barriers a national responsibility. The CRPD emphasizes core values such as equality and non-discrimination, accessibility, self-determination, inclusion, and reasonable accommodation. Article 19 further highlights the importance of universally accessible community services to realize these values (Chou & Lin, 2020).

Meanwhile, post-World War II Indigenous policies in many countries have exhibited similar trends, focusing on self-determination and autonomy while preserving cultural and social structures through geographic boundaries. Despite facing similar challenges, such as small populations, economic disadvantage, and social discrimination, Indigenous peoples and persons with disabilities diverge in policy implementation: persons with disabilities prioritize social inclusion, while Indigenous peoples emphasize autonomy. Additionally, while the CRPD advocates for community support services to enhance the self-determination and inclusion of persons with disabilities, these services rely heavily on robust welfare systems. In the context of Indigenous studies, welfare states are often critiqued as tools of continued colonialism (Wang, 2010).

Globally, research on Indigenous persons with disabilities often adopts the "Southern disabled standpoint," which critiques the CRPD model for being overly Western-centric, lacking multicultural considerations, and neglecting the impacts of colonialism on the Global South. Although Taiwan is not a member of the United Nations, it enacted the *Act to Implement the Convention on the Rights of Persons with Disabilities* in 2014, progressively aligning its policies with the CRPD. However, there remains limited exploration of how the CRPD's core values and goals for community services are realized within Taiwan's Indigenous societies, particularly regarding their significance for Indigenous persons with disabilities.

In Taiwan, research on Indigenous peoples has made significant strides in areas such as long-term care and cultural rights. However, studies focusing specifically on Indigenous persons with disabilities remain scarce, with only limited discussions by Wang (2014) and Tsai (2009). Moreover, there is a notable lack of literature examining the implementation of the CRPD in Indigenous tribe. To address this gap, this study uses a case study of an Atayal tribe in Datong Township, Yilan County, employing secondary data analysis, field observations, and qualitative interviews to explore the implications of the CRPD's Article 19 on community services and the removal of social barriers for Atayal persons with disabilities. This article aims to examine whether the construction of universally accessible community services in Indigenous Peoples, as a means of implementing the CRPD, reflects the criticisms raised by the "Southern disabled standpoint" regarding insufficient multicultural perspectives.

II. Literature Review

1. Core Values of the CRPD and Accessibility of Community Services

a) Core Principles and Values of the CRPD

The medical model of disability views disability as an individual problem that requires medical treatment or rehabilitation for correction or recovery (Wu, 2007). Under this model, persons with disabilities (PWDs) are expected to adapt to society, rather than society accommodating them. In contrast, the social model of disability, introduced in the 1980s, asserts that disability arises from societal structures and systemic exclusion rather than individual impairments. According to this perspective, disability is socially constructed and results from environmental barriers and discrimination. Therefore, social and cultural changes, such as improving accessibility, can enable PWDs to move beyond isolation and fully participate in society. Building upon the social model, the rights-based model goes further by framing the removal of societal barriers as a fundamental human right and a state responsibility. This model advocates for PWDs to have legal standing to claim their rights and demand systemic changes. The Americans with Disabilities Act (ADA) of 1990 and the United Nations Convention on the Rights of Persons with Disabilities (CRPD) adopted in 2006 represent key milestones in the implementation of the rights-based approach.

The CRPD requires States Parties to implement legislative and policy measures to protect the rights of PWDs, submit periodic reports for international review, and ensure that disability rights are not merely an advocacy issue but a legally enforceable state responsibility. The core values of the CRPD include equality and non-discrimination, community inclusion, and independent living. To achieve these goals, States Parties must ensure accessibility, reasonable accommodation, sufficient community services, and deinstitutionalization. Article 2 of the CRPD defines "disability discrimination" as any distinction, exclusion, or restriction based on disability that impairs or denies PWDs the equal recognition, enjoyment, or exercise of all political, economic, social, cultural, civil, or other rights and freedoms. This definition includes the refusal to provide reasonable accommodation. While the rights-based model incorporates elements of the social model by emphasizing the elimination of societal barriers, its primary focus remains on protecting individual rights through legal mechanisms.

b) Accessible Community Services for PWDs: The Implementation of CRPD Core Values

Article 19 of the CRPD, "Living Independently and Being Included in the Community," explicitly affirms the right of PWDs to choose to live in the community and receive necessary support services (Chou & Lin, 2020). To ensure the exercise of this right, States Parties must establish diverse community support services that prevent PWDs from being isolated or institutionalized. The General Comment No. 5 of the CRPD further clarifies the practical implementation of Article 19, emphasizing the significance of community-based services, independent living arrangements, and personal assistance. The universal availability and accessibility of community support services serve as a key indicator of the institutionalization of disability rights protection, aligning with the core values of the CRPD (Chou & Lin, 2020).

When PWDs have access to community services, they are more likely to live within their communities rather than being placed in institutions. Such services not only promote equality and independent living but also safeguard PWDs from exploitation and inhumane treatment. The CRPD views community support services as a model institutional framework, influencing various aspects of PWD rights, including education, healthcare, mobility, employment, rehabilitation, and adequate living standards. The successful implementation of CRPD principles and the rights-based model requires a robust welfare system and social policy framework. In contemporary society, accessible community services are a crucial benchmark for evaluating the effectiveness of CRPD implementation, directly impacting whether PWDs can truly integrate into their communities and achieve independent living.

2. CRPD Perspectives on Disability Policies vs. Indigenous Policies

a) The Impact of Capitalist Exploitation on the Global South

Indigenous peoples worldwide generally face socio-economic disadvantages, particularly in education, employment, and health. They experience higher rates of alcohol addiction, suicide, mental illness, and infant mortality compared to non-Indigenous populations (Huang 2014; Chen 2014). These challenges stem from the capitalist exploitation of Indigenous lands, cultures, and resources, exacerbating their social marginalization. Soldatic & Biyanwila (2006) argue that disabled individuals in the Global South are particularly vulnerable due to inadequate infrastructure and medical services, leading to preventable impairments becoming permanent disabilities. Furthermore, the global pharmaceutical and rehabilitation markets are dominated by multinational corporations, restricting the autonomy of Southern nations in managing their disability policies. Despite claims of assisting developing countries, global development policies—such as World Bank initiatives—often facilitate further resource extraction, intensify internal conflicts, and degrade the environment, thereby worsening the living conditions of disabled individuals in the Global South.

b) CRPD and the Social Model May Not Be Universally Applicable

Meekosha (2004) notes that while the social model of disability originated in Western metropolitan contexts, it has become dominant in shaping disability discourse worldwide. Grech (2011) criticizes the social model for monopolizing the discourse on disability, often imposing Northern perspectives on the Global South without considering local cultural contexts. Jenks (2017) further argues that while CRPD is perceived as a human rights tool in the North, scholars from the Global South question its actual capacity to achieve equality. Haang'andu (2018) found that despite extensive European Union-led efforts to promote disability rights in Sub-Saharan Africa, many local governments have struggled to implement effective policies, highlighting the disconnect between Western disability frameworks and Southern realities. Soldatic & Biyanwila (2006) assert that Global South nations should develop their own "Southern Disabled Standpoint" rather than wholly adopting Northern models. Cleaver (2016), in a study of Zambia, found that while local disability policies remained influenced by Northern agendas, disabled individuals in the South were capable of articulating their own needs and priorities.

3. Indigenous Studies vs. Disability Studies: Core Conceptual Differences

Comparing "Indigenous Studies" with "Disability Studies," which is largely based on the social and rights-based models, reveals several fundamental differences.

a) Social Disability vs. Social Suffering

Meekosha (2011, 2008) criticizes Northern disability scholars for overemphasizing "social disability" while ignoring the colonial impact on the Global South. Imperialism, colonial rule, warfare, land dispossession, and poverty have all contributed to high disability rates among Indigenous populations. Kleinman et al. (1997) introduced the concept of "social suffering," emphasizing that colonial histories have inflicted both physical and psychological trauma, making it a crucial factor in disability formation beyond mere environmental barriers. Ghai (2002) argues that Northern disability research fails to acknowledge the harsh socio-economic realities faced by disabled individuals in the Global South. Tsai (2009), in her study of the Yami (Tao) people in Taiwan, found that the high prevalence of mental disorders among the population was closely linked to historical and cultural oppression, further validating the relevance of "social suffering."

b) Individual Rights vs. Collective Rights

CRPD prioritizes individual rights and self-determination, advocating that disabled individuals should have the legal means to challenge discrimination. However, Indigenous self-determination emphasizes collective rights, contrasting with the individualistic framework of CRPD. Chung (2017) argues that Western human rights discourse is rooted in European individualism, which, when applied to Indigenous contexts, can inadvertently undermine collective cultural rights. Since Indigenous societies operate based on communal decision-making rather than individual autonomy, directly transplanting individual rights frameworks may be inappropriate. Kuan (2017) contends that when an entire ethnic group faces systemic discrimination, focusing solely on individual rights is insufficient. Instead, collective rights must be recognized to ensure meaningful inclusion. Shih (2017) further notes that while CRPD upholds personal liberty, it does not adequately consider Indigenous social structures, potentially creating tensions between group equality and individual freedoms.

c) Universal Welfare vs. Anti-Welfare Colonialism

CRPD advocates for universal welfare to ensure non-discriminatory access to essential services for disabled individuals. However, this approach may not be entirely applicable to Indigenous Peoples. Meekosha (2008) warns that welfare policies formulated in the North can erode Indigenous cultural and political autonomy, resulting in a form of "welfare colonialism." Wang (2010), in examining Taiwan's post-Typhoon Morakot permanent housing policies, criticizes government welfare interventions for disregarding Indigenous cultural traditions, effectively imposing a form of cultural colonization. Kuan (2017) argues that social welfare policies that focus solely on individual benefits, without incorporating Indigenous social support networks, risk fragmenting traditional communal care structures, pushing individuals into an atomized welfare system. Jenks (2021) also critiques CRPD's heavy reliance on state mechanisms, arguing that it lacks a pluralistic cultural perspective. If CRPD implementation fails to account for Indigenous understandings of disability, it risks being counterproductive. These critiques highlight the tension between CRPD's pursuit of universal rights and the need to respect Indigenous cultural specificities.

d) The Challenges of Implementing CRPD in Indigenous Peoples

While CRPD seeks to establish a universal framework for disability rights, its applicability in the Global South and Indigenous regions remains contested. Adopting a purely CRPD-based social model for disability policy may overlook the cultural and historical contexts of Indigenous Peoples. For example, designing community-based services without considering Indigenous lifestyles and social structures can result in ineffective implementation. To successfully implement CRPD in Indigenous territories, a deep understanding of local disability perspectives is essential. Indigenous experiences of disability must be analyzed through lenses of social suffering, collective rights, and cultural identity, rather than simply applying Northern frameworks. CRPD focuses on removing social barriers, but Indigenous disability issues often stem from deeper historical, cultural, and socio-political struggles. Disability experiences in the Global South cannot be fully addressed using Northern social models alone. To ensure CRPD's effectiveness in Indigenous Peoples, policies must be adapted to local cultural and socio-political contexts, avoiding another layer of colonial imposition. Research and policy development should prioritize Indigenous perspectives, rather than relying on a one-size-fits-all approach, to genuinely advance the rights and well-being of Indigenous persons with disabilities.

4. Indigenous Peoples and the Implementation of the CRPD in Canada, Australia, and New Zealand

Indigenous peoples in Canada, Australia, and New Zealand face systemic disadvantages in social, economic, and health indicators, a common phenomenon across all three countries (Huang, 2020). Australia ratified the **Convention on the Rights of Persons with Disabilities (CRPD)** in 2008. Its

Indigenous population, including Aboriginal Australians and Torres Strait Islanders, comprises approximately 3.3% of the national population (Ross, 2021). Among Indigenous Australians, 23.9% have disabilities—a higher proportion than among non-Indigenous Australians. Jakubowicz and Meekosha (2012) highlight that during early institutionalization processes in Australia, many Indigenous children with disabilities were forcibly removed from their cultural communities, resulting in long-term consequences. Chisholm et al. (2017) found that **Fetal Alcohol Spectrum Disorder (FASD) among Indigenous Australians** is closely linked to community trauma. They advocate for Indigenous-led solutions, noting that the CRPD framework may create tensions in Indigenous Peoples. Gooding et al. (2017) also point out that, despite years of CRPD implementation, research on Indigenous Australians with intellectual and cognitive disabilities remains insufficient.

New Zealand ratified the CRPD in 2008. The Māori, New Zealand's Indigenous people, comprise approximately 17% of the national population. Among Māori, 32% have disabilities, compared to 24% among non-Indigenous New Zealanders. To address these disparities, New Zealand implemented the **Māori Disability Action Plan (2012–2017)** in consultation with Māori communities. The plan is aligned with the **Whānau Ora** approach, which emphasizes **family-centered well-being and self-management**, allowing families to set their own goals and design strategies to enhance the well-being of Māori persons with disabilities. Canada ratified the CRPD in 2010, with Indigenous peoples—including **First Nations, Inuit, and Métis**—comprising approximately 4.3% of the national population (Hahmann et al., 2019). Hoffman et al. (2016) highlight a critical gap between CRPD principles and Canadian disability policies, particularly in Indigenous Peoples, where **substitute decision-making** is more common than the **supported decision-making** model advocated by the CRPD. Stienstra (2018) further argues that Canada's disability policies are significantly shaped by **colonial legacies and neoliberalism**, resulting in a gap between human rights protections and the actual realization of **decolonized inclusion** for Indigenous persons with disabilities.

Overall, the proportion of Indigenous persons with disabilities in all three countries is higher than that of non-Indigenous populations. While Canada, Australia, and New Zealand have signed and ratified the CRPD, the legacy of colonialism has left structural inequalities and discrimination, making CRPD implementation in Indigenous Peoples particularly challenging. Although New Zealand's Māori have relatively stronger recognition of land rights and Indigenous sovereignty, all three Indigenous groups face deep structural barriers that require more effective decolonization policies to address. Avery (2022), in discussing the intersectional identity of Indigenous persons with disabilities, highlights that the two most relevant human rights instruments for their protection are the CRPD and the United Nations Declaration on the Rights of Indigenous Peoples (UNDRIP). The CRPD was adopted by the United Nations in 2006, followed by the UNDRIP in 2007. Despite their temporal proximity and some conceptual similarities, these two frameworks operate independently within international human rights law and exhibit significant differences in their application and impact within national social policies. The CRPD, as a legally binding convention within the international human rights system, imposes legal obligations on state parties, requiring them to implement its provisions through domestic coordination mechanisms (Article 33). In contrast, UNDRIP fundamentally differs from the CRPD in its legal status. As a declaration, UNDRIP is not legally binding under international human rights law. Instead, its primary purpose is to guide states in recognizing and promoting Indigenous self-determination and cultural preservation. As an aspirational document, UNDRIP lacks the legal authority to hold states accountable, meaning that while it symbolically supports Indigenous rights, its practical implementation remains weak and unenforceable.

This distinction underscores a critical gap in the protection of Indigenous persons with disabilities, as the legally binding nature of the CRPD does not fully encompass the unique cultural and self-determination rights emphasized in UNDRIP. The absence of enforceable mechanisms for UNDRIP weakens its ability to effectively challenge systemic injustices, leaving Indigenous persons with disabilities in a precarious position where their disability rights are legally recognized, but their Indigenous rights remain largely aspirational. Consequently, meaningful decolonization efforts must ensure that both disability rights and Indigenous sovereignty are upheld within national legal frameworks.

5. CRPD-Implementation in Taiwan's Indigenous Peoples

In Taiwan, there is limited research on the implementation of CRPD-mandated community services for Indigenous persons with disabilities. Most existing studies focus on the long-term care (LTC) system in Indigenous Peoples, which provides valuable insights into the challenges of implementing modern social services in these areas. In practice, before the Taiwanese government significantly expanded disability-specific community services, most persons with disabilities relied on LTC services, making it a key reference point for understanding other emerging community-based services.

LTC services in Indigenous regions face accessibility challenges, including insufficient coverage, transportation barriers, and resource scarcity (Tung & Huang, 2010). Lin and Huang (2020) highlight that Indigenous Peoples often lack adequate training and employment opportunities, leading to low participation in caregiver training programs. As a result, many LTC workers come from outside the community, lacking cultural and linguistic competency, which affects service quality (Chen & Chan, 2015). Additionally, whether care coordinators have strong community ties significantly impacts service effectiveness (Wang, 2019; Lai, 2017). Hsu and Lin (2011) argue that LTC needs assessments are designed based on mainstream values, leaving Indigenous groups with limited participation and a passive role in the system. Wang (2019) further critiques that LTC policies and assessments are not neutral, but rather reflect political and cultural power dynamics. Existing LTC systems in Taiwan are largely urban-centered and Han-dominated, making them ill-suited to Indigenous geographic and cultural realities (Lin, 2019). Policies such as land and building regulations restrict the establishment of LTC facilities in Indigenous Peoples, while centralized food services and copayment structures create additional cultural barriers for Indigenous elders (Hsu, 2020). Scholars have proposed "culturally competent care" and "cultural safety" as alternative frameworks to avoid the cultural colonialism of LTC services (Ru, 2018; Lai, 2017). The integration of cultural competence and Indigenous self-determination into LTC policy is crucial for enabling aging-in-place and sustaining community-based eldercare (Hsu & Lin, 2011).

Existing studies on Indigenous persons with disabilities in Taiwan remain scarce. Tsai (2009) explores the historical and social origins of mental disorders among the Tao people in Lanyu, while Wang (2014) examines independent living among Indigenous persons with disabilities aged 50 and above in Nantou and Taichung. Chou (2023), in a study on Indigenous Tayal persons with disabilities in Yilan, found that local Indigenous Peoples do not perceive ableist language as discriminatory and are generally resistant to formal community services. Chang et al. (2024) conducted a systematic review of the intersection of state welfare systems and Indigenous persons with disabilities, arguing that recognizing Indigenous cultural contexts and social structures is essential for effective care and support. Similarly, Chiu (2024) analyzed case studies of individuals from three different Indigenous groups in Taiwan, demonstrating that variations between Indigenous and mainstream cultures influence how disabilities are defined, perceived, and addressed. Chiu further emphasized that Indigenous cultures are not static but continuously evolving and redefining themselves in response to broader social changes.

Overall, Taiwan's LTC policies have failed to fully account for Indigenous geographic and cultural diversity, leading to significant implementation challenges. These difficulties parallel the multicultural challenges faced in CRPD implementation in Global South contexts. This study will further explore whether CRPD-based community services for persons with disabilities in Yilan's Tayal communities exhibit similar cultural dissonance as Taiwan's LTC policies in Indigenous Peoples, highlighting potential gaps in cultural contextualization.

III. Research Methodology

This study focuses on the Atayal communities in Yilan County, Taiwan, to explore the construction and utilization of community services for persons with disabilities. The following research methods were employed:

1. Secondary Data Analysis

Secondary data from the past two decades, including books, journal articles, and publications by public and private institutions, were collected and analyzed to address the following:

1. Definitions and interpretations of key concepts, such as community services, disability, community, individual, and family, as shaped by Atayal culture;
2. Atayal attitudes toward persons with disabilities and their perspectives on community services;
3. The distribution of community service resources for persons with disabilities in Yilan County's indigenous areas.

The referenced secondary data sources are listed in the bibliography.

2. Qualitative Interviews

To validate findings from secondary data analysis and gain deeper insights into the construction and utilization of community service resources, qualitative interviews were conducted between 2021 and 2022. Participants were recruited with assistance from local service organizations in Yilan County and met the following criteria:

1. Aged 18 or older;
2. Residents of Atayal communities in Yilan County;
3. Holders of disability identification cards issued to indigenous persons.

A total of 16 adult Atayal persons with disabilities and two family members of persons with disabilities were interviewed. The Atayal participants were coded by gender as A1-A6 and B1-B10, while the two family members, both female, were coded as C1 and C2. The interviews focused on three main dimensions:

1. Causes of disability;
2. Perceptions and approaches to disability;
3. Current usage and perspectives on community services.

Using the core concepts of the CRPD as a framework, this study conducted a comparative analysis of secondary data and interview findings. The aim was to examine the causes of disability among Atayal individuals, the construction and utilization of community service resources, and the alignment and discrepancies between the two datasets.

IV. Research Findings

This study addresses three primary questions: First, does the "social suffering" perspective from Southern research apply to indigenous persons with disabilities in Taiwan's Atayal communities? Second, how do the Atayal people understand disability, and does their experience reflect the social barriers, such as discrimination and environmental inaccessibility, highlighted by the CRPD? Third, how do the Atayal perceive community service needs, and do these align with the CRPD's advocacy for accessible services?

1. Harms Caused by Capitalism and State Hegemony

a) The Impact of Capitalism and Colonialism on Indigenous Disadvantage

Wang (2014) notes that the homogenizing development of global capitalism has led to crises for Taiwan's Indigenous peoples, including community disintegration, cultural erosion, and ethnic disappearance. Wang (2006) describes the influence of capitalism on Indigenous economies and perspectives: During the Qing dynasty, resource-sharing was practiced under material exchange policies; under Japanese colonial rule, wage systems and commercialized agriculture disrupted subsistence economies, introducing capitalist market values into Indigenous Peoples. After the 1960s, the Atayal began cultivating cash crops, but global economic pressures and market fluctuations undermined local economies, prompting youth migration and weakening community support systems.

Wang (2023) further reveals how labor commodification and quantification under capitalism have impacted social relationships among Indigenous peoples. Using Mignolo's concepts of "post-Occidentalism" and "border thinking", Wang highlights the mutual permeation of colonial and Indigenous cultures and the resulting systemic disadvantages in education, health, and socioeconomic indicators. Educational issues include high teacher turnover, cultural gaps, and resource shortages, which reduce learning motivation and opportunities (Tsai, 2004). Moreover, class structures shaped by capitalism contribute to addiction behaviors among Indigenous populations (Chen, 2014). Chi (2005) identifies historical ethnic power inequalities as the root cause of Indigenous challenges, calling for structural resource investments to address these issues. Tsai (2004) advocates for affirmative policies to compensate for cultural disadvantages and promote equitable development opportunities for Indigenous peoples.

b) The Absence of Community Services in Atayal Peoples in Yilan

The Karandala tribe (pseudonym) in Datong Township, Yilan County, is home to about 800 Atayal residents. It lacks essential facilities such as early intervention, day care, family respite care, and personal assistance services, requiring residents to travel to Yilan City or Luodong for such services. Even the nearest clinic is a 20-minute drive from the tribe. Despite being a major Atayal settlement, Datong and neighboring Nan'ao Township have only one day service center and two respite care facilities during the study period.

The uneven distribution of resources, shaped by administrative decisions and capitalist priorities, leaves remote tribes under-resourced in healthcare, transportation, and community services. The absence of affirmative policies to balance urban-rural disparities exacerbates the "social suffering" experienced by Atayal persons with disabilities. Interviews reveal that this structural inequality plays a decisive role in causing disabilities, underscoring the far-reaching impact of resource allocation disparities.

c) The Main Causes of Acquired Disabilities: Beyond the Social Model—The Experience of Social Suffering in Indigenous Peoples

Among the 16 Atayal persons with disabilities interviewed in this study, except for A6 and B9, nearly all had acquired disabilities. The causes of their disabilities included illness, traffic accidents, strokes, substance abuse, and alcohol consumption, reflecting the impact of inadequate medical resources and the structural social suffering within the tribe.

d) Disabilities Caused by Illness

Several interviewees, including A1, A2, A3, A4, B3, B4, B6-B8, developed disabilities due to untreated illnesses. Examples include:

- A2 (Paralysis): As an infant, A2 suffered from a high fever of 40° C. Due to living in a remote mountainous area with limited transportation, medical care was delayed, leading to central nervous system damage and paralysis in the right side of the body.
- A3 (Severe Hearing Impairment): An untreated childhood ear infection resulted in a ruptured eardrum, which was only diagnosed and treated in adulthood.
- A4 (Intellectual Disability, Epilepsy): Suffered from a high fever as a child, but due to the father's busy work schedule, medical attention was delayed, affecting cognitive development.
- B4 (Physical Disability): A bacterial spinal cord infection required surgery, leaving B4 permanently unable to feel the lower body, necessitating lifelong use of crutches.

These cases illustrate how limited transportation and inadequate healthcare access in Indigenous communities lead to preventable illnesses developing into permanent disabilities.

e) Disabilities Caused by Traffic Accidents

B1, B5, and B10 sustained disabilities due to traffic accidents:

- B1 (Severe Visual Impairment): Suffered a head injury and eye damage in a motorcycle accident while returning from work early in the morning.
- B5 (Brain Injury): After graduating from junior high school, B5 moved to Taipei for temporary work. While crossing the road, they were hit by a motorcycle, resulting in a left-brain injury. Though rehabilitation allowed standing, walking remains unstable, and they have lost all memories before junior high.

- B10 (Spinal Cord Injury): A truck driver involved in an accident, leading to paraplegia.

Many traffic accident survivors were commuting long distances or engaging in high-risk jobs due to economic pressures, highlighting the lack of local employment opportunities and occupational safety measures.

f) Mental Disabilities and Substance Abuse

- B2 (Schizophrenia): Started using amphetamines in junior high school after parental divorce and abandonment. Overuse led to a severe mental disorder.
- A5 (Mental Illness): Struggled with significant life stress and alcohol abuse in youth, eventually diagnosed with a mental disorder before turning 30.

These cases indicate that family breakdown, inadequate social support, and economic hardships contribute to higher risks of substance abuse and mental health crises among Indigenous persons.

g) Alcohol Consumption and Strokes

- A6 (Mental Illness): Engaged in excessive drinking due to economic stress but later stopped after being diagnosed with a mental illness.
- B8, B9 (Strokes): Both suffered early strokes in middle age due to excessive alcohol consumption, which led to their disabilities.

The high prevalence of alcohol-related disabilities among Indigenous persons suggests that alcohol consumption may serve as a coping mechanism for stress within the tribe, yet it significantly contributes to deteriorating health and increased disability risks.

Among the 14 interviewees with acquired disabilities, the primary causes were insufficient healthcare access, limited transportation, poverty, and fragile social support systems. Compared to Taiwan's overall population with disabilities, Indigenous persons are disproportionately affected by illness- and accident-related disabilities (Ministry of Health and Welfare, 2023). Furthermore, interview findings show that alcohol consumption is closely linked to life stress, further exacerbating disability risks. These findings indicate that the primary causes of disability among Atayal persons are not merely physical impairments or social barriers but stem from a deeper structure of "social suffering." This differs from the social model of disability emphasized in CRPD, as disabilities in Indigenous communities often result from long-term social marginalization, poverty, and health disparities rather than solely environmental barriers or social discrimination.

To effectively support persons with disabilities in Indigenous areas, disability policies must go beyond the traditional social model and incorporate perspectives of social suffering and structural inequality. Addressing the unique challenges faced by Indigenous persons with disabilities requires comprehensive healthcare access, employment security, and culturally appropriate support services, rather than simply applying Western disability frameworks without adaptation.

h) A Tribe Lacking Support: Social Exclusion Beyond the Concept of Social Barriers?

The Atayal people with disabilities in Kaladala Village, Datong Township, Yilan, face multiple challenges, including limited public transportation, disrupted education, poverty, and a lack of family support. These difficulties reflect a broader issue of social exclusion, rather than simply a matter of social barriers as defined by CRPD.

i) Inconvenient Transportation and Lack of Resources

Datong Township lacks community-based disability services and large hospitals, with only one health clinic available. For medical examinations or surgeries, residents must travel to Luodong or Yilan, while the nearest small clinic requires a 40-minute motorcycle ride. Public transportation remains underdeveloped, with bus schedules unchanged for decades, offering only three trips per day (morning, noon, and evening). For those unable to purchase or drive a vehicle, transportation becomes a significant economic burden. B3, who is severely visually impaired, cannot drive and must pay NT$1,000 per trip to hire someone to transport him to the nearest hospital for medical check-ups. Both A2 and A1 noted that local transportation and service resources have remained stagnant for years, forcing many residents to buy their own vehicles to compensate for the lack of public transit.

j) Interrupted Education

Most interviewees had low educational attainment, with only A2, A3, and B1 having attended high school (without completing it), while the rest had only finished elementary or middle school. Many recalled frequent absenteeism due to various challenges:

- Transportation barriers: "The school was too far to walk."
- Financial difficulties: "Dormitory fees were too expensive for my family."
- Family responsibilities: "My parents had to work, so I had to take care of my younger siblings and help on the farm."

B6 shared: "As a child, I had to tend cattle and dig sweet potatoes. Since we couldn't afford boarding, I couldn't continue my education after elementary school." This situation—education being cut short due to economic and family constraints—was common among the interviewees.

k) Informal Labor and Poverty

Except for A3, who had stable employment in a factory in Taoyuan, all other interviewees had never left the village or held long-term, contract-based employment. Most sustained themselves through informal jobs such as farming, bamboo harvesting, weeding, and temporary construction work. Even before becoming disabled, they had unstable incomes and lived in economic hardship.

Most respondents relied on government subsidies of approximately NT$5,000 per month, with only A2, A3, and B4 not classified as low-income households. Furthermore, many did not own their homes but were allowed to live in properties temporarily provided by relatives. This reflects a longstanding structural issue in which Indigenous communities struggle with poverty and employment instability.

l) Family Separation and Social Isolation

Among the interviewees, A2 and A3 lived with their spouses or children, while others either lived alone or with elderly mothers:

- A1 and B3 were divorced, now living alone, with children working elsewhere.
- B1, B2, B4, and B5 never married; B2 and B4 lived alone, while B1 and B5 resided with their mothers.
- Many experienced parental separation, the early death of family members, or the loss of a spouse, resulting in diminished social and emotional support.

A1 shared: "My husband was abusive, so I divorced him. I've lived alone ever since, taking care of my parents by myself. I even had to go to the hospital alone for surgeries … Eventually, I developed depression and was hospitalized in a psychiatric ward multiple times." The lack of a family support system intensifies the difficulties faced by Indigenous persons with disabilities, not only in daily life but also in accessing medical and emotional support.

The Atayal persons with disabilities in Kaladala Village experience barriers in education, poverty, family separation, inadequate transportation, and a lack of medical and social support services. Many acquired their disabilities due to delayed medical treatment, traffic accidents, or substance abuse, all of which are closely linked to the structural inequalities and social suffering of indigenous communities. Compared to the CRPD's focus on social discrimination and accessibility, the struggles of the Atayal people are more aligned with poverty, educational inequality, resource shortages, and social isolation. This suggests that a CRPD-based framework alone may not fully address the needs of Indigenous persons with disabilities. Instead, policies must incorporate perspectives of social suffering and structural inequality to effectively improve their living conditions.

2. The Concept of Social Discrimination: Absent from the Lives of Atayal Persons with Disabilities

a) Compassion vs. CRPD's Concept of Social Barriers

The Atayal worldview is shaped by gaga, a set of ancestral customs, taboos, and social contracts that dictate behavior. Violating gaga is believed to bring divine punishment (Wang, 2006). However, no historical or contemporary research explicitly documents Atayal perspectives on disability. An early Japanese colonial report (1996) classified Atayal persons with disabilities into two categories:

- "Mnquciq" (idiocy) and "liqun utux" (spiritually possessed): Considered incapable of decision-making, but their actions were often forgiven. Families were responsible for restraining them to prevent harm to others.
- Persons with sensory and physical disabilities (e.g., blind, deaf, mute, or physically impaired): They retained legal capacity and were viewed with pity and compassion. Publicly mocking them was strictly forbidden and punishable.

This suggests that historically, the Atayal people showed sympathy and acceptance toward persons with disabilities, rather than discrimination. Do these attitudes persist today, or has modern industrial society introduced a discriminatory view of disability as unproductive?

Interviews with Atayal persons with disabilities indicate that, apart from B2, most felt accepted rather than discriminated against. C1, the sister of an intellectually disabled man, explained: "For those born with disabilities, our people believe it's due to past misfortunes in the family. Is that discrimination? For those who acquire disabilities later, we take it lightly and even joke about it."

Other interviewees shared similar views:

- B5: “People in the village help me, they send me food. They don’t see me as different—we’re all family.”
- A3: “We don’t discriminate. Maybe people think things, but we help each other more.”
- B4: “People in the village still support me. They even help park my four-wheel scooter.”

Overall, Atayal communities do not strongly associate disability with discrimination as framed by the CRPD. Instead, family and social ties promote mutual aid and inclusion, reducing the relevance of Western notions of social barriers.

b) The Use of the Term "Disabled": Does Language Matter?

In mainstream Taiwanese discourse, the term “handicap” has been replaced by “disabilities” to avoid negative connotations. However, in the interviews, many respondents continued to use “handicap” without perceiving it as derogatory:

- B4: “Only government offices use ‘persons with disabilities’. At home, we just say ‘handicap’! To me, ‘handicap’ and ‘disability’ mean the same thing.”
- A1: “It doesn’t matter what you call it, we’re talking about the same people.”
- A3: “Whether it’s ‘handicap’ or ‘disability,’ isn’t it the same thing?”

For Atayal persons with disabilities, these terms are external labels with little impact on their daily lives. The notion that terminology itself constitutes social discrimination—central to CRPD’s framework—is largely irrelevant in their lived experiences.

CRPD emphasizes social discrimination as a key factor in disabling persons with impairments. However, for the Atayal people, discrimination is not a defining aspect of their experience of disability. Instead, their challenges are shaped by economic hardship, lack of infrastructure, and family circumstances, rather than societal attitudes. This suggests that applying CRPD’s concept of social barriers directly to Indigenous communities may overlook their unique cultural perspectives and lived realities.

3. Unnecessary CRPD Community Services: As Long as There Is Family, No Outside Help Is Needed

a) Western Community Services vs. The Needs of Atayal Persons with Disabilities

CRPD prioritizes accessible community services for persons with disabilities. However, the Atayal villages in this study lack CRPD-designated disability services. This absence raises questions:

- Is it due to local government resource allocation based on population size?
- Or does the individual rights-based model of CRPD services fail to align with the Atayal collective cultural values and actual needs?

Previous studies on long-term care in Indigenous communities indicate cultural and practical differences in caregiving. CRPD assumes a fixed boundary between "society" and "individuals", emphasizing personal rights. In contrast, Atayal identity and gaga traditions define individuals through social relationships and collective experiences (Wang, 2023).

Unlike Western notions of fixed communities, Atayal alang refers to "a group of people who gather and support each other," bound by rituals, cooperation, and shared responsibilities. The community is fluid and flexible, shaped by social interactions rather than rigid geographic boundaries. In this context, applying a standardized community service model designed for urbanized societies may not align with Atayal social structures.

b) "As Long as Family Is Here, We Don't Need Outside Help"

Most respondents were unaware of community-based disability services such as personal assistants or supported employment. Instead, they prioritized family presence over formal services:

- A3: "The real problem is when children leave the village. If they stay, we don't need government help."
- B1: "My mom takes care of me. If she gets sick, my brother will take over."
- B4: "I'd rather have my nieces come help me than strangers from a service program."
- B6: "I just hope my son won't forget about us when I can no longer move."

Rather than advocating for disability services as a right, respondents valued family support more. A2 summarized this sentiment:

"I don't need to demand my rights or ask society to change for me. If my family or friends can help, I don't need these services."

c) Survival First: Financial Aid Over Services

Many respondents asked: "Can your research help us get more financial aid from the government?" Most receive about NT$5,000 per month, with low-income individuals receiving NT$7,000–8,000—insufficient even in rural areas.

- B6 borrows rice from neighbors, and B7–B9 rely on elder care centers for free meals.
- B1: "Cash is more helpful than services. I can't go out, but with money, I can ask someone to buy things for me."
- B2: "There are many disabled people in our village. Most apply for disability benefits, not services, because we can barely survive."

For Atayal persons with disabilities, economic survival outweighs accessibility to community services. They do not expect the government to improve infrastructure or medical resources, as long as cash aid is sufficient to cover transportation and essential needs.

CRPD emphasizes universal access to disability services, but Atayal respondents prioritize family care and financial aid. The assumption that government services must replace family support does not align with Atayal social structures. Instead of imposing Western community service models, policies should focus on economic stability and culturally adapted support systems.

V. Conclusion and Discussion

1. Perceptions of Social Discrimination and Barriers Among Atayal Persons with Disabilities

The CRPD, based on the social model of disability, emphasizes the state's responsibility to eliminate social discrimination and environmental barriers faced by individuals with impairments. However, this study found that Atayal communities inherently practice compassion toward persons with disabilities, discouraging mockery or insults. Strong kinship bonds within the tribe make discrimination against persons with disabilities rare. Furthermore, terms such as "disability" or "handicap" are perceived by most Atayal persons with disabilities as external language constructs without inherent discriminatory connotations. Consequently, the social discrimination and barriers defined by the CRPD do not appear to be prevalent within Atayal communities.

2. Social Suffering as a Primary "Disabling" Factor

Indigenous peoples, long affected by capitalism and colonialism, often reside in resource-deficient rural areas, facing challenges such as poor transportation, health inequities, and economic poverty. These conditions constitute a state of social suffering. The study revealed that most Atayal persons with disabilities acquired their impairments due to untreated illnesses, traffic accidents, or excessive alcohol consumption—problems closely linked to the lack of medical resources and high stress levels within their communities. Data from Taiwan's Ministry of Health and Welfare indicate that Indigenous peoples have significantly higher rates of disability caused by illness and accidents compared to the general population. This highlights how social suffering creates an alternative "disabling" environment distinct from the CRPD's focus on post-impairment discrimination.

3. Limited Priority for Accessibility to CRPD Community Services

While the CRPD advocates for accessible community services, this study found that most Atayal persons with disabilities place greater importance on support from family or community members rather than assistance from professional service providers. They do not perceive the absence of community services as a violation of their rights but are more concerned about the lack of family presence and support. Instead of prioritizing community service infrastructure, respondents expressed a preference for financial assistance to address transportation and healthcare needs, which would more effectively alleviate their living challenges.

4. Indigeneity and Poverty Outweigh Disability-Related Inconveniences

The challenges faced by Atayal persons with disabilities stem more from the systemic deprivation of Indigenous Peoples than from post-impairment social discrimination. Insufficient infrastructure in education, transportation, and healthcare presents more urgent issues than the lack of community services. Grech (2011) asserts that reducing poverty is more critical than implementing CRPD community services, a perspective echoed by the Atayal respondents.

5. Tailoring CRPD Implementation to Indigenous Contexts

The CRPD shifts the focus from the medical model to a human rights model. However, directly abandoning the medical model in Indigenous areas may be overly abrupt, ignoring the historical and systemic social suffering faced by these communities. Indigenous populations require improvements in healthcare and living conditions to prevent disadvantaged environments from producing more persons with disabilities. To effectively implement the CRPD, it is essential to incorporate Indigenous cultural and geographical specificities, integrating concepts such as "cultural care" and "cultural safety" rather than directly transplanting the CRPD framework.

The challenges faced by Tayal persons with disabilities stem from the historical impacts of capitalism and colonialism, with social suffering playing a crucial role in the disablement process. The applicability of the CRPD's frameworks on social discrimination and community services is limited in Indigenous areas. Therefore, priority should be given to improving infrastructure and economic support in Indigenous communities while integrating Indigenous cultural characteristics to promote the genuine well-being and social inclusion of persons with disabilities. However, this paper focuses on the relationship between Indigenous persons with disabilities living in Indigenous communities and community services. In Taiwan, Indigenous people living in tribal communities and those residing in metropolitan areas may have different perceptions of Indigenous collective culture and the individual rights emphasized by the CRPD. Further research is needed to better understand the experiences and needs of Indigenous persons with disabilities living in different regions of Taiwan.

References

Chang, H.-H., & Su, F.-S. (2019). The history and culture of Western disability perspectives. In K.-Y. Wang, C.-Y. Lin, & H.-H. Chang (Eds.), *Disability Studies: Theory and Policy Applications* (pp. 11–42). Kaohsiung: Chu Liu.

Chen, L.-J., & Chan, Y.-C. (2015). Exploring the implementation model of the Tribal Elders Day Care Center Project (Tribal Cultural Health Station) in Nantou's indigenous areas. *Taiwan Indigenous Studies Quarterly, 8*(1), 43–76.

Chen, M.-H. (2014). Indigenous health issues in Taiwan and the world: A historical and political-economic perspective. *Taiwan: A Radical Quarterly in Social Studies, 97*, 209–246.

Chi, C.-J. (2005). Indigenous research and Han-Indigenous relations: A postcolonial review. *National Policy Quarterly, 4*(3), 5–28.

Chisholm, R., Tulich, T., & Blagg, H. (2017). Indigenous young people with foetal alcohol spectrum disorders: The Convention on the Rights of Persons with Disabilities and reform to the law governing fitness to stand trial in Western Australia. *Law in Context, 35*(2), 85-107.

Chiu, T. (2024). Exploring Indigenous Disability Experiences in Taiwan. *The International Journal of Disability and Social Justice, 4*(1), 82–98.

Chou, Y.-C., & Lin, H.-F. (2020). *2020 Research on the Adaptation of Disability Welfare Institutions to Article 19 of the CRPD.* Social and Family Affairs Administration, Ministry of Health and Welfare: Parents' Association for Persons with Intellectual Disabilities, R.O.C.

Chou, Y.-C. (2023). When CRPD and indigenous people with disabilities intersect: A preliminary study on community services for Atayal tribe members in Yi-Lan County. *Taiwanese Journal of Sociology, 73*, 105–148.

Chung, H.-H. (2017). The design of collective and individual rights in Taiwan's indigenous policies. *Indigenous Education Journal, 27*, 6–7.

Cleaver, S. R. (2016). *Postcolonial encounters with disability: Exploring disability and ways forward together with persons with disabilities in Western Zambia.* Canada: University of Toronto.

Ghai, A. (2002). Disabled women: An excluded agenda of Indian feminism. *Hypatia, 17*(3), 49–66.

Grech, S. (2011). Recolonising debates or perpetuated coloniality? Decentring the spaces of disability, development and community in the global South. *International Journal of Inclusive Education, 15*(1), 87–100.

Haang'andu, P. (2018). Transnationalizing disability policy in embedded cultural-cognitive worldviews: The case of sub-Saharan Africa. *Disability and the Global South, 5*(1), 1292–1314.

Hahmann, T., Badets, N., & Hughes, J. (2019). *Indigenous people with disabilities in Canada: First Nations people living off reserve, Métis and Inuit aged 15 years and older.* Canada: Statistics Canada.

Chang H.H., Lin J.-J., Ru H.-Y., & Chen M.-C. (2024). Welfare State Regimes Encountering Indigenous People with Disabilities: A Systematic Literature Review. *NTU Social Work Review, 50*, 141–177.

Hoffman, S. J., Sritharan, L., & Tejpar, A. (2016). Is the UN Convention on the Rights of Persons with Disabilities impacting mental health laws and policies in high-income countries? A case study of implementation in Canada. *BMC International Health and Human Rights, 16*(1), 1–18.

Hsu, C.-T. (2020). The current situation and challenges of local long-term care workforce in indigenous communities: Insights from a local participant. *Community Development Quarterly, 169*, 209–218.

Hsu, C.-T., & Lin, T.-L. (2011). Exploring the urban living experiences of the Paiwan elderly. *Journal of Social Development Studies, (9)*, 19–39.

Huang, Y.-H. (2014). *Indigenous Social Welfare: Problem Analysis and System Construction*. Taipei: Shuang-Ye Books.

Huang, Y.-H. (2020). Trends in international indigenous social welfare development: Implications for Taiwan. *Community Development Quarterly, 169*, 19–36.

Jakubowicz, A., & Meekosha, H. (2002). Bodies in motion: Critical issues between disability studies and multicultural studies. *Journal of Intercultural Studies, 23*, 237–252.

Jenks, A. B. (2017). *Rights Enabled or Disabled? The UN CRPD and Fixing Meanings of Disability in the Global South* [Unpublished doctoral dissertation]. University of Delaware.

Kleinman, A., Das, V., & Lock, M. M. (Eds.). (1997). *Social suffering*. California: University of California Press.

Kuan, D.-W. (2017). Individual and collective rights of indigenous peoples. *Indigenous Education Journal, 27*, 12–16.

Lai, L.-Y. (2017). The development process and cultural considerations of indigenous community care services: A case study of Haiduan Township, Taitung County. *Taiwan Journal of Community Work and Community Studies, 7*(2), 149–181.

Liao, F.-T. (2017). Historical development and the connotation of power. In N.-Y. Sun & F.-T. Liao (Eds.), *Convention on the Rights of Persons with Disabilities* (pp. 3–24). Taipei: Taiwan New Century Cultural and Educational Foundation.

Lin, M.-J. (2019). A tribal care paradigm or the Sisyphean boulder? Reflections on Atayal eldercare services through pilot projects in remote areas. *Taiwan Journal of Community Work and Community Studies, 9*(1), 37–82.

Lin, Yi-Ying, & Pei-Ting Huang. (2020). The development of human resources empowerment in Aboriginal Village. *Development Journal, 109*, 234–242.

Meekosha, H. (2004). Drifting down the gulf stream: Navigating the cultures of disability studies. *Disability & Society, 19*(7), 721–733.

Meekosha, H. (2008). Contextualizing disability: Developing southern/global theory. *Keynote presented at the 4th Biennial Disability Studies Conference, Lancaster University, UK, September 2nd-4th.*

Meekosha, H. (2011). Decolonising disability: Thinking and acting globally. *Disability & Society, 26*(6), 667–682.

Ru, H.-Y. (2018). Cultural safety issues in Taiwan's indigenous long-term care policy. *Taiwan: A Radical Quarterly in Social Studies, 109*, 199–214.

Shih, C.-S. (2017). The dilemma between freedom and equality: A discussion on the dialectics of indigenous group rights and individual freedom. *Indigenous Education Journal, 27*, 8–9.

Soldatic, K., & Biyanwila, S. J. (2006). *Disability and development: A critical southern standpoint on able-bodied masculinity.* Presented at the TASA Conference, University of Western Australia & Murdoch University, December 4–7.

Tsai, W.-S. (2004). Reflecting on the educational situation and prospects of Taiwan's indigenous students from the perspective of equal educational opportunities. *Journal of Education and Social Research, 6*, 109–144.

G. The Right to Housing and Forced Evictions – Recent Developments

Lukas Romberg[1]

Abstract:

This article addresses the ongoing challenge of securing adequate housing and the occurrence of forced evictions.[2] While it is not intended to provide an exhaustive analysis of the right to housing – which has already been widely discussed in the literature – this overview seeks to present its legal basis and key components in a clear and accessible way, without tracing every one of its many branches and ramifications. In addition, it highlights recent developments and identifies emerging areas for further research in this constantly evolving field.

Keywords:

human rights; right to housing; forced eviction; socio-economic rights; eviction and human rights; housing; adequate alternative housing; proportionality analysis; right to land; General Comment No. 26

I. Introduction

To underline the vital importance of the right to housing (to be precise: *adequate* housing) and the protection against forced evictions, I must begin this article with the following anecdotal experience: I had the great opportunity to assist the members of the International Review Committee during the review of the Republic of China (Taiwan)'s Third National Report on the International Covenant on Economic, Social and Cultural Rights (ICESCR) in the spring of 2022. During the proceedings, a considerable discrepancy became apparent, particularly in how the right to adequate housing was interpreted and assessed in its function as protection against forced evictions. On the one hand, numerous directly affected

1 Research Assistant, Chair of Public Law, Economic Analysis of Law and Public Commercial Law, University of Mannheim (Germany), lukas.romberg@uni-mannheim.de

2 Parts of this publication are based on a lecture the author gave during an event organized by the National Human Rights Commission (NHRC) of Taiwan at National Chengchi University in Taipei on October 25, 2023.

citizens took the floor, sharing deeply emotional accounts of their traumatic experiences with forced evictions. On the other hand, the Taiwanese government stated that there had been no forced evictions for development projects during the period in question at all (Republic of China (Taiwan) 2022, 39–40). There is much to suggest that this is due to a very different understanding of the term "*forced eviction*", which is also reflected in para. 53 of the Concluding Observations issued by the International Review Committee (International Review Committee 2022, 10).

Considering the foregoing, there is sufficient reason to shed some light on the right to housing as a "crucially important human right" (Donnelly et al. 2020, 209) and to analyze recent developments in this area on an international level by making references to the situation in Taiwan and Germany.

II. Forced Evictions as a Worldwide Problem

1. Numbers and Facts

To begin with, it must be emphasized that – as is so often the case with violations of human rights – collecting relevant data proves difficult due to the frequent absence of systematic reporting. Nonetheless, it can be assumed that all the key indicators relevant to the right to housing have worsened in recent years. According to *UN-Habitat*, more than 1.6[3] billion people worldwide currently live in inadequate housing conditions (UN-Habitat 2023, 17). While it was assumed at the time of the adoption of General Comment No. 4 in 1991 that there were around 100 million homeless people (CESCR 1991, 2), today, that figure is believed to have risen significantly to around 150 million (UN-Habitat n.d.).

Interestingly, the figures for annual evictions vary widely, ranging from 2 million (UN-Habitat n.d.) to as many as 15 million (UN 2019, 3). The truth probably lies somewhere in between, although once again, much depends on the definitional boundaries of what constitutes a "forced eviction". There is broad consensus that forced evictions are a pressing issue in both developed and developing countries (CESCR 1997, 2; Kothari 2015, 6). However, it is noticeable that some states stand out in particular. According to the former UN Special Rapporteur on adequate housing *Kothari*, China and India are especially striking: between approximately 1950 and 2000,

3 Whereby the website of UN-Habitat refers to 1.8 billion people (UN-Habitat n.d.).

each country displaced nearly 50 million people due to development projects, often in violation of international legal standards (Kothari 2015, 6).

2. Reasons for Evictions

The reasons for evictions are manifold and reflect a wide range of structural, political, and socio-economic dynamics. Reasons for large-scale evictions are often urban and rural development projects, such as dams or roads, but also mining, extractive industries and other industrial activities. Other examples include armed conflicts, refugee movements or mass migration. The clearing of informal settlements ("slums") – often framed as part of the so-called "criminalization of poverty"– also contributes significantly to the phenomenon. Importantly, events that may appear positive at first glance, such as major international sporting events[4], have also been associated with large-scale evictions and displacement (UN-Habitat and OHCHR 2014[5], 4; CESCR 1997, 2–3). In the last few decades, more people have been displaced by development projects than by conflicts or natural disasters (Kothari 2015, 6).

In everyday life, however, the most visible and widespread cause of eviction remains the inability to pay rent or service mortgage debt. A recent OECD study shows just how virulent the issue is for tenants: in 2023 alone, at least 2.4 million eviction proceedings were initiated against tenants in OECD member states. The United States recorded the highest rates, with approximately 4.6% of rental households affected (OECD 2024, 2–3).

3. Impact on Human Rights

Living somewhere safe constitutes one of the fundamental human needs. The impact on human rights is very diverse, as housing is what enables the realization of a whole range of human rights. Examples include the rights to health, work and education (UN-Habitat and OHCHR 2014, 5).

As is often the case with structural human rights violations, certain groups are disproportionately affected. Ethnic, religious, racial, and other minorities face a significantly higher risk of being subjected to forced evictions. Indigenous peoples, whose property rights to land are frequently insufficiently recognized or protected, are also disproportionately affected (Kolocek 2017, 158–59). The same applies to women due to physical inferiority and the lack

4 Detailed on this issue (Heerdt 2023).

5 This fact sheet contains a very comprehensive list of possible reasons for evictions.

of legal ownership of land in some states. Although evictions are psychologically stressful for most people, children are particularly vulnerable (UN-Habitat and OHCHR 2014, 16). Crucially, forced evictions can result in homelessness, thereby violating the very essence of the right to adequate housing. In many instances, eviction does not resolve the underlying structural issues but merely displaces them geographically or socially. Due to these far-reaching consequences, the former United Nations Commission on Human Rights (UNCHR) stated in a resolution in 1993 that forced evictions are a "gross violation of human rights" (UNCHR 1993, 2)[6].

III. The Right to Housing in (Inter)national Law

Although some states – including certain federal states within Germany (Guckelberger 2016, 350–51) – have incorporated references to the right to adequate housing into their constitutions, these provisions generally amount to programmatic state objectives rather than enforceable rights. A notable exception is South Africa, where Art. 26 of the Constitution explicitly guarantees the right to adequate housing and establishes corresponding state obligations (Hohmann 2021, 15). Nevertheless, the focus should be on provisions in international treaties.

First, there is no explicitly written "human right against forced eviction" as such in international human rights law. However, there is a *right to adequate housing*, which is closely linked to protection against forced evictions. Of particular importance is Art. 25 (1) of the Universal Declaration of Human Rights (UDHR), adopted by the United Nations General Assembly on 10 December 1948 in the aftermath of the Second World War. According to the UDHR, everyone has a right to an adequate standard of living, which includes housing. Nonetheless, the UDHR is not legally binding. Rather, it was the consensus from the outset that this declaration should be followed by legally binding treaties (Riedel 2017, 25–26).

The right to adequate housing has since been incorporated into a range of international treaties. The most important of these are Art. 11 (1) International Covenant on Economic, Social and Cultural Rights (ICESCR, 1966), Art. 5 (e) iii) International Convention on the Elimination of All Forms of Racial Discrimination (ICERD, 1965), Art. 14 (2) (h) Convention on the

6 Repeated in 2004: *Resolution 2004/28: Prohibition of Forced Evictions.* Adopted April 16, 2004, 56th Meeting, 60th Session. UN Doc. E/CN.4/RES/2004/28, https://undocs.org/en/E/CN.4/RES/2004/28.2004/28.

Elimination of All Forms of Discrimination Against Women (CEDAW, 1979), Art. 27 (3) Convention on the Rights of the Child (CRC, 1989) and Art. 28 (1) Convention on the Rights of Persons with Disabilities (CRPD, 2006). The International Covenant on Civil and Political Rights (ICCPR, 1966) does not directly mention the right to housing. However, Art. 17 of the ICCPR is understood by the UN treaty body in its General Comment (more on this below) in such a way that, although it does not grant a positive right to housing, it does establish a right to protection against state interference with existing habitations (CCPR 1988, 1).

Even though the right to housing is, as shown, recognized in numerous treaties, its essential interpretation is found in Art. 11 (1) ICESCR, as also reflected in para. 3 of General Comment No. 4. Accordingly, this article will focus primarily on Art. 11 (1) ICESCR.

Compared to other countries such as Germany, where the ICESCR has been in force since its ratification in 1973, the situation in Taiwan is markedly different. Taiwan has been excluded from the UN since the adoption of General Assembly Resolution 2758 in 1971 and is therefore not a State Party to the ICESCR or other core UN human rights treaties. Nevertheless, in a unilateral effort to strengthen its domestic human rights protection framework, Taiwan incorporated both the ICESCR and the ICCPR, along with other key treaties, into national law through the Act to Implement the ICCPR and the ICESCR in 2009 (Shope 2012).[7] According to Art. 1 of the Act, the purpose of the legislation is explicitly to enhance the country's human rights protection system. More significantly, Art. 3 of the Act stipulates that the interpretation of the Human Rights Committee should be taken as a basis. As a result, the substantive interpretation of the rights enshrined in the ICESCR and ICCPR in Taiwan closely mirrors international standards, despite the country's exclusion from formal UN mechanisms.

A textual reading of Art.11 (1) ICESCR reveals a high degree of vagueness, as the provision merely refers to the right to "adequate housing" without elaborating on its specific normative content (Donnelly et al. 2020, 216). The content is mainly illuminated by General Comments of the Committee on Economic, Social and Cultural Rights (CESCR), reports and guidelines issued by successive UN Special Rapporteurs on adequate housing, Concluding Observations issued in the framework of the periodic state reporting procedure and, – more recently – views adopted in the context of individual communications under the Optional Protocol to the ICESCR

7 See about the review process in Taiwan (Nowak 2019).

(OP-ICESCR)[8]. Over time, this interpretative framework has contributed to an increasingly precise and operational understanding of the right to adequate housing. The development of this process up to the current developments is described in the following.

IV. General Comments as a Cornerstone

The General Comments are an essential and indispensable tool for the interpretation of the ICESCR. In these authoritative statements, the Committee elaborates its interpretation of specific rights and obligations under the Covenant in relation to thematic issues or legal standards. Although General Comments are not considered legally binding in a formal sense, they are widely accepted and de facto followed, so that their legal recognition and justiciability in the narrower sense are not of overwhelming importance (Riedel 2017, 31).

Among the 26 General Comments adopted since 1981, two of the earlier ones even deal particularly with the right to housing and the issue of forced evictions. General Comment No. 4 from 1991 (CESCR 1991) contains a basic description of the right to adequate housing and was the first General Comment devoted to a substantive right under the ICESCR. In para. 8, it identifies seven core elements that are considered essential for the realization of the right to adequate housing: (1) legal security of tenure, (2) availability of services, materials, facilities and infrastructure, (3) affordability, (4) habitability, (5) accessibility, (6) location and (7) cultural adequacy. This comprehensive framework underscores that the right to housing entails far more than mere "bricks and mortar". Even if in many areas the affordability criterion has recently become of utmost importance[9], it is the first criterion – legal security of tenure – that is most directly relevant in the context of forced evictions. Although the remaining criteria are not genuinely associated with eviction, they certainly influence it indirectly. They become particularly relevant again when addressing the issue of accommodation after an eviction. Moreover, para. 18 states that "forced eviction are prima facie incompatible with the requirements of the Covenant and can only be justified in the most excep-

---

8 UN-General Assembly. 2008. *Optional Protocol to the International Covenant on Economic, Social and Cultural Rights.* A/RES/63/117, adopted 10 December 2008. https://treaties.un.org/doc/source/docs/A_RES_63_117-Eng.pdf

9 See for Taipei (Rietdijk 2024).

tional circumstances, and in accordance with the relevant principles of international law" (Saul, Kinley, and Mowbray 2014, 933).

Due to many reports on forced evictions, General Comment No. 7 (CESCR 1997) was explicitly dedicated to this issue. As *Leckie* observes, it constitutes "the most authoritative pronouncement on forced evictions" (Leckie 2001, 165). Even though there are various definitions of the term *forced eviction*[10], the one in para. 3 of General Comment No. 7 has gained widespread acceptance. There, forced evictions are defined as the "permanent or temporary removal against their will of individuals, families and/or communities from the homes and/or land which they occupy, without the provision of, and access to, appropriate forms of legal or other protection". Although the CESCR itself acknowledges in para. 3 that this definition may not be entirely satisfactory,[11] it sometimes even uses the terms "eviction" and "forced eviction" synonymously (Litschke and Sumski 2022, 4).

Further, para. 11 clarifies that – of course – not all evictions constitute human rights violations. Evictions may be justified if there are exceptional circumstances, such as rent (but also mortgage) arrears or unjustified damage to the rented property. However, the list is rather rudimentary and by no means exhaustive. For instance, other legitimate interests of landlords – such as repossession for personal use – are not explicitly addressed. The same applies to lawful development projects, although General Comment No. 7 describes possible negative effects of these initiatives, including those launched by major international aid organizations like the World Bank (paras. 17–18). It goes without saying that these reasons must actually exist and not serve merely as pretexts, as is often the case with the eviction of informal settlements (UN-Habitat and OHCHR 2014, 5). Moreover, the mere existence of one of the aforementioned circumstances does not automatically render an eviction lawful per se. As emphasized in para. 14, evictions must be "carried out in strict compli-

---

10 E.g. UN Special Rapporteur Kothari on Housing (A/HRC/4/18) 2007, para. 4: "*acts and/or omissions involving the coerced or involuntary displacement of individuals, groups and communities from homes and/or lands and common property resources that were occupied or depended upon, thus eliminating or limiting the ability of an individual, group or community to reside or work in a particular dwelling, residence or location, without the provision of, and access to, appropriate forms of legal or other protection.*"

11 As an example, I refer to the terminology in Germany: the term "forced eviction" is translated as "Zwangsräumung" and is also understood in legal language as the enforcement of an eviction order by enforcement officers. However, this says nothing about whether the eviction complies with national law, let alone international human rights law. Furthermore, nothing is said about whether physical force was actually used. The exercise of force can be against (human) rights, but it can also be in accordance with them.

ance with the relevant provisions of international human rights law and in accordance with general principles of reasonableness and proportionality". Para. 15 outlines eight procedural requirements, which can essentially be divided into those applicable before, during, and after the eviction. They include, for instance, an assessment of avoidability, sufficient prior consultation and information, the presence of government officials during the eviction, the possibility of seeking legal protection and asserting claims for compensation, and the provision of adequate alternative accommodation (Saul, Kinley, and Mowbray 2014, 937). According to para. 9 of General Comment No. 7, national legislation must be designed and implemented in such a way that these human rights obligations are fulfilled.

In addition to the General Comments, the *guidelines and reports of the UN Special Rapporteur on the right to adequate housing* – a mandate established in 2000 – have exerted significant influence on the evolving interpretation of the right to housing. Even if they are not legally binding either, they contribute to the formation of a widely recognized body of soft law and serve as important reference points for both states and civil society actors.

One particularly influential document is the *Basic Principles and Guidelines on Development-Based Evictions and Displacement* of 2007 (UN HRC 2007), which has been widely acknowledged and cited in both academic and policy contexts. The latest guidelines issued by former Special Rapporteur *Farha* from 2019 (UN HRC 2019) summarize the core problems regarding the right to housing once again and also address more recent challenges, such as the impact of climate change on the right to housing.

V. The CESCR's Jurisprudence on Housing Rights

A new dimension in the interpretation and enforcement of the right to adequate housing has emerged through the introduction of the individual communications procedure under the OP-ICESCR.

1. Implementation of the Optional Protocol

There was – and, some would argue, still is – a large gap between the enforcement of economic, social and cultural (ESC) rights and civil and political (CP) rights, resulting from a lack of political will to harmonize the two systems (Haque 2021, 39).[12]

12 On the drafting process, see Riedel (2011, 577–78).

While the first Optional Protocol to the ICCPR (OP-ICCPR), which entered into force in May 1976, has long provided individuals with the right to submit complaints regarding violations of CP rights, the enforcement of ESC rights was limited primarily to observations in the state reporting procedure and elaborations in General Comments (Riedel 2011, 575). In contrast to that, the OP-ICESCR, which came into force nearly 40 years later in May 2013, now also takes a more individualistic approach, reflecting a shift towards the equal recognition and enforceability of economic, social and cultural rights vis-à-vis civil and political rights (Riedel 2011, 586–87).

In accordance with Art. 2 OP-ICESCR, individuals or groups may submit so called communications[13] to the Committee on Economic, Social and Cultural Rights (CESCR) claiming to be victims of a violation of their Covenant rights by a State Party. However, the admissibility of such communications requires the prior exhaustion of domestic remedies (Art. 3), ensuring subsidiarity in the protection of rights. Upon examination of the communication (Art. 8), the Committee issues its views and, where appropriate, recommendations to the parties concerned (Art. 9). While the Committee's views are not legally binding in the formal sense, they carry considerable moral and interpretative authority, particularly in guiding national jurisprudence and influencing policy development.

In Germany, it took until July 2023 for the ratification of the OP-ICESCR – a step that was widely considered long overdue (Scherrieb 2023, 1). In contrast, the situation in Taiwan remains fundamentally different: as discussed above, Taiwan is excluded from the UN treaty, and the International Review Committee established by Taiwan itself does not have the authority to adjudicate individual complaints.

As of August 2025, 46 states have signed and 31 have ratified the OP-ICESCR.[14] The proportion of states that have ratified the corresponding optional protocol in relation to the state parties is the lowest compared to the six other core human rights treaties (Di 2024, 1442). *Di* offers several explanations for this. For one, the ratification process itself can be very time-consuming and politically sensitive. It must also be taken into account that the OP-ICESCR is still quite young compared to other optional protocols. But more fundamentally, there is ongoing skepticism regarding the justiciability of economic, social and cultural rights, which are often

13 On the development of the term, see Riedel (2011, 580–81).

14 United Nations Treaty Collection, *Optional Protocol to the International Covenant on Economic, Social and Cultural Rights*, https://treaties.un.org/pages/ViewDetails.aspx?src=TREATY&mtdsg_no=IV-3-a&chapter=4, accessed August 4, 2025.

perceived as vague or overly dependent on progressive realization (Di 2024, 1442–44). Unlike civil and political rights – which largely take the form of negative obligations (e.g. the prohibition of torture) – economic, social and cultural rights frequently entail positive duties on the part of the state, such as the allocation of resources or the creation of social programs. These obligations are often seen as more difficult to quantify or predict, and thus as potentially more intrusive for States Parties (Vols 2023, 3). This must not obscure the fact that the precise scope of CP rights is just as contested in detail as that of ESC rights.

So far, the individual complaints procedure has not seen widespread use among potential victims. A large number of the current cases share similar factual backgrounds and legal issues, often directed against the same state (Di 2024, 1445). Still, the OP-ICESCR holds significant potential to foster a more diverse and evolving "committee jurisprudence" (Riedel 2011, 587–88) in the future.[15]

2. Right to Housing as a Core Competence of the CESCR

It is no overstatement to claim that the right to adequate housing – particularly in the context of forced evictions – has emerged as the core area of jurisprudential focus for the CESCR under the individual communications procedure. The vast majority of the 121 cases that have been closed since the entry into force of the OP-ICESCR relate to the right to adequate housing, and more specifically (forced) evictions.[16] The number of proceedings that resulted in a decision on the merits is currently relatively low at 16. As of March 2025, a total of 204 cases remain pending, some of which were submitted as early as 2018 and 2019.[17] Among the 204 pending communications, 192 involve evictions, including 136 against Spain – a particularly significant proportion.

The question therefore arises as to why the Spanish eviction cases are so prominently represented. One factor could be the severe Spanish housing crisis resulting from the financial crisis (Scherrieb 2023, 3 fn. 15). The second reason given by *Alston* is the 2018 ruling of the Spanish Supreme Court, which held that individual decisions by UN treaty bodies are legally

15 More critical is Di (2024, 1460): "has not been accepted and welcomed by states as expected."

16 Office of the High Commissioner for Human Rights juris database, filtered by CESCR, https://juris.ohchr.org, accessed August 4, 2025.

17 Table of pending cases as of March 2025 published on the website of the Office of the High Commissioner for Human Rights, https://www.ohchr.org/en/treaty-bodies/cescr/individual-communications, accessed August 4, 2025.

binding on the State[18] –, thereby increasing the attractiveness of the CESCR as a forum for dispute resolution. He also states that in an early view of the committee it was held that eviction without the provision of adequate alternative housing violates the right to housing, so that communications were submitted with the requests for interim measures under Art. 5 OP-ICESCR (Alston 2020, 458–59). In 2023, however, the Spanish judiciary clarified – or arguably narrowed – this precedent. The Supreme Court held that while the views of treaty bodies do not possess direct executive effect, they may nonetheless serve as a basis for state liability under domestic law (Pineda 2023, 211). Yet, the decline in communications assumed by Scherrieb (2023, 3 fn. 15) did not materialize in view of the number of open proceedings from the following years. It remains to be seen whether this dominance of Spanish eviction cases will continue, or whether the future will bring a broader geographical and substantive diversification of the Committee's caseload – potentially involving new States Parties or communications concerning other ESC rights beyond housing.

3. The Views of the Committee as a Concretization of the Right to Housing

As previously noted, the right to adequate housing is the core area of the CESCR's jurisprudence under its individual communications mechanism. While the primary function of these proceedings is to assess specific individual complaints and – where appropriate – offer redress to victims of violations, their significance goes well beyond the resolution of isolated disputes. At the same time, they also serve as an effective tool for the Committee to further specify the scope of protection under Art. 11 (1) ICESCR (Grohmann 2022, 2).

a) The State as the Duty-Bearer Under the Covenant

To begin with, it is essential to examine the personal scope of protection under the Covenant – that is, who is protected by the right to adequate housing and who bears the corresponding obligations.

The protection under Art. 11 (1) ICESCR is initially independent of the ownership rights to the land or building. Thus, both owners and tenants, whether in the private rental market or public/social housing, are enclosed. Importantly, the absence of formal legal title – a situation frequently encountered by indigenous peoples and informal settlers – does

18 María de los Ángeles González Carreño v. Ministry of Justice, Judgment No. 1263/2018.

not, in itself, constitute a legitimate justification for forced eviction (Kolocek 2017, 158–59). Respect for human rights requires that residents of emergency or transitional housing or even informal settlements enjoy protection against arbitrary or forced eviction (General Comment No. 4, para. 8 (a)).

This principle was reaffirmed in the case *López Albán v. Spain*[19]. The complainant had entered into a rental agreement with an individual who, unbeknownst to her, was neither the legal owner nor otherwise authorized to lease the premises. When the actual owner initiated eviction proceedings, the Spanish courts ruled against her, citing her lack of legal title. The CESCR however, held that while the absence of legal title may constitute a legitimate basis for initiating eviction procedures, such actions must still comply with all other Covenant guarantees, including the requirements of necessity, proportionality, and the provision of adequate alternative housing (para. 6.2).

In this context, the communication *Infante Díaz v. Spain*[20] should also be mentioned. The Venezuelan national Infante Díaz and her son were undocumented migrants in Spain and were evicted without the provision of alternative housing. The Committee, referring to General Comment No. 20 (ICESCR 2009) on non-discrimination, stated that Covenant law applies equally to everyone, regardless of nationality, legal status and documentation (para. 7.6). This reinforces the universalist character of ICESCR obligations. Nonetheless, the protective scope is not unlimited. A limitation can be found in the communication *Pankka & Pérez vs. Spain*[21], in which the CESCR emphasized that the Covenant does not protect against evictions that do not relate to the primary residence, but to real estate investments (para. 8.4).

On the other side of the legal relationship stands the state as the primary duty-bearer under the Covenant. However, in practice, states sometimes attempt to evade responsibility by portraying forced evictions as the result of purely private legal relationships. This line of argument became particularly visible in *Ben Djazia et al. v. Spain*[22] – the first communication in which the CESCR substantively addressed the issue of forced evictions. In that case, a family had been living in a rented accommodation in Madrid. When their rental agreement expired, it was not possible to extend the lease due to arrears. As they had no alternative accommodation, they refused to move out,

19 López Albán v. Spain, E/C.12/66/D/37/2018.

20 Infante Díaz v. Spain, E/C.12/73/D/134/2019.

21 Pankka & Pérez v. Spain, E/C.12/65/D/9/2015.

22 Ben Djazia et al. v. Spain, E/C.12/61/D/5/2015.

so the lessor took legal action to evict them. In response to the communication, Spain argued that it bears no responsibility in the termination of a private-law tenancy, but merely acts as an intermediary in the dispute between the private parties (para. 4.2). However, such a restrictive reading of state obligations is incompatible with the Covenant. Human rights obligations are not limited to direct state actions but also entail positive duties to protect individuals from rights violations committed by third parties. This principle of horizontal effect (*Drittwirkung*) requires states to adopt legislative and administrative measures ensuring that private actors – such as landlords, real estate developers, landowners, and businesses – do not carry out evictions in a manner that violates Covenant standards (paras. 14.1–14.2). From the residents' perspective, it makes no difference whether the landlord is the State, a company or a private individual (Casla 2022, 260), nor whether they are tenants rather than owners themselves.

Nonetheless, the public-private divide can give rise to complex legal and accountability issues. The *Grenfell Tower fire* in the United Kingdom is a prominent example, illustrating how the "boundaries between public accountability and private unaccountability" in the housing context may become ambiguous and contested (Hohmann 2019, 25). Such cases highlight the urgent need for clear regulatory frameworks and effective enforcement mechanisms to ensure that human rights are upheld, regardless of the legal form or actor involved.

b) Concretization of the Requirements for a Lawful Eviction Towards a Proportionality Test

While General Comment No. 7 acknowledges that evictions may be lawful if they are conducted "in accordance with the law and in conformity with the provisions of the International Covenants on Human Rights" (para. 3), the precise criteria for such conformity remained largely undefined. Already in the Ben Djazia case (supra note 22), the individual requirements that must be met to avoid a violation of Art. 11 (1) ICESCR were outlined in para. 15.1 – albeit not yet as clearly defined as in later communications. Such a detailed breakdown of the individual requirements can finally be found in the case of *Rosario Gómez-Limón Pardo v. Spain*[23], whereby these requirements presumably relate to the limitation of all Covenant rights (Grohmann 2022, 9). In para. 9.4 of that view the Committee identifies Art. 2 (1) ICESCR in conjunction with Art. 11 (1) ICESCR as the normative basis for a five-step proportionality test.

---

23 Rosario Gómez-Limón Pardo v. Spain, E/C.12/67/D/52/2018.

The *first* requirement is that the eviction must be determined by law. This principle also derives from Art. 4 ICESCR. The same applies to the *second* condition, according to which an eviction may only take place for a legitimate reason and must serve "the general welfare in a democratic society". The *third* requirement is that it must be suitable for the legitimate purpose cited. Further, the *fourth* condition is that "the limitation must be necessary, in the sense that if there is more than one measure that could reasonably be expected to serve the purpose of the limitation, the least restrictive measure must be chosen" (necessity). Finally, the *fifth* requirement is a weighting of the benefits of the limitation in promoting the general welfare against the impacts on the enjoyment of the limited right (proportionality in a narrow sense). The analysis of this proportionality "must be carried out by a judicial or other impartial and independent authority with the power to order the cessation of the infringement and provide an effective remedy".

Although property as such is not a right specifically protected under the ICESCR, the proprietary interests assigned to individuals by domestic legal systems can of course be taken into account on the "general welfare" side of the proportionality analysis (Di 2024, 1455). As *Grohmann* has analyzed correctly, it is noteworthy that the criteria of the proportionality analysis were adopted almost verbatim from the case law of the German Federal Constitutional Court (Grohmann 2022, 9). Various factors must be taken into account when weighing up the interests. As previously discussed, the protection afforded by Art. 11 (1) ICESCR applies irrespective of the legal status or identity of the lessor. However, this is not entirely irrelevant when it comes to weighing up the interests involved. A distinction is drawn between individual landlords, who may require the property for personal use or as essential income, and institutional actors, such as financial institutions or corporate owners (López Albán v. Spain (supra note 19, at para. 11.5)). Other factors to be considered in the proportionality test are the "availability of suitable alternative housing, the personal circumstances of the occupants and their dependents and whether they have cooperated with the authorities in seeking suitable solutions" (supra note 23, at para. 9.5). Greater requirements for justification are made, for example, in the case of Ben Djazia (supra note 22), as the eviction affects young children, in other words particularly vulnerable groups of people (para. 16.6).

The depth of the committee's own proportionality analysis varies depending on the procedural quality of the national-level assessment. Where domestic courts have conducted a comprehensive and reasoned proportionality review, the Committee tends to exercise restraint in re-evaluating the case, regardless of whether it agrees with the outcome. In contrast, where national courts fail to engage in a meaningful balancing of interests, the Committee assumes a more active role in the proportionality test (Grohmann 2022, 12–13).

In the latest case *Hamid Saydawi and Masir Farah v. Italy*[24], the criteria for justification of an eviction and the proportionality test are also described in detail (paras. 8.1–8.7). However, the CESCR then quite quickly jumps to the conclusion – presumably due to the clarity of the violation on the merits – without conducting a full examination (i.e., an assessment of reasonableness), resulting in a finding that a violation of the right to housing had occurred (Kreller 2024, 139).

c) Adequate Alternative Housing and Procedural Requirements

In addition to the proportionality analysis, some procedural requirements must be met. As described above, these were already outlined in General Comment No. 7 (see IV.) and were subsequently reaffirmed in Ben Djazia et al v. Spain (supra note 22, at para. 15.1). The CESCR addressed these issues as early as in its first-ever decision, *I.D.G. v. Spain*[25]. In that case, the complainant was not properly notified of mortgage enforcement proceedings, as the notification had been issued via public posting. The Committee found that this form of notice was inadequate under the circumstances and violated the complainant's right to due process, as she was unable to effectively contest the eviction (para. 14). Spain was therefore urged to amend its legislation on public notification (para. 17), a step it subsequently took.

Of particular importance is the obligation to provide suitable alternative housing. This has consistently emerged as the central concern in the Committee's case law on evictions (Di 2024, 1453). Already in General Comment No. 7 (CESCR 1997) the Committee emphasized that an eviction must not result in homelessness, as this in itself would constitute a violation of Art. 11 (1) ICESCR (para. 16).

In the case of Ben Djazia et al. vs. Spain (supra note 22), the requirements were repeated and further specified, one could also say tightened. Thus, for example, it is emphasized that states have a positive obligation "to take reasonable measures to provide alternative housing to persons who are left homeless as a result of eviction" (para. 15.2). The same paragraph re-

24 Hamid Saydawi and Masir Farah v. Italy, E/C.12/75/D/227/2021.

25 I.D.G. v. Spain, E/C.12/55/D/2/2014.

fers not only to alternative housing but also emphasizes the need for *adequate* alternative housing. The State Party "must take all necessary steps, to the maximum of their available resources, to uphold this right" (para. 15.3). Although it is left to the State Parties to decide how exactly they will uphold this right, the states should "take consistent and coordinated measures to resolve institutional shortcomings and structural causes of the lack of housing" (para. 15.3). The State Party is allowed to set criteria or conditions for access to public housing with a view to rationalizing social services resources. However, such criteria must remain reasonable, proportionate, non-discriminatory and must avoid stigmatization (para. 17.2).

Another right developed in this context is that family members have a right not to be separated from each other, as was the case of the complainant López Albán (supra note 19, at para. 9.3). With regard to state obligations, the Committee interestingly even goes so far as to accuse Spain of exacerbating the housing shortage itself by selling almost 3,000 houses and other properties to private investors in 2013 to boost the public budget (Ben Djazia et al. vs. Spain (supra note 22, at para. 17.5)). This suggests an evolving standard of macro-level accountability, where states may be held responsible not only for individual violations, but also for broader policy choices that restrict the availability of affordable housing.

If the State Party does not manage to provide alternative accommodation, it must first demonstrate that "it has considered the specific circumstances of the case" and, moreover, that "despite having taken all reasonable measures, to the maximum of its available resources, it has been unable to uphold the right to housing of the person concerned" (para. 15.5). As *Kreller* notes, the Committee has yet to develop a consistent threshold for reviewing such resource-based justifications under Art. 2(1) ICESCR. The standard of review remains unclear, and future clarification – potentially in the form of a dedicated General Comment – would be highly desirable to ensure legal certainty and comparability (Kreller 2024, 141).

A review of the requirements relating to adequate alternative housing reveals that the corresponding obligations imposed on States are extensive in scope. This is reflected in the majority of views in which the CESCR found that the State Party had failed to take all appropriate measures to ensure such housing (Vols 2023, 14). Against this background, *Vols* analyzed whether these strict requirements with their far-reaching protection could lead to moral hazard concerns. Specifically, he notes that if the obligation to provide adequate alternative housing were interpreted as implying that evictions are impermissible even in cases of non-payment, tenants or mortgage holders might be incentivized to deliberately default, knowing that the state would be obliged to rehouse them. Taken further, this could undermine the property rights of owners and create risks for financial institutions, which could ultimately also be a reason why states are hesitant to sign the Optional Protocol (Vols 2023, 15, 25; Kreller 2024, 142). To this end, he analyzed the very far-reaching national eviction protection in Poland and South Africa and the moratoria introduced during the COVID-19 pandemic. Even if there is no clear, reliable empirical evidence for this, he rightly calls for a restrictive, reasonable interpretation of Art. 11 (1) ICESCR, so that only people who are actually in need must be provided with alternative, adequate housing (Vols 2023, 24).

VI. General Comment No. 26 and (the Right to) Land

A proper consideration of the right to housing necessarily entails an examination of land-related issues, as both are inherently interconnected. Access to land is essential for the realization of many rights, particularly for rural populations such as peasants and Indigenous Peoples. A right to land is therefore explicitly enshrined for peasants and rural communities in Art. 17 of the UN Declaration on the Rights of Peasants and Other People Working in Rural Areas (UNDROP, 2018) and for Indigenous Peoples in Art. 26 of the UN Declaration on the Rights of Indigenous Peoples (UNDRIP, 2007).

However, there is still no such recognition in the Core International Human Rights Instruments[26]. Nonetheless, *De Schutter* has argued that such a right is "emerging" in international law (De Schutter 2010). Aware of the importance of land, the CESCR has issued 2022 General Comment No. 26 on land and economic, social and cultural rights (CESCR 2022). Its stated aim is to clarify the "States' obligations to the impact of access to, use of and control over land" (para. 4). In para. 3, the Committee also notes that various groups such as scholars, civil society organizations and special rapporteurs are demanding the recognition of the right to land. Nevertheless, their demands were denied and the right to land was explicitly not recognized in General Comment No. 26.

Interestingly, the academic reception of this General Comment was rather restrained and there are hardly any articles on it. In one of the few articles

26 https://www.ohchr.org/en/core-international-human-rights-instruments-and-their-monitoring-bodies, accessed August 4, 2025.

dealing with it, *Wadlig* criticizes that the Committee missed the opportunity to consider land as more than a resource and human-land relations as property relations and did not focus on the "rights of nature" (Wadlig 2023).

However, the main reason for mentioning this General Comment is that it also contains some remarks on the right to housing. This shows once again how closely the two issues are connected.[27] Para. 22 restates the state's obligation to respect tenure rights, including the prohibition of arbitrary forced evictions and the demolition of housing as a punitive measure. Para. 23 reaffirms the importance of security of tenure from General Comment No. 4 and the well-known statement from General Comment No. 7, according to which forced evictions are prima facie incompatible with the requirements of the Covenant. It is noteworthy, however, that the elements of the examination of the justification of an eviction (proportionality analysis) developed in the case of Ben Djazia et al. v. Spain (supra note 22) and further refined in the case of Gómez-Limón Pardo v. Spain (supra note 23, see VI. 3. b.) are now set out in a General Comment. The following paragraph 24 once again states that the alternative housing provided in the event of an eviction must meet the requirements of General Comment No. 4, from which it follows that the alternative accommodation must be *adequate* as well.

In this sense, General Comment No. 26 consolidates and summarizes the key legal standards developed in the CESCR's communications jurisprudence. It thus provides a valuable interpretive tool for assessing the human rights compatibility of eviction practices. It should be considered whether in the future the strong focus on evictions in rural areas should be shifted more towards urban areas and the alternative housing that is available there. This is supported by the empirical reality that evictions regularly occur more frequently in urban areas (Gershenson and Desmond 2024, 92) and that, in many regions, rising rents and rent arrears are main drivers of housing loss (e.g., Germany: Statista 2025), highlighting the particular challenges posed by urban housing markets.

VII. Enforcement and Monitoring Problems

As in virtually every field of human rights, the monitoring and enforcement of the right to adequate housing faces significant challenges. These

27 At the time this article was written, the special rapporteur for housing also called for input on "Land and the right to adequate housing", https://www.ohchr.org/en/calls-for-input/2025/call-input-land-and-right-adequate-housing, accessed August 4, 2025.

are particularly evident in two main areas: the lack of reliable data and problems regarding enforcement.

1. Lack of Data

A fundamental precondition for the protection and enforcement of human rights is transparency and access to reliable data.[28] However, in the field of housing – and especially evictions – such data is often incomplete, fragmented, or entirely absent. The current situation in Germany serves as an illustrative example.

Even though Germany is frequently regarded as a country with a well-developed legal system and administrative infrastructure, significant data gaps remain. The German Institute for Human Rights, the independent national human rights institution, has explicitly criticized the current data collection practices. First, it notes that the data on the annual number of evictions is incomplete as several federal states fail to submit reports. Moreover, even where data is available, it lacks crucial qualitative information. For instance, the social background of those affected is not captured: neither the reasons for the eviction nor the involvement of children nor the post-eviction housing situation are documented. Furthermore, the extent to which court-ordered evictions were prevented by appeals is likewise not recorded (Litschke and Sumski 2022, 6).

The answer to a written question from a member of parliament in January 2025 also reveals that there is still no distinction between evictions affecting households with children and those without.[29] However, it is precisely this data that would be needed to monitor whether the human rights requirements are all being complied with in Germany. It would therefore be welcome if the enforcement officers (Gerichtsvollzieher), as those who carry out the eviction and are in actual contact with the evicted persons, were required to collect and report this data.

Similar criticisms have been raised in Taiwan, where critical voices have long pointed out that the country's housing statistics fail to reflect social differentiation – particularly by class, gender, nationality, or ethnicity (Chen 2016, 652). As described above, this did not change in the last review process either, as no reliable figures about evictions could be pre-

28 For a proposal for the monitoring process, see (Riedel 2007).

29 German Bundestag. 2025. Printed Matter 20/14451: Written Questions with the Answers of the Federal Government. 20th Legislative Period. Berlin: German Bundestag. https://dserver.bundestag.de/btd/20/144/2014451.pdf, p. 49.

sented. This is also the reason why the International Review Committee, in its concluding observations 2022, recommended that a further investigation in this area should be conducted by the National Human Rights Commission in Taiwan (International Review Committee 2022, 10).

Without such data, both national oversight bodies and international human rights mechanisms are hindered in their efforts to ensure that states meet their obligations. Moreover, the lack of transparency undermines public accountability and limits the ability of civil society and researchers to assess the true scope and nature of housing rights violations.

2. The Enforceability Problem

It is well known that human rights are notoriously inadequately enforced. This holds particularly true for ESC rights. In countries such as Spain, which have ratified the OP-ICESCR, the protection of human rights, especially the right to housing, has in any case become much more visible in recent times as a result of the committee's adopted views. However, this could be counteracted by the long duration of proceedings and the large number of cases that have now piled up. In order to continue the committee's work in a meaningful way and also out of respect for the victims, it will therefore probably be necessary to increase funding and, above all, staffing, as the committee itself has stated (Di 2024, 1434).[30] One way or another, the committee does not have any powers to enforce its decisions on individual states. The international treaties on human rights have predominantly no "real teeth" (Hohmann 2019, 20). *Leijten* assumes that, despite the entry into force of the OP-ICESCR, the ICESCR still only serves as a "touchstone for the international monitoring process" (Leijten 2015, 24).

Thus, for example, the problem arises when recommendations of the committee are not taken seriously. An illustrative example of this is described by Kolocek (Kolocek 2017, 161–62): In Hong Kong there was already a large number of bed-space apartments or so-called "cage homes" in the early 2000s. In the committee's understanding, these are an "affront to human dignity"[31]. The Chinese government, in contrast, thanked the committee for its concerns, but did not want to follow them. Rather, they believed their approach was the right one: People who lived in these bed-space apartments would do

30 On the current problems of treaty bodies, see (Grohmann 2024).

31 CESCR_CHN (2001) Consideration of reports submitted by States Parties under Articles 16 and 17 of the Covenant. Concluding Observations of the Committee on Economic, Social and Cultural Rights. China: Hong Kong Special Administrative Region. E/C.12/1/Add.58, para. 25.

so "largely out of choice for convenience, economic and other personal reasons"[32]. However, this completely disregards the state's duty to protect its citizens, which arises from human rights.[33] Asian countries in specific are accused of paying too little attention to the issue of adequate housing (Kolocek 2017, 218).

VIII. Conclusion

No other human right enshrined in the ICESCR receives as much attention as the right to adequate housing in Art. 11 (1) ICESCR. This can be seen from the number of General Comments dedicated to this topic alone, but also from the fact that it has so far been the dominant topic in the individual complaint procedures. Over the past decades, the right to adequate housing has become increasingly concretized, particularly through the development of a proportionality analysis for evictions and the elaboration of procedural and substantive requirements for ensuring adequate alternative accommodation. It has been shown that one focus of the committee's work, as well as that of many scholars, is the examination of the right to adequate alternative housing after an eviction. In order to ensure the success of human rights, it is important not to lose sight of the fact that there must be tangible improvements for the people actually affected. It will be the responsibility of the CESCR to further sharpen the requirements for adequate housing but not to overstretch them so that they can be fulfilled appropriately and do not end in a Pyrrhic victory.

References

Alston, Philip. 2020. „The Committee on Economic, Social and Cultural Rights." In *The United Nations and Human Rights: A Critical Appraisal*, 2nd ed., edited by Frédéric Mérégret and Philip Alston, 439–76. Oxford: Oxford University Press.

Casla, Koldo. 2022. "Unpredictable and Damaging? A Human Rights Case for the Proportionality Assessment of Evictions in the Private Rental Sector." *European Human Rights Law Review* 2022 (3): 253–272.

32 People's Republic of China (2003) Initial reports submitted by States Parties under Articles 16 and 17 of the Covenant. E/1990/5/Add.59, para. 592 (c).

33 However, a rethink is currently taking place and a bill (Basic Housing Units Bill, C3411) has been presented to regulate the letting of subdivided units (SDUs) in residential buildings, https://www.news.gov.hk/eng/2025/06/20250620/20250620_103706_270.html, accessed August 4, 2025.

Chen, Yi-Ling. 2016. "Gender and the Housing 'Questions' in Taiwan." *ACME: An International Journal for Critical Geographies* 15 (3): 639–658.

Committee on Civil and Political Rights (CCPR). 1988. *General Comment No. 16: Article 17 (Right to Privacy)* (HRI/GEN/1/REV.9(VOL.I)). Geneva: United Nations Civil and Political Council.

Committee on Economic, Social and Cultural Rights (CESCR). 1991. *General Comment No. 4: The Right to Adequate Housing (Art. 11 (1) of the International)* (E/1992/23). Geneva: United Nations Economic and Social Council. https://undocs.org/E/1992/23.

Committee on Economic, Social and Cultural Rights (CESCR). 1997. *General Comment No. 7: The Right to Adequate Housing (Art. 11 (1) of the Covenant): Forced Evictions* (E/C.12/1997/4) Geneva: United Nations Economic and Social Council. https://docs.un.org/en/E/C.12/1997/4

Committee on Economic, Social and Cultural Rights (CESCR). 2009. *General Comment No. 20: Non-discrimination in economic, social and cultural rights (art. 2, para. 2, of theInternational Covenant on Economic, Social and Cultural Rights)* (E/C.12/GC/20). Geneva: United Nations Economic and Social Council. https://docs.un.org/E/C.12/GC/20

Committee on Economic, Social and Cultural Rights (CESCR). 2022. General Comment No. 26 on Land and Economic, Social and Cultural Rights. E/C.12/GC/26. https://digitallibrary.un.org/record/4002081.

De Schutter, Oliver. 2010. "The Emerging Human Right to Land." *International Community Law Review* 12: 303–334.

Di, Lei. 2024. "The Justiciability of Economic, Social and Cultural Rights in International Law: Balancing International Supervision and National Sovereignty." *Journal of Human Rights* 23 (6): 1434–1461.

Donnelly, Dessie, Joe Finnerty, Cathal O'Connell, and Albie Sachs. 2020. "The Right to Housing." In *International Human Rights, Social Policy & Global: Critical Perspectives*, edited by Gerard McCann and Féilim Ó hAdhmaill, 1st ed., 209–22. Bristol University Press. https://doi.org/10.46692/9781447349228.018

Gershenson, Carl, and Matthew Desmond. 2024. "Eviction and the Rental Housing Crisis in Rural America." *Rural Sociology* 89 (1): [86–105]. https://doi.org/10.1111/ruso.12528.

Grohmann, Nils-Hendrik. 2022. "Tracing the Development of the Proportionality Analysis in Relation to Forced Evictions under the ICESCR." *Human Rights Law Review* 22 (1): 1–24. https://doi.org/10.1093/hrlr/ngac025.

Grohmann, Nils-Hendrik. 2024. *Strengthening the UN Human Rights Treaty Bodies: An Analysis of the Committees' Legal Powers and Possibilities for Reform.* Tübingen: Mohr Siebeck. https://doi.org/10.1628/978-3-16-162826-9.

Guckelberger, Annette. 2016. "Schutz der Wohnung." In *Handbuch der Grundrechte in Deutschland und Europa*, vol. 8: *Landesgrundrechte in Deutschland*, edited by Detlef Merten and Hans-Jürgen Papier, § 235, 321–355. Heidelberg: C.F. Müller.

Haque, Muhammad Ekramul. 2021. "Justiciability of Economic, Social and Cultural Rights under International Human Rights Law." *Dhaka University Law Journal* 32 (Centennial Special Issue): 39–54.

Heerdt, Daniela. 2023. *Addressing human rights abuses at mega-sporting events – A shared responsibility in theory and practice.* Front. Sports Act. Living 4:1067088. https://doi.org/10.3389/fspor.2022.1067088.

Hohmann, Jessie M. 2021. "Housing as a Right." In *Oxford Handbook on Economic, Social and Cultural Rights*, edited by Katharine Young and Malcolm Langford. Forthcoming 2022. https://ssrn.com/abstract=3928225.

Hohmann, Jessie. 2019. "The Right to Housing." In A *Research Agenda on Housing*, edited by Markus Moos. Cheltenham: Edward Elgar Publishing.International Review Committee. 2022. *Review of the Third Reports of the Government of Taiwan on the Implementation of the International Human Rights Covenants: Concluding Observations and Recommendations adopted by the International Review Committee.* Taipei.

Kolocek, Michael. 2017. *The Human Right to Housing in the Face of Land Policy and Social Citizenship: A Global Discourse Analysis.* Palgrave Macmillan.

Kothari, Miloon. 2015. *The Global Crisis of Displacement and Evictions – A Housing and Land Rights Response* New York: Rosa-Luxemburg-Stiftung – New York Office. https://rosalux.nyc/wp-content/uploads/2020/11/RLS-NYC_displacement_and_evictions.pdf.

Kreller, Gregor. 2024. "Der UN-Sozialausschuss und das Recht auf Wohnen in der Sache Saydawi und Farah gegen Italien." *MenschenRechtsMagazin* (MRM) 29 (2): 131–142. https://doi.org/10.60935/mrm2024.29.2.12.

Leckie, Scott. 2001. "The Human Right to Adequate Housing." In *Economic, Social and Cultural Rights: A Textbook*, 2nd ed., edited by Asbjørn Eide, Catarina Krause, and Allan Rosas, 149–168. Dordrecht, Boston, and London: Martinus Nijhoff Publishers.

Leijten, Ingrid. 2015. "The German Right to an Existenzminimum, Human Dignity, and the Possibility of Minimum Core Socioeconomic Rights Protection." *German Law Journal* 16 (1): 23–48. https://doi.org/10.1017/S2071832200019416.

Litschke, Peter, and Lara Sumski (2022). Zwangsräumungen als Menschenrechtsverletzung: Vorgaben des Ausschusses zum UN-Sozialpakt und anderer Menschenrechtsgremien zu Räumungen. (Information / Deutsches

Institut für Menschenrechte, 43). Berlin: Deutsches Institut für Menschenrechte. https://nbn-resolving.org/urn:nbn:de:0168-ssoar-85047-2.

Nowak, Manfred. 2019. "Personal Reflections on the Taiwan Human Rights Review Process." In *Taiwan and International Human Rights: A Story of Transformation*, edited by Jerome A. Cohen, William P. Alford, and Chang-fa Lo, 321–327. Economics, Law, and Institutions in Asia Pacific. Singapore: Springer. https://doi.org/10.1007/978-981-13-0350-0.

OECD. 2024. *Indicator HC3.3. Evictions.* OECD Affordable Housing Database, http://oe.cd/ahd.

Pineda, Eduardo Jiménez. 2023. "The legal value of the decisions given by the United Nations Human Rights Treaty Bodies in light of the Judgments of the Spanish Supreme Court of 13 June 2023 (STS 786/2023) and of 29 November 2023 (STS 1597/2023): End of Story?" *Spanish Yearbook of International Law 27:* 191–216. https://doi.org/10.36151/SYBIL.2024.008.

Republic of China (Taiwan). 2022. *Replies to the List of Issues to be taken up in connection with the consideration of its Third Report (ICESCR).* Taipei: Government of the Republic of China (Taiwan).

Riedel, Eibe. 2007. "Measuring Human Rights Compliance – IBSA Procedure as a Tool of Human Rights Monitoring." In *Les droits de l'homme et la constitution: Études en l'honneur du Professeur Giorgio Malinverni*, edited by Andreas Auer, Alexandre Flückiger, and Michel Hottelier, 251. Geneva: Schulthess.

Riedel, Eibe. 2011. "New Bearings in Social Rights? The Communications Procedure under the ICESCR." In From Bilateralism to Community Interest: Essays in Honour of Judge Bruno Simma, edited by Ulrich Fastenrath, Rudolf Geiger, Daniel-Erasmus Khan, Andreas Paulus, Sabine von Schorlemer, and Christoph Vedder, 574–89. Oxford: Oxford University Press. https://doi.org/10.1093/acprof:oso/9780199588817.003.0037.

Riedel, Eibe. 2017. "Best of UN: Aus der Arbeit des UN-WSK-Ausschusses." *Zeitschrift für Menschenrechte* 2017 (1): 24–40.

Rietdijk, Chantalle Elisabeth. 2024. "Adequate Housing in Taipei City's Private Rental Market: A Visual Content Analysis of Online Rental Unit Advertisements." *Housing Studies*, published June 14, 2024. https://doi.org/10.1080/02673037.2024.2363928.

Saul, Ben, David Kinley, and Jacqueline Mowbray. 2014. "Article 11: The Right to an Adequate Standard of Living." In *The International Covenant on Economic, Social and Cultural Rights: Commentary, Cases, and Materials*, online ed. Oxford: Oxford University Press. https://doi.org/10.1093/law/9780199640300.001.0001.

Scherrieb, Asita Maria. 2023. *Individualbeschwerden beim UN-Ausschuss für wirtschaftliche, soziale und kulturelle Rechte: Eine Handreichung für Betroffene, Zivilgesellschaft und Anwaltschaft.* (Information / Deutsches Institut für Menschenrechte, 45). Berlin: Deutsches Institut für Menschenrechte. https://nbn-resolving.org/urn:nbn:de:0168-ssoar-87866-5.

Shope, Mark L. 2012. "The Adoption and Function of International Instruments: Thoughts on Taiwan's Enactment of the Act to Implement the ICCPR and the ICESCR." *Indiana International & Comparative Law Review* 22: 159–192. https://ssrn.com/abstract=3265739.

Statista. 2025. "Wohnungslose in Deutschland nach Gründen und Art der Wohnungslosigkeit 2024." accessed August 4, 2025, https://de.statista.com/statistik/daten/studie/590569/umfrage/gruende-fuer-den-letzten-wohnungsverlust-von-wohnungslosen-in-deutschland/.

UN-Habitat and OHCHR. 2014. *Forced Evictions, Fact Sheet No. 25/Rev.1.* United Nations, New York and Geneva. www.ohchr.org/Documents/Publications/FS25.Rev.1.pdf.

UN-Habitat. 2023. *Rescuing SDG 11 for a Resilient Urban Planet: SDG 11 Synthesis Report 2023.* Nairobi: UN-Habitat. https://unhabitat.org/sites/default/files/2023/11/sdg_11_synthesis_report_2023.pdf.

UN-Habitat. n.d. Housing Rights. https://unhabitat.org/programme/housing-rights, accessed August 4, 2025.

United Nations Commission on Human Rights (UNCHR). 1993. *Resolution 1993/77: Forced Evictions.* Adopted March 10, 1993, 49th Meeting, 49th Session. UN Doc. E/CN.4/RES/1993/77. https://undocs.org/en/E/CN.4/RES/1993/77.

United Nations HRC. 2007. *Report of the Special Rapporteur on Adequate Housing as a Component of the Right to an Adequate Standard of Living, Miloon Kothari.* A/HRC/4/18, Annex 1, Geneva: United Nations Human Rights Council. https://docs.un.org/en/A/HRC/4/18.

United Nations HRC. 2019. *Guidelines for the Implementation of the Right to Adequate Housing, Leilani Farha.* A/HRC/43/43, Geneva: United Nations Human Rights Council. https://docs.un.org/en/A/HRC/43/43.

Vols, Michel. 2023. „The Optional Protocol to the ICESCR, Homelessness and Moral Hazard: The Alternative Adequate Housing Requirement in the CESCR's Jurisprudence – an Incentive Not to Pay for Housing?" *International Human Rights Law Review* 12 (1): 1–25. https://doi.org/10.1163/22131035-12010001.

Wadlig, Gabriele. 2023. "Beyond Property Relations: Why the Committee on Economic, Social and Cultural Rights' Narrow Understanding of Land Limits the Protection of Human-Land Relationships." *Völkerrechtsblog.* https://doi.org/10.17176/20230419-084352-0.

H. The Concluding Report of Taiwan's Transitional Justice Commission - A Holistic Approach to Transitional Justice?

Jau-hwa Chen[1]

Abstract

This article investigates the following questions: (1) why the United Nations have urged member states to take a holistic approach to transitional justice; (2) how Taiwan's Commission on Promoting Transitional Justice came to understand the aforementioned approach and expresses this position in its Concluding Report; and (3) what challenges Taiwan's transitional justice faces and what lessons can be drawn from the Concluding Report. Bo Yang's case study and confrontation with the offenders who tortured him highlighted the victims' critical situations. The issues outlined in this scenario represent the holistic approach's ambitions.

Keywords

Holistic Approach; Transitional Justice; Bo Yang; Justice; Truth: Reparation; Victim-centered approach, Prosecution; Truth Commission; The Act on Promoting Transitional Justice; The Commission on Promoting Transitional Justice; transitional injustice.

I. Introduction

In 2017, Taiwan's parliament approved *The Act on Promoting Transitional Justice* (hereinafter referred to as "the Act"), and the Commission on Promoting Transitional Justice (hence referred to as "the commission") was founded the following year. The panel was tasked with restoring historical truth and faith in society, removing authoritarian symbols, and exonerating erroneous convictions, among other things. The Act specifically stated that "functioning on a task-oriented basis under the executive branch" (aka the

1 Prof. Jau-hwa Chen is a Taiwanese professor in Soochow University's Master's Program in Human Rights. She spent 2006–2007 as a visiting scholar at the German Institute for Human Rights. She teaches and conducts research on human rights philosophy, gender and human rights, and transitional justice. jhchen@scu.edu.tw

Executive Yuan), the commission must give its final report to the Executive Yuan within the next two years. The commission will cease to exist after submitting its final report. This independent organization indicated two delays in completing the report; however, the report was eventually delivered to the government in May 2022.

In contrast to the *Concluding Repor*t, which claimed to adopt an internationally recognized 'holistic approach' to transitional justice processes in accordance with the Act (*Concluding Report* 2022, volume I, 5), the commission's approach was haphazard and piecemeal, and thus the recommendations and stance outlined in the report stood in stark contrast to the stated aims of both the Act and the commission. It is worth noting that the *Concluding Report* did not suggest trials for perpetrators or an investigation into their alleged crimes. Nor did it even imply that such actions were necessary components of an integrated and complementary whole, as the holistic approach required. There was no explicit relationship between the chores and the aim they wanted to achieve.

Taiwan finds itself in an unusual circumstance since the Kuomintang regime's henchmen have not been brought to justice and continue to operate with impunity. The delivery of reparations by the Memorial Foundation of 228 appears to exceed accountability and justice. This, in turn, gives the idea that victims' complaints are motivated largely by financial concerns, rather than a desire to remedy injustices.

To understand how this situation arose, we must investigate the following key questions: (1) why the United Nations have urged member states to take a holistic approach to transitional justice; (2) how the commission came to understand the aforementioned approach and express this position in its Concluding Report; and (3) what challenges Taiwan's transitional justice faces and what lessons can be drawn from the *Concluding Report.*

This article is divided into four parts to address the aforementioned questions. The first section discusses the case of Bo Yang, which represents Taiwan's transitional injustice scenario and the serious issues that develop as a result of a lack of victim-centered approaches to transitional justice. The second section of this article discusses the importance of a comprehensive approach to transitional justice processes, as advocated by the United Nations. The third section exposes the commission's misinterpretation of the holistic approach and its consequences. Such a misinterpretation is inexorably linked to the recommendations made by the *Concluding Report.* This section aims to demonstrate the significant difference between a truly holistic strategy and the commission's piecemeal approach. Building on the three preceding sections, the final section of this article examines and draws lessons from important issues concerning Taiwan's transitional justice, as detailed in the *Concluding Report*. It aims to help readers reconsider the future of Taiwan's transitional justice.

II. The Case of Bo Yang and the Challenges it Posed to Taiwan's Transitional Justice

After Taiwan began its transition to democracy, Bo Yang, a pseudonym for Guo Yidong, published a series of articles in a newspaper in 1996. Mr. Bo, a dissenting writer, was a political prisoner from 1968 to 1977. His sentence was commuted from 12 years to eight years, although he was not released until April 1977. Following his release, he, like other political prisoners, remained under government supervision.

What was his crime? He was court-martialed for implying that Popeye the Sailor and his kid were Chiang Kai-shek and his eldest son, Chiang Ching-kuo. This event began in 1967, shortly after Bo took over as editor of the China Daily Family Supplement. He ran a series of the comic strip "Popeye the Sailor" from Monday to Friday, which he translated himself. It was one of the comic strips published in January 1968 that put him in trouble. The tale goes like this. Popeye and his son, Sweep Pea, bought an island. When Popeye arrived on the desolate island, he promptly addressed 'the island country' and began campaigning for president in an uncontested election. Bo Yang was later arrested for his (satirical) humor, court martialed and sentenced to 12 years in prison.

Bo Yang's book series included an account of his detention and interrogational torture at the hands of two interrogators, Gao Yi-ru and Liu Zhanhua, in Taipei's Investigation Bureau Guest House. Bo Yang highlighted his pain at the degrading appearance of the immediate torturers, whom he had seen on a few occasions. They exhibited no regret for their acts. They continued to deny using torture or other forms of pressure to extract a forced confession. Disputing the accuracy of his account, Liu insisted that, while he was present when Bo Yang confessed, Bo was not tortured during interrogation. Liu went on to say that he had been a "law-abiding civil servant" who had remained faithful to the country for three decades. He obeyed the law. He should not have been chastised for simply performing his job. Being deeply outraged by the claimed crime of torture, Liu stated unequivocally that he would "consider filing a defamation suit against Bo Yang should he continue to mislead the public" (Bo and Zhou 1996, 408–409).

Following Liu's protest, Bo Yang and his wife had supper with him. Bo Yang's wife, who did not mince words, asked Liu why he tormented Yang. Liu leaned over to Bo Yang, grabbed his right arm with both hands, and smiled: "Mr. Bo, we didn't torture people, did we?" Bo was stunned with outrage after Liu's outright denial.

A similar scene occurred during Bo's meal with Gao Yi-ru (Bo and Zhou 1996, 407-408). Gao did not deny that Bo had made the confession under duress and offered a toast to Bo as a mark of apologies. To Bo's surprise, Gau stated that it was Bo's "blow-by-blow account" of his misdeeds that eventually proved him guilty, not coercion, and that Bo's forthrightness rendered additional pressure unnecessary. Bo was completely speechless after hearing his weasel comments.

It is worth mentioning that Bo's memoir includes a story of remorse and reconciliation told by his friend Chen Bao-chuan. A Japanese military police officer seized Chen and smacked him for his anti-Japanese actions. Decades later, the retired Japanese military police officer set out in quest of Chen, eventually finding him. Kneeling on the ground, the former police officer freely stated, 'It was my responsibility to arrest you, but I should never have been so brutal' (Bo and Zhou 1996, 407). He then requested Chen for forgiveness. Bo fell into tears after learning about this story.

Bo Yang sought a genuine apology from perpetrators for their wrongdoings. He was taken aback by the offenders' brazen lies, which not only denied his charges outright but also shifted all responsibility to him. Liu and Gao's flagrant manipulations of facts represent a terrible reality in Taiwan. That is, proximate offenders feel no regret for the torture and human rights violations they have previously committed against victims. In their opinion, those who makes false claims should be profoundly ashamed of themselves. It's no surprise that non-governmental human rights organizations have referred to Taiwan's transitional justice as "transitional injustice"[2].

It would be overly simplistic to define Taiwan's transitional justice system as having "only victims, no perpetrators". As previously stated in Bo's case, he had clearly identified the abusers. The case of Bo is not a unique instance. Many victims, like Bo, provided detailed (and stomach-churning) recollections of their interrogation experiences and identified torturers during oral

2 https://www.tahr.org.tw/activity/307.

history interviews. These accounts could have been verified had the government compared them to existing archive materials. Similarly, many victims have met abusers on numerous occasions since Taiwan began its journey to democracy. Although successive Taiwanese governments have passed a series of acts to facilitate processes and mechanisms of transitional justice, such as the February 28 Incident Disposition and Compensation Act (1995), Act Governing the Recovery of Damage to Individual Rights during the Period of Martial Law (2000), Compensation Act for Wrongful Trials on Charges of Sedition and Espionage during the Martial Law Period (2006), and the Act in 2017, none of them had dealt with the perpetrators' issues that were recorded by the victims. Those activities have thus far failed to address victims' legitimate grievances and sense of injustice. They have also not advised that the government conduct an investigation into alleged misdeeds committed by culprits.

In other words, a culture of impunity prevails. While victims may be exonerated and get damages for unjust convictions and jail, they have no remedy if they demand an apology from the offenders. Victims are not given a role in promoting accountability for past wrongs or contributing to a narrative of healing and reconciliation. Victims who come out to identify perpetrators may face vengeance and character assassination. Abusers may deny claims as smears, defamation, monetary gain, or hate speech.

Victims want the government to take their claims seriously and alter the entire transitional justice system accordingly. Making an investigation an intrinsic aspect of transitional justice, together with legal prosecution, truth-telling, compensation, and institutional transformation, would restore victims' dignity and reduce their sense of injustice and impotence. If the overall goal of transitional justice is to create a just society in the long run, the commission's activities should be viewed as building bricks of transitional justice. Victims' allegations against offenders are thus critical to the process of truth-telling, investigation, prosecution, restitution, and so on; they also help victims overcome a sense of unfairness. Some allegations may be false or only partially true. To vindicate victims, all allegations should be documented, examined, and compared to other available evidence.

Bo Yang's story exemplifies Taiwan's transitional (in)justice crisis. Given that successive administrations have paid scant attention to victims' testimonies and feelings of unfairness, it is necessary to investigate ways in which victims can play an important role in creating and implementing transitional justice systems.

III. The Significance of a Holistic Approach to Transitional Justice as Underscored by the UN

Nelson Mandela and international specialists working on transitional justice are well aware of the obstacles that post-authoritarian countries would face. While totalitarian regimes no longer exist, no new order has emerged to fill the hole (Boraine 2006, 17–18; Arbour 2006, 1–3). The memory of past abuses and transgressions has become so ingrained that perpetrators and the institutions to which they belong can admit no wrongdoing and enjoy total impunity.

Some of them continue to command the state's police, military, and intelligence apparatuses, as well as numerous government institutions. So, how can societies address this legacy and then establish transitional justice? The conventional explanation can be found in the principles of international criminal justice established in the Nuremberg Trials, a paradigm of transitional justice based on retribution that predates the phrase "transitional justice" itself. However, relying solely on retributive justice and conducting full-fledged criminal investigations and prosecutions, whether national, domestic, or international, would be practically impossible.

To come to terms with the large-scale abuses, the United Nations and international experts, therefore, recommend that other complementary measures should be brought in and be incorporated into transitional justice, such as truth commissions, remedial actions, vetting process, particularly in societies that are characterized by

> *a lack of political will for reform, a lack of institutional independence within the justice sector, a lack of domestic technical capacity, a lack of material and financial resources, a lack of public confidence in Government, a lack of official respect for human rights and, more generally, a lack of peace and security.*[3]

A significant step toward transitional justice[4] was highlighted in the report presented by Kofi Annan on August 3, 2004. The report, entitled, "the UN Secretary-General Report on the Rule of Law and Transitional Justice

3 Report of the UN Secretary General on the Rule of Law and Transitional Justice in Conflict and Post-Conflict Societies (S/2004/616), 3.

4 The term "transitional justice" and its development please compare: Arthur, Paige 2009. "How 'Transitions' Reshaped Human Rights: A Conceptual History of Transitional Justice" in Human Rights Quarterly 31. 321–367; Naomi Roht-Arriaza. 2006. "The new landscape of transitional justice", in: Transitional Justice in 21. Century, Cambridge & Malden:

in Conflict and Post-Conflict Societies" (hereafter referred to as "the 2004 Report"), defined transitional justice as:

The full range of processes and mechanisms associated with a society's attempts to come to terms with a legacy of large-scale past abuses, in order to ensure accountability, serve justice and achieve reconciliation. (p. 4, emphasis added)

This definition of transitional justice shows discontent over the retributive justice model, recognizes its one-sidedness and draws important lessons from it. Regarding processes and mechanisms, the 2004 Report accentuated that

> *where transitional justice is required, strategies must be holistic, incorporating integrated attention to individual prosecutions, reparations, truth-seeking, institutional reform, vetting and dismissals, or an appropriately conceived combination thereof. (p. 9, emphasis added)*

It is necessary to ask why the 2004 Report emphasized a holistic approach. A basic response to this question is that fragmented initiatives to transitional justice have consistently failed. Various remedies, such as prosecution, truth commissions, corrective acts, the vetting process, and so on, have relative strengths and limits, as well as distinct social, legal, and moral consequences. Given this, various measures should be devised and planned as a whole to ensure that they are intimately intertwined with one another and so serve as necessary and mutually complimentary components of the whole.

It would be impossible to prosecute all abusers, tell just the truth, undo victims' damages and losses, and purge and indict all ex-perpetrators in the current system (De Greiff 2012, 36). The catchphrases: "No Peace without Justice", "No Truth without Justice", "No Reparation without Truth and Justice" illustrate this: "The weakness of each of these measures provides a powerful incentive to seek ways in which each can interact with the others in order to make up for their collective limitations" (De Greiff 2012, 35).

The Nuremberg Trials paradigm has been attacked for its selectivity, imposition of victor's justice, and ineffectiveness in promoting reconciliation. In contrast, South Africa's truth and reconciliation commission has been chastised for conflating justice and reconciliation and for rushing to award amnesty to individuals who perpetrated atrocities during apartheid. Adopting a holistic approach indicates that both the Nuremberg Trials and Truth

Polity, 1–16; Teitel, Ruti. 2003. "Transitional Justice Genealogy", in Harvard human rights journal, Vol. 16, No. spring, 69–94.

Commission models should be considered, complementing and supplementing one another.

Some studies are highly pessimistic regarding the efficiency of partial measures of justice in coping with massive state violence and human rights violations when dictatorships ended (Sikkink & Walling 2007, 428–429). They claim that full-fledged prosecutions would threaten political stability in newly democratic countries. However, Sikkink and Walling's quantitative analysis of perpetrator trials in Latin American countries revealed a totally different pattern. The number of offender prosecutions had increased throughout Latin America in response to appeals from victims and their families. They also emphasized that the execution of several complementing measures for human rights and democratic reform does not preclude trials and retributive justice, and that the importance of trials in establishing accountability should not be dismissed out of hand.

According to Arendt (2003, 29–36), postwar trials of war criminals brought previously overlooked moral questions to the forefront, sparking arguments about the (im)morality of the accused's actions under totalitarian control. For starters, judicial processes separated responsible individuals from the war engines and bureaucratic institutions to which they belonged.[5] Second, in the face of totalitarian or authoritarian government, victims of systematic murder, brutality, and atrocities were more likely to remain silent. Trials alleviated the agony of past violations and abuses, as long as they were carried out in compliance with the rule of law, due process, and proportionality. Third, trials compelled ordinary people to reconsider their individual actions and obligations in the face of tyranny, as well as their social, political, and moral consequences.

The 2004 Report underscored the critical role victims play in developing and implementing transitional justice measures. Victims should be consulted and actively participate in decision-making processes, regardless of the measures used (for example, prosecutions, trials, truth commissions, compensation, or institutional reform initiatives). Their interests must be carefully examined, and their rights must be protected through appropriate procedures. Victims and their grieving families could reclaim the agency that perpetrators had previously denied them, allowing them to move on from feelings of loss, trauma, worry, and humiliation.

5 The division of individual and collective guilts please see: Karl Jaspers. 1946. *Die Schuldfrage*, Heidelberg: Lambert Schneider. 31–34.

To lay the foundations for transitional justice, it requires a post-authoritarian society to come to terms with its past wrongs inflicted on victims. In this regard, as key actors, victims could make a substantial contribution to the implementation of such comprehensive programs. Instead of being disregarded as smears and innuendo, the evidence provided by victims has the potential to give considerable light on the historical underpinnings of past abuses. Furthermore, by restoring victims' agency, post-authoritarian cultures can gradually overcome collective trauma. Thus, transitional justice is not something that falls from the sky or is bestowed by the authorities; rather, it is something that victims and the new community work together to create. That is why the 2004 Report emphasized the victims of vulnerable, marginalized, or disadvantaged groups, such as ethnic minorities, people with disabilities, the elderly, children, women, prisoners, refugees, and so on, and proposed a differentiated approach to ensure their equal participation in transitional justice decision-making.

IV. The Misreading of a Holistic Approach by the Commission and its Impact on the Concluding Report

The Concluding Report's fundamental text includes an introduction, four volumes, and three appendices. In volume I's General Remarks (總論), the Concluding Report briefly mentioned and discussed a holistic approach. It expressly stated that

> *When a country promotes a transitional justice process, from specific goals to the strategies it adopts, it cannot rely on a single approach or follow a single model. Rather, it must situate transitional justice in a specific historical and political context and make comprehensive arrangements for dealing with multiple goals and strategies. This is because each approach or model has its limitations. Taken together, these approaches and models may be at odds with one other (volume I: 2).*

The *Act* entrusted the commission with the following tasks: (1) declassifying political files; (2) removing symbols of authoritarianism and preserving sites of persecution; (3) exonerating wrongful convictions and incarcerations, restoring historical truth, and promoting reconciliation; (4) dealing with ill-gotten assets of the KMT; and (5) tackling other transitional justice matters.

The Concluding Report stated that the implementation of these tasks was the result of the adoption of numerous solutions devised and developed with Taiwan's distinctive historical and political situation in mind. Volume I of the Concluding Report declared that the commission's transitional justice was indeed holistic. However, the Concluding Report did not explain how the Act-enumerated tasks constituted interrelated pieces and achieved various goals, nor did it describe what made those tasks context-specific and mutually beneficial.

It is unclear why the Concluding Report associated truth commissions and criminal prosecution with narrow focus measures, "a single approach" and then prohibited "the use of a single model" (Vol. I, 5). They are not, if they work together to find the truth, justice, and compensation for the victims. Similarly, readers, victims, and concerned citizens are perplexed by comments that "identifying perpetrators and holding them accountable" and "personnel investigation and handling" were not crucial to the purposes of transitional justice. Rather, they came under the category of "restoring the historical truth" and "resolving judicial misconduct".

The Concluding Report stated that "due to some careful contemplation," the commission, not the court system, was designated to preside over the rectification of past illegality. But this very official document did not explain what that "careful contemplation" was, who made such "contemplation," for what purposes, why such "careful contemplation" could not be subjected to close scrutiny and public debate, or how such "careful contemplation" could be justified in the eyes of tens of thousands of victims who have, thus far, lived under traumas.

In other words, such procedures would ensure that no prosecutions were filed, that all culprits were granted amnesty, and that civil personnel and authorities were never vetted. This would allow the state and government agencies to disavow responsibility, effectively ruling out any future constitutional, legal, and personnel reforms.

It is somewhat unusual to find sentences in the Concluding Report couched in terms of "Taiwan's specific political context," yet the Concluding Report neglected to clearly out exactly what that specific context was. This "specific political context" could therefore refer to anything. One might reasonably assume that the government could easily relegate authoritarianism, institutional settings of abuse and violence, the underlying social tensions, violations of human rights, and oppression that still exist in post-authoritarian society to the past, rather than something that is ongoing and unresolved today. Alternatively, China's threat of force may be utilized to argue that prosecuting and trying the perpetrators is against Taiwan's political stability and national security.

The report acknowledged that gender justice was an important component of transitional justice (Vol. I, 3), but claimed without more explanation that the commission was not mandated by the Act to promote it (Vol. I: 6). It is worth noting that the Act did not charge the commission with determining monetary compensation. This decision was based on the fact that the 228 Memorial Foundation has previously awarded compensation to victims. This raises questions about whether the Act assigned those obligations to the commission arbitrarily and whether the panel carried them out at its own discretion.

The Concluding Report, to some extent, left more unsolved questions than it answered. Without clarifying the rationale behind the commission's work, it is difficult to determine what function the declassification process fulfilled. How does this approach relate to and strengthen the commission's other duties, such as removing authoritarian symbols and protecting places of injustice, addressing judicial malpractice, and restoring historical truth? What good or negative effects did the aforementioned activities have on other duties, and what corrective actions were taken? In other words, had the actual holistic approach been implemented, the tasks and the processes for their implementation would have been more mutually complementary.

The tasks claimed to be completed by the commission, such as providing access to declassified political files and planning the removal or renaming of authoritarian symbols (Vol. III: 62), enumerated in volume III, did not explain how each task was an essential component of the integrated and mutually reinforcing whole. It also didn't explain how each individual part worked or how multiple elements interacted with each other. In fact, practically all of the aforementioned activities were continuations of past work conducted by Taiwan's public and corporate sectors, academic studies, and non-governmental transitional justice organizations. Their individual efforts began even before the Act was enacted in 2017 and the commission was established in 2018. Through the mobilization of administrative resources, the commission put together numerous tasks while paying little attention to the interconnected nature of its tasks, current resources, and the type of transition justice that diverse stakeholders would like to establish.

The Concluding Report paid more attention to the injustices perpetrated against indigenous peoples. However, there was a lack of awareness to the diverse nature of victims among disadvantaged groups,[6] such as children, women, and persons with disabilities, despite the fact that diversity was meant to be a prominent theme of the official report. Instead of being integrated, these activities fractured and hollowed out the claimed goals of Taiwan's transitional justice. The execution of those duties and their corollaries, as detailed in the Concluding Report, appeared to contradict the commission's ostensible commitment to transitional justice.

V. Challenges of Taiwan's Transitional Justice

Based on a clarification of the major features of the holistic approach as outlined in the Concluding Report, as well as the commission's misinterpretation of this approach, we believe that Taiwan's transitional justice faces significant obstacles.

The Concluding Report shows that the commission paid insufficient attention to the importance of victims' testimonies on the perpetrators as individuals in the design and implementation of transitional justice systems. Volume II focused heavily on the establishment and transformation of a single-party state into an authoritarian state, as well as an assessment of the criminality of government agencies during martial law. However, volume II was a rehash of the known, including no new information. Everything stated and pieced together in Volume II can be found in academic publications, oral histories, and/or reports prepared by victim assistance organizations. Surprisingly, the crime of systematic persecution against victims such as Bo Yang and other dissidents was largely ignored, despite the fact that presidents Chiang Kai-shek and Chiang Ching-kuo were directly blamed for establishing and preserving the party-state regime. Similarly, similar blame was assigned to respective heads of the KMT, the repressive state apparatus, and the judicial system, despite the

6 Comparing with: Yang, Tsui 2014 (楊翠, 2014). "Women and the White Terror Incidents" (女性與白色恐怖事件), In *The Symposium of Human Rights and Political Events* (台灣人權與政治事件學術研討會), the Compensation Foundation for Wrongful Trials on Charges of Sedition and Espionage during the Martial Law Period (財團法人戒嚴時期不檔審判補償基金會); Wu, Pei-ju 2021 (吳佩儒, 2021). *Invisible White Terror: Representation of Persons with Disabilities and Human Rights Museums* (看不見的白色恐怖:再現身心障礙者與人權博物館) Taipei: Soochow University.;National Human Rights Museum. 2015. https://www.nhrm.gov.tw/WebUPD/nhrm/Learning/03獄外之囚_展覽手冊.pdf (獄外之囚:白色恐怖受難者女性家屬口述記錄成果展展覽手冊); Jau-hwa Chen (ed. 2019). *In Search of an Unnamed Rose: Memory, White Terror and Torture* (尋找一株未命名的玫瑰:記憶、白色恐怖與酷刑). New Taipei City: National Human Rights Museum.

fact that their political standing was more concerned with bureaucratic roles and/or political responsibilities in general than with the culpability of being direct perpetrators in specific cases.

The Concluding Report considers Chiang Ching-kuo to be the mastermind behind Taiwan's intelligence services and authoritarian settings, when he began to serve as the secretary-general and director of the "information unit of the confidential office of the presidential office" (總統府機要室資料組) in 1950. Being in charge of secret intelligence, he could have penetrated any Taiwanese government institution he wanted; he was accused in a large number of political cases. However, the Concluding Report emphasized his role as the head of the authoritarian regime rather than his actions against victims. According to Liu Shih-ming (Liu 1999), Chiang Ching-kuo directed secret services to create cases against political opponents. Victims were detained and imprisoned not because they posed a threat to national security, but because Chiang Ching-kuo was upset by what they had said. Lei Cheng (雷震) was among them. Charges of sedition were made up in response to his criticism of the government.

Bo Yang, a victim of white terror, revealed that Chiang Ching-kuo wanted him killed (Bo Zhou 1996, 331–333), and the 2004 report of the Control Yuan confirmed such a claim based on achieve materials of the Taiwan Garrison Command (台灣警備司令部), which was presented to Chiang Ching-kuo by National Security Bureau Director Zhou Zhong-feng (周中峯) (Li 2021, 59). The commission may find it instructive to investigate the culpability of people inside the oppressive state machinery, as well as the circumstances surrounding torture, systematic violence and terror, and execution of specific victims. Its failure to investigate the alleged violations perpetrated by Chiang Ching-kuo individually, much alone specify viable legal remedies, was a farce of transitional justice.

The importance of an investigation into the criminals' responsibility cannot be overstated. Victims' suffering at the hands of proximate offenders must be understood as a genuine cause of grievances. As the state has proved victims' innocence and eventually cleared them of all accusations, it is unreasonable to claim that those who tortured and subjected victims to other cruel, inhuman, or humiliating treatment should be exonerated. Government agencies, such as judicial and prosecution offices or an independent truth commission, must uncover the truth about the cases and hold the criminals accountable for what they have done to the victims. Any transitional justice approach that fails to act on the truth revealed in testimonies merely diminishes victims' pain and perpetuates the status quo. Truth, justice, and reparation must be united and implemented simultaneously through the coordination and collaboration of government organizations.

Taiwan's transitional justice had a rough ride since victims' statements were largely rejected and dismissed. The Concluding Report clearly questions the responsibility of perpetrators. This means that the party-state system, rather than eager participants or vicious henchmen, should bear blame for the horrors. If Taiwan's transitional justice is to live up to its name and expectations, victims and their families must be involved in designing and implementing truth-finding processes, as well as developing a clear vision of a just society. This cannot be accomplished in the absence of victim-centered measures and procedures.

The commission acknowledged indigenous peoples' suffering. However, it excluded much more victims from vulnerable categories than it included. The Concluding Report did not explain why it included some victims of vulnerable groups while excluding others, such as women, children, and people with disabilities; what prevented them from identifying other vulnerable groups and addressing their legitimate grievances, concerns, and needs; or why those perspectives of the victims were not included in justice, truth, and reparation programmes, highlighting that transitional justice is relevant to the most discriminated.

If Taiwan is to allow victims to reclaim their dignity, heal psychological trauma, and ultimately achieve genuine peace, the government's transitional justice initiatives must go beyond compensation. The Concluding Report dealt with victims in terms of compensation, property restitution, political trauma recovery, and eventual criminal record erasure. In terms of compensation, in addition to passing the *Act to Restore Victims' Rights Infringed by Illegal State Acts During the Period of Authoritarian Rule* (2025), the commission stated that membership in "communist organizations" would not affect the government's recognition of one's status as a political prisoner. The commission was fully aware of the multiplicity of victims and the anti-communist political ideas that pervaded Taiwan; the commission's approach deserves to be praised. However, as Pablo de Greiff (2012, 36) reminded us, any compensation granted to victims must be used in conjunction with other transitional justice measures, such as truth-telling or institutional transformation. In the absence of these measures, transitional justice measures are, at best, nominal and symbolic, and at worst, ineffective and intolerant. Similarly, restoring victims' dignity demands an examination into abusers' involvement. Expunging victims' criminal records is not a gift bestowed upon them; rather, it is historical and factual.

The 2004 Report focuses on "the centrality of victims in the design and implementation of transitional justice." Victims' narratives and tales are critical for restoring a country's historical memory and initiating a learning process to right past wrongs, preserve human rights, and establish the groundwork for justice in post-authoritarian societies. To go forward, post-authoritarian countries must investigate the conditions that arose from the past and conduct a thorough examination of past atrocities. "The centrality of victims" does not entail that criminals have no rights. Rather, it means that their rights should not be prioritized over those of victims, and that any investigation into alleged wrongdoing must adhere to human rights standards and due process of law. This is especially true for victims and their bereaved families of the February 28 incident and the White Terror.

VI. Concluding Remarks

The commission failed to explain why these tasks were chosen, owing to a lack of a holistic approach to integrating various components of an interlocking whole. This resulted in the fragmentation of transitional justice mechanisms. It is debatable whether the decisions to implement fragmented and haphazard measures sprang from Taiwan's unique circumstances or from transitional justice examples established by other nations. Because the commission failed to articulate the very rationale behind its work, it not only undermined the commission's legitimacy and credibility in implementing transnational justice, but it also rendered the commission's efforts to execute individual tasks ineffective and incomplete. Extensive consultation processes are required to gather varied perspectives (such as government and non-governmental organizations, victims and vulnerable groups of victims, the general public, and so on) and achieve the commission's stated goals.

Based on previous experience, the UN concluded that isolated and fragmentary measures may achieve nothing. Under certain conditions, they may leave victims worse off than they were. If the commission had considered the declassification of political files to be a crucial component of an integrated and holistic approach, it would have been linked with the prosecution of criminals, amnesty, and compensation plans, among other things. Similarly, follow-up agencies should have considered the following: which files should be made public, which cases should be thoroughly probed, and whether public or private hearings should be convened.

Coordination between governmental agencies, such as the Ministry of Justice, Ministry of Culture, and Ministry of the Interior, for a truth-finding mission, justice restoration in some specific cases that had been compensated, and the possibility of prosecution in those cases, should be recommended and implemented. In this regard, the various tasks for the agencies will be combined to achieve a shared objective and become integral aspects of that aim. Opening political files does not always imply truth-telling. It is also not necessary to tell the truth. Verifying multiple (even opposing) narratives, comparing archival materials to victims' testimony, and conducting a truth-seeking investigation into sequences of events and affected groups or persons all require a significant amount of effort.

References

Chinese:

台灣人權促進會 (2011年10月7日)。〈船過水無痕?國慶枉斷魂! ~從江國慶案看臺灣的轉型不正義〉。https://www.tahr.org.tw/ activity/307 (Taiwan Association for Human Rights. [2011, October 7]. *Nothing left after the case? The National Day is in vain: Taiwan's transformational impropriety as seen from the Chiang Kuo-Ching case.*)

李福鐘 (2021)〈兩蔣威權體制特性再探 從柏楊案談起〉,《國史館 館刊》,第69期 (2021/9), 39–76頁。(Li, Fu-chung. 2021. Reappraising the Characteristics of the Authoritarian Regimes of chiang Kai-shek and Chiang Ching-kuo: The Sedition Case of Bo Yang. In *Bulletin of academia Historica*. Vol. 69. 39–76.)

柏楊 (1996)。《柏楊回憶錄》(周碧瑟訪)。遠流。(Bo, Y. [1996]. *Memoirs of Bo Yang* [P. Chou, Interviewer]. Yuan-Liou.)

吳佩儒 (2021)《看不見的白色恐怖:再現身心障礙者與 人權博物館》台北:東吳大學人權碩士學位學程碩士論文。(Wu, Pei-ju. 2021. *Invisible White Terror: Representation of Persons with Disabilities and Human Rights Museums*. Taipei: Soochow University.)

國家人權博物館籌備處 (2015)。《獄外之囚:白色恐怖受難者女性 家屬口述記錄成果展展覽手冊》。(National Human Rights Museum. 2015. *Prisoners outside: Oral records of female victims of the White Terror*, Exhibition brochure.)

陳瑤華 (2019) 主編。《尋找一株未命名的玫瑰:記憶、白色恐怖與 酷刑》, 20-43。新北市:國家人權博物館。 (Jau-hwa Chen. 2019 ed. *In Search of an Unnamed Rose: Memory, White Terror and Torture*. New Taipei City: National Human Rights Museum.)

楊翠(2014)。〈女性與白色恐怖事件〉。收在《台灣人權與政治事件學術研討會》。財團法人戒嚴時期不檔審判補償基金會。(Yang, Tsui. 2014. "Women and the White Terror Incidents". In *The Symposium of Human Rights and Polit-*

ical Events. the Compensation Foundation for Wrongful Trials on Charges of Sedition and Espionage during the Martial Law Period.)。

監察院 (2016年12月8日)。《調查報告》(093國調0002字號)。 https://www.cy.gov.tw/CyBsBoxContent.aspx?n=133&s=65 (Control Yuan. [2016, December 8]. *Investigation report* [national decree no. 093-0002].)

劉熙明 (1999) 〈蔣中正與蔣經國在戒嚴時期不當審判中的角色〉,《台灣史研究》,第6卷, 第2期, (Liu Shih-ming. 1999. "The role of Chiang Kai-shek and Chiang Chin-kuo during the Period of the White Terror". *Taiwan Historical Research*. Vol. 5 No. 2 139–187)

轉型正義促進委員會 (2022)。《任務總結報告》(The Commission. 2022. *Concluding Report*, Book I, II, III, and VI, Appendix I, II and III.)

The Act Governing the Recovery of Damage to Individual Rights during the Period of Martial Law. 2000.

The Act on Promoting Transitional Justice. 2017.

The Act to Restore Victims' Rights Infringed by Illegal State Acts During the Period of Authoritarian Rule. 2025.

Arbour, Louise. 2006. "Economic and Social Justice for Societies in Transition". In International Law and Politics. Vol.: 40:1. 1–27.

Arendt, Hannah. 2003. *Responsibility and Judgment*. Ed. By Kohn, J. New York: Schocken Books.

Arthur, Paige. 2009. "How 'Transitions' Reshaped Human Rights: A Conceptual History of Transitional Justice" in *Human Rights Quarterly* 31 (2009): 321–367.

Boraine, Alexander L. 2006. "Transitional Justice: A Holistic Interpretation". In *Historical Reconciliation*. Vol. 60. No. 1. 17–27.

Compensation Act for Wrongful Trials on Charges of Sedition and Espionage during the Martial Law Period. 2006.

De Greiff, P. 2012. "Theorizing Transitional Justice". In *Transitional Justice*. Ed. By Williams, M. 31–77. http://www.jstor.org/stable/24220123. (9.6.2023)

The February 28 Incident Disposition and Compensation Act 1995.

Jaspers, Karl. 1946. *Die Schuldfrage*, Heidelberg: Lambert Schneider.

Roht-Arriaza, Naomi. 2006. "The new landscape of transitional justice", in: *Transitional Justice in 21. Century*, Cambridge & Malden: Polity, 1–16.

Sikkink, K., & Walling, C. B. 2007. "The Impact of Human Rights Trials in Latin America". In Journal of Peace Research, 44(4), 427–445. http://www.jstor.org/stable/27640539. (9.6.2023)

Teitel, Ruti. 2003. "Transitional Justice Genealogy", in *Harvard human rights journal*, Vol. 16, spring, 69–94.

UN Secretary General. 2004. Report of the UN Secretary General on the Rule of Law and Transitional Justice in Conflict and Post-Conflict Societies (S/2004/616).

I. Assessing a Delayed Truth Commission: Progress and Challenges of the Taiwanese Transitional Justice Commission and Its Follow-up Mechanism

Yi-Li Lee[1]

Abstract

This chapter assesses Taiwan's transitional justice process by analyzing the mandate, operations, and limitations of the Transitional Justice Commission and its subsequent institutional arrangements. Until its dissolution in 2022, the Commission made progress in truth recovery, reparations, and promoting historical reckoning. After its closure, the transitional justice conference, chaired by the prime minister, supported by the Office of Human Rights and Transitional Justice, was introduced. Additionally, implementation tasks were delegated to various governmental ministries. Despite these advancements, challenges remain, including the absence of a centralized coordinating body, ambiguities regarding the role of National Human Rights Commission, lacking gender-sensitive perspective to transitional justice process, and insufficient civil society participation. This chapter argues that Taiwan's experience illustrates both the potential and limitations of implementing truth commissions in post-authoritarian settings. The analysis contributes to broader debates on delayed transitional justice and the relationship between legal frameworks and political will in confronting historical injustice.

Keywords:

Transitional justice, Truth commission, Transitional Justice Commission, National human rights commission, Follow-up mechanisms, Authoritarian legacies, Institutional design, Regime change, Civic Engagement, Democratization, Political archive, Authoritarian symbol, International human rights law, Incorporation

1 Yi-Li Lee is an Associate Professor at the Institute of Law for Science and Technology of National Tsing Hua University. Her academic interests cover a variety of topics, including transitional justice, digital rights and AI governance, comparative constitutional law, international human rights law, international humanitarian law and international criminal law.

I. Introduction

Transitional justice poses a vast array of political, legal, and social challenges during a shift from authoritarianism to democracy (Kritz 1995; Teitel 2002, 11–26; Teiltel 2014, 3–10; Hansen 2014, 105–106; Chang and Lee 2021), a transformation that Taiwan and several other Asian countries have undergone after nearly four decades under authoritarian rule (Wu 2005, 77–102; Caldwell 2018, 449–83; Rowen and Rowen 2017, 92–112; Chang-Liao and Chen 2019, 619–43; Huang 2021, 209–33). Since the late 1980s and early 1990s, Taiwan's successive democratically elected governments have struggled with the complexity of transitional justice and faced challenges similar to those encountered in the constitutional histories of other nations (Wu 2005, 81–90; Caldwell 2018, 462–67; Chang-Liao and Chen 2019, 633–34; Lee and Chang 2023, 685). At the onset of democratization, Taiwan introduced various mechanisms toward transitional justice. However, apart from compensation and limited effort to reveal truths, many of these mechanisms have failed or faced significant obstacles. This limited effectiveness has impeded the progress of Taiwan's constitutional democracy and contributed to societal division. The lack of comprehensive and accurate historical accounts and identification of responsible parties has enabled the easy exploitation of the past for political gains (Chang-Liao and Chen 2019, 640–41; Su 2019).

In January 2016, the Democratic Progressive Party in Taiwan achieved an unprecedented victory by winning presidential and parliamentary elections. With high hopes for reform, victims of previous human rights violations expressed strong demands for truth, justice, and reparation. A new era of transitional justice commenced when President Tsai Ing-wen assumed office on May 20, 2016. Since then, President Tsai has initiated a few initiatives, including advancing the Act on Promoting Transitional Justice, which established an institutional framework for addressing issues related to transitional justice. In December 2017, this Act established the Transitional Justice Commission within the Executive Yuan. The Commission was vested with the authority to recover and categorize political archives, eliminate authoritarian symbols, rectify judicial wrongs, and promote social reconciliation. Upon the completion of its mandate, the Commission was dissolved on May 31, 2022, after the release of a final report that recommended a series of follow-up mechanisms and policies to be implemented by the Executive Yuan. Subsequently, transitional justice programs were assigned to various ministries within the Executive Yuan. Furthermore, the Human Rights and

Transitional Justice Office was established under the Prime Minister of the Executive Yuan.

Against this background, this chapter aims to examine the achievements of the Taiwanese Transitional Justice Commission and the challenges it currently faces with regard to its follow-up mechanisms. The chapter argues that the Commission has made significant progress by overturning criminal judgments rendered by military tribunals during the White Terror period. Moreover, the current follow-up arrangement could facilitate the acquisition of administrative or political resources for the implementation of the recommendations of the final reports of the Commission. However, concerns persist, including whether the Human Rights and Transitional Justice Office has sufficient capacity to coordinate and integrate the ministries and officials in charge of these ministries possess the professional knowledge and ability necessary to address transitional justice issues.

II. Transitional Justice Commission and Its Follow-up Mechanisms

1. Creation of the Transitional Justice Commission

Since January 2016, calls from victims for truth, justice, and reparation have accelerated the implementation of various initiatives toward transitional justice in Taiwan, particularly after the DPP secured the presidency and a parliamentary majority for the first time. This shift in political dynamics has incited reforms in transitional justice. From May 2016 onward, the administration of President Tsai Ing-wen has introduced a series of transitional justice mechanisms. For instance, in August 2016, President Tsai formally apologized to the indigenous populations in Taiwan (Office of President 2016) followed by the enactment of the DPP government of several laws and policies intended to address the authoritarian past of the nation. Within the same month, the Legislative Yuan passed the Act on Governing the Handling of Illegally Seized Assets by Political Parties and Their Affiliated Organizations (Illegally Seized Party Assets Act), which led to the formation of the Ill-Gotten Party Assets Settlement Committee under the Executive Yuan to manage assets that were unlawfully acquired by the KMT during its authoritarian regime (Ill-Gotten Party Assets Settlement Committee 2016). In March 2017, the Indigenous Historical Justice and Transitional Justice Commission was formed under the leadership of President Tsai to address historical injustices against indigenous communities and to establish guidelines for land distribution to these groups (Presidential Office Indigenous Committee 2016).

One of the most significant strides in transitional justice occurred through the enactment of the Act on Promoting Transitional Justice in December 2017. This legislation led to the establishment of a transitional justice commission under the Executive Yuan (Transitional Justice Commission 2018), which was tasked with investigating abuses on human rights from the end of Japanese colonial rule on August 15, 1945, to the cessation of Martial Law in Kinmen and Matsu on November 6, 1992 (Act on Promoting Transitional Justice 2017, Art. 7). The Transitional Justice Commission, which comprised nine members nominated by the Prime Minister and approved by the Legislative Yuan (Act on Promoting Transitional Justice 2017, Art. 8), was empowered to recover and categorize political archives, dismantle authoritarian symbols, rectify judicial errors, and foster societal reconciliation (Act on Promoting Transitional Justice 2017, Art. 2). Additionally, it possesses the authority to rename symbols that glorify dictators to uphold democratic principles and constitutionalism (Act on Promoting Transitional Justice 2017, Art. 5). The Commission is also authorized to conduct extensive investigation into abuses on human rights during the authoritarian era, which required the public and private sectors to submit pertinent documents and unlock archives (Act on Promoting Transitional Justice 2017, Art. 16). Moreover, it can probe and manage ill-gotten political party assets, although it does not address assets identified by the Ill-Gotten Party Assets Settlement Committee (Act on Promoting Transitional Justice 2017, Art. 7). Lastly, a groundbreaking power of the commission is its ability to overturn the conviction of civilians judged by military tribunals during the White Terror period (Act on Promoting Transitional Justice 2017, Art. 6).

To facilitate the operation of related businesses, based on the Act on Promoting Transitional Justice, the Transitional Justice Commission has divided its internal staff into four task groups. These groups are respectively responsible for restoring historical truth, handling authoritarian symbols, rectifying judicial injustices, and rebuilding social trust (Transitional Justice Commission 2022). As per the first provision of Article 11 of the Transitional Justice Act, the Commission for Transitional Justice needed to submit a summary report on the aforementioned tasks within two years. The same article allows an extension of the term by the Premier if the tasks are not completed within two years. The Commission applied for extensions of its term twice, in April 2020 and April 2021 (Transitional Justice Commission 2022) due to operational needs. After these extensions, at the end of May 2022, the Commission for Transitional Justice completed its mission and submitted its final report to the Premier (Transitional Justice Commission 2022).

2. Follow-up Mechanisms Since 2022

To continue the work of transitional justice, the arrangement of a successor mechanism became an institutional issue in the era after the Transitional Justice Commission. In early 2022, when it was confirmed that the Transitional Justice Commission would no longer be extended, the discussion on the integration of relevant systems became a focus across sectors. Experts and scholars proposed different solutions, such as transferring the relevant operations to the Human Rights Committee of the Control Yuan (Pan 2022), thus establishing a dedicated agency (Li 2022) or forming a permanent institution (Lai 2022). As the responsible agency, the Transitional Justice Commission proposed two transition plans in its final report. The first plan involved the dispersion of a few of the Commission's tasks to existing ministries and the establishment of a time-limited level-3 independent agency responsible for investigating oppressive regimes and holding perpetrators accountable. This agency would be a specialized body. The second plan entailed the delegation of tasks to different ministries based on the nature of such tasks without creating a dedicated agency (Transitional Justice Commission 2022).

In May 2022, after the official dissolution of the Transitional Justice Commission, the Executive Yuan adopted a transition mechanism in which the Premier of the Executive Yuan served as a convener of the Transitional Justice Conference and established a Human Rights and Transitional Justice Office within the Executive Yuan to coordinate work related to human rights and transitional justice (Lee 2022). Additionally, operations related to the Transitional Justice Commission were transferred to various ministries of the Executive Yuan.

On May 27, 2022, the Legislative Yuan revised the Act on Promoting Transitional Justice to implement this plan. According to the newly amended Article 11-1 of the Act, after the dissolution of the Transitional Justice Commission, the Executive Yuan established the Conference on Promoting Transitional Justice, which is responsible for integrating, coordinating, and supervising the tasks outlined in Article 2, Paragraph 2 of the Act and the final report. The Premier of the Executive Yuan served as the convener of this conference, while the Human Rights and Transitional Justice Office of the Executive Yuan acted as the staff unit to continue the promotion of transitional justice policies (Lee 2022). According to Article 17-2 of the Executive Yuan's Procedures, the major responsibilities of the Human Rights Office include (1) planning, drafting, and reviewing policies, plans, and legislation related to transitional justice and coordinating and supervising the (2) opening of political archives and the identification and handling of perpetrators, (3) handling of authoritarian symbols, preservation of unjust sites, and education on transitional justice, (4) the rectification of judicial and administrative injustices, restoration of victims' rights, and mental health services for victims of political violence and their families, and (5) the Transitional Justice Fund.

Furthermore, according to the newly amended Article 11-2 of the Act, after the dissolution of the Transitional Justice Commission, the relevant operations were transferred to six main ministries: the National Development Council, Ministry of the Interior, Ministry of Culture, Ministry of Justice, Ministry of Education, and Ministry of Health and Welfare. For instance, the responsibilities of the Ministry of Justice include rectifying judicial and administrative injustices and identifying and handling perpetrators. The Ministry of the Interior conducts the removal of authoritarian symbols, while the Ministry of Culture addresses unjust sites. The Ministry of Health and Welfare facilitates healing among victims of political violence and their families, and the Ministry of Education provides education on transitional justice. Lastly, the National Development Council manages the income, custody, and application of the Transitional Justice Fund.

III. Progress and Challenges

This section analyzes what progress that Transitional Justice Commission and its follow-up mechanisms have made and what challenges they encountered. Until its dissolution in 2022, the Transitional Justice Commission achieved some success in truth recovery, symbolic reparations, and advancing historical reckoning. Following the Commission's closure, the implementation of transitional justice was transferred to a new structure. The prime minister chaired the transitional justice conference, with assistance of the human rights and transitional justice office. Additionally, transitional justice implementation was delegated to the various governmental ministries, allowing more direct access to administrative or political resources. Despite this progress, challenges remain, including the need for a centralized coordinating body, clearer institutional roles for human rights commissions, more gender-sensitive perspectives and stronger civil society involvement.

1. Progress

a) Transitional Justice Commission

At the end of May 2022, the Transitional Justice Commission officially concluded its term and submitted its final report to the Premier of the Executive Yuan. According to the closure report of the Commission, its main achievements included the following:

aa) Political archive collection and public access

Archives are crucial to the pursuit of justice and all mechanisms of transitional justice because they provide indispensable evidence for the identification of perpetrators of severe human rights abuses in the past. Without access to these archives, holding wrongdoers accountable becomes exceedingly challenging. Additionally, archives are essential for revealing the truth. For victims of human rights violations, archives typically represent the sole means of understanding actual events. Importantly, families hold the right to learn the fate of their relatives and ascertain any violations, and every citizen possesses the right to know their shared history. This right compels the state to locate missing archives and maintain them to enhance public understanding and help establish an accurate historical account of Taiwan's past. To improve the management of archives, the Legislative Yuan enacted the Act on Political Archives in July 2019.

Notably, this law expands the definition of political archives to include records from government bodies, political parties, and affiliated organizations (Act on Political Archives 2019, Art. 3). It requires officials from these entities to transfer their political archives to the National Archives Administration (Act on Political Archives 2019, Art. 6). The law also streamlines the process for declassifying records such as automatically publicizing any confidential archive older than 30 years (Act on Political Archives 2019, Art. 5). The Commission collected 137,511 political files from 33 government agencies and declassified more than 10,000 records (Transitional Justice Commission 2022, 7). Subsequently, the Taiwan Transitional Justice Database was established (Transitional Justice Commission 2022, 40).

bb) Handling of authoritarian symbols

Under Article 2, Paragraph 2 of the Act on Promoting Transitional Justice, one of the mandates assigned to the Commission is the removal of authoritarian symbols. Article 5, Paragraph 1 of the Act further stipulates that the purposes of such removal are: (1) to establish a constitutional order based on freedom and democracy; (2) to reject the legitimacy of authoritarian rule; and (3) to draw lessons from past human rights violations. Since its establishment in 2017, the Commission has removed authoritarian symbols across Taiwan. By the time of its dissolution, thousands of such symbols had been removed (Transitional Justice Commission 2022, 72).

cc) Preservation of sites of injustice

According to reports, injustice sites associated with the White Terror, including locations where victims were arrested, interrogated, tortured, tried, imprisoned, executed, and buried, are aiming to enhance public understanding of the historical sites related to White Terror. More than a thousand sites of injustice were officially preserved, while relevant legal recommendations were proposed (Transitional Justice Commission 2022, 209). These sites included the Garrison Command Security Office Detention Center, Secret Service Northern Office, Investigation Bureau, Ministry of Defense Military Law Detention Center, Machangding Execution Grounds, and Ankeng Execution Grounds. According to a report, mechanisms for promoting historical education at these injustice sites will be established based on inventory results. Ongoing plans include the Injustice Sites Virtual Museum Development Project and the Injustice Sites Identification System Project. These initiatives involve the use of a virtual online museum to connect individual and scattered locations, thereby comprehensively recreating the landscape of White Terror and the development of democracy and human rights in Taiwan.

dd) Rectification of judicial injustices

In 1949, after facing defeat in the civil war against the Communist Party, the KMT government retreated to Taiwan (Yeh 2016, 32). On May 20, 1949, it declared Martial Law in mainland China and Taiwan to solidify its rule and legitimacy (Yeh 2016, 32). Moreover, in 1947, shortly after the ROC Constitution came into effect, it was suspended by the Temporary Provisions Effective During the Period of National Mobilization for the Suppression of Communist Rebellion, which was introduced in 1948.[2] These provisions facili-

2 It is important to note that the ROC Constitution after becoming effective was not applied to Taiwan as requested by the Chen Yi government.

tated a presidential rule under the party-state system, which was retained until May 1991. Martial Law, which endorsed human rights violations, was not lifted until July 1987. These legal frameworks were the main sources of state-sanctioned terrorism from the 1950s to the late 1980s. Additionally, several laws were enacted under the guise of the Mobilization for Suppression of Communist Rebellion. Among the most oppressive laws were the Statute for the Eradication of Communist Espionage in 1950 (effective from June 13, 1950, to May 16, 1991), Statute for the Punishment of Treason in 1949 (effective from June 21, 1949, to May 22, 1991), and National Mobilization Law in 1942 (effective from March 29, 1942, to January 6, 2004). The White Terror began during the 1950s and 1960s and continued to a lesser extent to the 1980s. The most important aspect about these terrors is that they were legally and judicially sanctioned by the apparatus of the KMT party-state regime.

Due to these laws and the Martial Law Decree, the military tried civilians and non-civilians. Suspects were frequently severely tortured during interrogation conducted by intelligence agents and military police. Initially, the legal affairs branch of the Taiwan Provincial Military Headquarters handled cases before they were forwarded to the Ministry of National Defense, which typically rubber-stamped decisions without substantial review. Particularly for those charged with treason, execution was carried out immediately after initial rulings, typically without an opportunity for appeal. These trials were conducted outside the norms of criminal procedure, which blatantly disregarded the rights to a fair trial and due process (Historical Research Commission 1995, 127).

Shortly after the 38-year-long Martial Law Decree was lifted in 1987, lawsuits that requested the examination of the legality of relevant laws implemented during the authoritarian regime were brought to courts. In 1989, the Constitutional Court of Taiwan was tasked to review the constitutionality of Article 9 of the National Security Act for the Period of National Mobilization for Suppression of the Communist Rebellion, which prohibited civilians convicted by the military tribunal during the Martial Law period from filing an appeal (Bowman 2012, 485–526).[3] In its notorious decision (*Interpretation No. 272*), the Court used "exceptional circumstances" and "difficulty in collecting and investigating evidence after such a prolonged period of time has elapsed and such changes in circumstances, and the need for maintaining the stability of judgment and social

3 During the "White Terror" Period, many victims, especially civilians, were detained and trialed by the military court without the due process.

order" as reasons for prohibiting the appeals of civilians persecuted by the military courts during Martial Law (Constitutional Court of Taiwan 1991). Conversely, this decision unfortunately blocked citizens who have been tried by the military courts during Martial Law from bringing their cases to ordinary courts.

To address the judicial injustice, Article 6 of the Transitional Justice Act specifically targets the correction of past judicial injustices, thus challenging the conservative mindset and practices outlined in the previous sections (Act on Promoting Transitional Justice 2017, Art. 6). On the date of its effectivity, Article 6(3) of the Transitional Justice Act mandates that convictions will be nullified and criminal records will be cleared for victims who received compensation or had their rights restored under the Act to Provide Monetary Reparations for Victims and Their Families of February 28 Incident (1995), Compensation Act for Wrongful Trials on Charges of Sedition and Espionage During the Martial Law Period (1998), and Act Governing the Recovery of Damage of Individual Rights During the Period of Martial Law (1995/2000).

The Transitional Justice Commission, through its initiative or upon petition from the individual, is authorized to reassess the criminal convictions of individuals not covered by these Acts, including those previously found guilty of subversive activities and, thus, ineligible for compensation. If these are deemed judicial errors, then they will be annulled and expunged. Regarding the return of confiscated properties after the clearing of records, the Transitional Justice Commission assessed the type and value of these properties, including land, buildings, or cash. Upon the competition of the Commission, a total of 5,902 cases of judicial injustice were rectified (Transitional Justice Commission 2022, 259).

b) Follow-Up Mechanism

To date, the Executive Yuan has convened the Conference on Promoting Transitional Justice three times. According to publicly available information on the website of the conference maintained by the Human Rights Office of the Executive Yuan, the office conducts quarterly tracking and surveys of progress made by various ministries allocated with specific tasks. Table 3 presents the self-assessed progress and outcomes of the responsibilities of each ministry. As of September 2023, all items were on schedule except for the Restoration of Victims' Rights and Disposal of Confiscated Property and Preservation of Sites of Injustice, which were lagging.

Responsible Ministry	Projects	Achievements
Ministry of Justice	Rectifying judicial and administrative injustice	Rectified 1,606 cases of injustice
	Identification and accountability of perpetrators	Drafted a special law for identifying and handling perpetrators
Ministry of the Interior	Restoration of victims' rights and disposal of confiscated property	Established the Foundation for the Restoration of Rights of Victims of Unlawful Acts During the Authoritarian Era in February 2023, which has processed 3,721 applications
	Elimination of authoritarian symbols	Conducted two nationwide surveys of authoritarian symbols in September 2022 and July 2023, thus identifying 930 existing statues and named spaces related to Chiang Kai-shek and Chiang Ching-kuo
National Development Council	Collection and application of political archives	Continued to collect and digitize political archives held by political parties
	Management of the Transitional Justice Fund	Continuously operated the fund
Ministry of Education	Education on transitional justice	Implemented the National Transitional Justice Education Action Guidelines and organized professional support community learning activities for transitional justice education
Ministry of Culture	Research, collection, and application of political archives (Archives Research and Transitional Justice Database)	Established the Authoritarian Era Political Case Integrated Search Platform
	Transformation of the Chiang Kai-shek Memorial Hall	Held a meeting of the Chiang Kai-shek Memorial Hall Transformation Task Force on May 29, 2023
	Preservation of sites of injustice	Completed the draft of the Preservation of Sites of Injustice Act and promoted educational activities about sites of injustice
Ministry of Health and Welfare	Mental health services of victims of political violence and their families	Promoted a political violence trauma awareness program and established support service locations for victims of political violence and their families

Source: Author

Table 1. Progress of the agency's business takeover

c) Impact of the Incorporation of International Human Rights Laws on Transitional Justice

The internalization of international human rights law has provided significant momentum for efforts toward advancing transitional justice in Taiwan. Despite its contested international status, Taiwan has exhibited notable progress in incorporating major international human rights instruments since the late 1990s. A key milestone occurred in 2009, when Taiwan ratified the International Covenant on Civil and Political Rights and the International Covenant on Economic, Social and Cultural Rights, which signaled a strong commitment to the alignment between its domestic legal framework and international human rights standards (Chang 2019 and Lee 2022).

International experts, who simultaneously urged the Taiwanese government to address unresolved transitional justice issues, particularly those that occurred during the White Terror period, welcomed these developments. In concluding observations on Taiwan's state reports in 2013 and 2017, independent review committees emphasized the importance of ensuring the rights of victims to truth, justice, and reparation (International Group of Independent Experts 2013, International Review Committee 2017). The committees called for the full disclosure of human rights violations in the past and guaranteed access to political archives.

These external pressures helped shape domestic policies on transitional justice and opened new opportunities for addressing long-term historical trauma, especially after the Democratic Progressive Party won the presidency and legislative majority for the first time in 2016. The most significant reform in Taiwan's efforts toward transitional justice came with the passage of the Act on Promoting Transitional Justice in December 2017. This legislation established the Transitional Justice Commission, which was granted extensive power, including the authority to declassify political archives, eliminate authoritarian symbols, rectify judicial injustices, and promote social reconciliation. Prior to its dissolution, the Commission regularly reported its progress on multiple fronts, including the establishment of the Transitional Justice Database, correction of judicial offenses, investigation of sites of injustice, elimination of authoritarian symbols, and provision of psychological healing and care for victims. It also annulled unjust criminal convictions, which underscores its commitment to redressing past injustices in accordance with international human rights standards.

The incorporation of international human rights treaties continues to shape Taiwan's transitional justice policies and practices. In response to follow-up monitoring mechanisms and concluding observations, government bodies responsible for transitional justice, such as the National Development Council, the Ministry of Justice, and the Commission for Promoting Transitional Justice, routinely review and report on related policies and actions. The incorporation has also positively influenced the judiciary's treatment of transitional justice cases. A notable example is a decision by the Taipei High Administrative Court, which cited Articles 2(1) and 2(3) of the International Covenant on Civil and Political Rights (ICCPR), along with General Comment No. 15 of the UN Human Rights Committee (Taipei High Administrative Court 2015). Drawing on these provisions, the Court affirmed that foreign victims of the February 28 Incident are entitled to the same right to compensation as domestic victims. The foundation responsible for administering reparations chose not to appeal the decision, and the plaintiff was ultimately awarded NTD 6 million in compensation. This case illustrates how the incorporation of international human rights norms has enabled Taiwanese courts to address transitional justice issues with greater assertiveness and progressiveness (Lee 2022).

2. Continuity and Challenges of Taiwan's Transitional Justice Process

a) Institutional Challenges

Taiwan uniquely employs the Premier of the Executive Yuan as the convener of the Transitional Justice Conference. The Human Rights and Transitional Justice Office of the Executive Yuan serves as a staff unit for coordinating efforts across the ministries involved in transitional justice. This structure is beneficial, because it elevates the administrative level to strengthen its enforcement of transitional justice policies. The President and the Premier, who have expressed support for related policies and bills, have publicly approved of this structure (Chen Z. H. 2023; Executive Yuan 2023).

As cited in the text about the second type of transition mechanism, one downside is its susceptibility to political changes, which can destabilize the implementation and continuity of policies and mechanisms in transitional justice. For instance, addressing transitional justice affairs may vary according to changes in political power, which potentially leads to delay or abandonment. This notion was evident in South Korea: the performance of the Ministry of Public Administration and Security, the Truth and Reconciliation Commission's successor organization, fell short of expectations, which prompted the establishment of a second-generation commission under President Moon Jae-in in 2020 (Truth and Reconciliation Commission of South Korea, 2021, pp. 7–8).

Furthermore, the current mechanism in Taiwan faces several challenges and potential weaknesses. First, although these mechanisms intend to normalize the function of transitional justice by distributing tasks to various ministries based on their nature, this approach may ignore practical factors. Burdened with daily tasks and constrained by various costs, routine administrative departments may neglect or delay issues related to transitional justice. Additionally, the division of work among departments could fragment the energy toward and discussion on the execution of transitional justice, thus preventing a systematic push for relevant activities. Moreover, as the Human Rights Office of the Executive Yuan merely acts as the staff unit, it lacks enforcement power to supervise the execution of duties among ministries; instead, it relies on soft mechanisms for monitoring progress (Chen Y. F. 2023, 5). Without a dedicated body, coordination and implementation of transitional justice policy and measures could suffer.

Lastly, despite the goal of these mechanisms to compel civil servants to confront and engage with issues in transitional justice in a sincere manner, the challenge remains of whether frontline administrative staff possess the necessary expertise and capability to address politically sensitive and complex issues. Although departments self-report satisfactory progress (Table 1), there remains a significant discrepancy between departmental assessment and public perception. For instance, concerns have emerged about the hesitation and sluggish progress displayed by the Ministry of Justice in identifying and holding perpetrators accountable (Lin 2023, 13). Given that holding perpetrators accountable has been a longstanding gap in Taiwan's legal framework for transitional justice (Lee 2016, 437), enhancing dialogue with various sectors and expediting the drafting of related bills are vital initiatives for the Ministry of Justice (Lee 2022, 182). Moreover, as recognized by Constitutional Court Interpretation No. 793, transitional justice is crucial to public interest that is closely tied to the realization of a democratic constitutional order. Nevertheless, the current performance of the mechanism exhibits a lack of a comprehensive policy for transitional justice within the government, which could lead to superficial and fragmented efforts across ministries. The nature of the Human Rights Office as a staff unit hinders it from effectively integrating the work directions and progress of the ministries. Therefore, the government should reconsider establishing an appropriate organization that can coordinate the overall direction and content of national transitional justice; in addition, in its institutional design, it should avoid the adverse impacts of political changes.

b) Insufficient Involvement of the National Human Rights Commission and Civil Society

On August 1, 2020, Taiwan established the National Human Rights Commission under the Control Yuan. Undeniably, since its inception, institutional issues have emerged such as vague responsibilities (Huang and Huang 2021, 108–09), vague division of tasks with the Control Yuan (Huang and Huang 2021, 110–11), issues in member selection (Wei 2020, 119; Li 2020, 114), and the ineffective exercise of authority (Wei 2020, 122–28; Chang 2021, 97; Huang and Huang 2021, 111–12). These issues have introduced doubts about whether the Commission can effectively protect and promote human rights. Addressing these institutional challenges requires the strengthening of relevant legislative work (Huang and Huang 2021, 114; Wei 2020, 122–28). Alternatively, a number of scholars recommend the transformation of the Control Yuan into a dedicated Human Rights Institution (Chang 2021, 93–101).

Apart from the organization of related visits, the National Human Rights Commission has not articulated its position on issues of transitional justice, which has been a regrettable aspect of transitional justice since its establishment. As Taiwan enters a new phase in the development of its mechanisms for transitional justice, this study argues that the Commission, as the official body responsible for human rights, plays a crucial role and function. Particularly, as demonstrated by international experiences, the National Human Rights Commission should step forward to protect and uphold human rights when existing mechanisms underperform. For example, in East Timor, the Office of the Provedor for Human Rights and Justice actively reached out to international and local human rights resources and networks to implement the recommendations of the Commission for Reception, Truth and Reconciliation after parliamentary committees failed to meet expectations (Kent, Kinsella and Tchailoro 2016). Furthermore, in front of the UN Human Rights Council in 2012, the Office utilized the Universal Periodic Review to highlight the failure of the Timorese government in implementing the final report of the Commission, which specifically affected rights to reparation, truth, and justice (Kent, Kinsella and Tchailoro 2016).

The current study posits that as the official human rights mechanism in Taiwan, the National Human Rights Commission is inseparable from the development and discussion of transitional justice. Therefore, it should proactively conduct engagement and monitoring to prevent human rights violations based on its mandate (Chang 2021, 98) and take concrete actions to participate in new projects in transitional justice. From the human rights perspective, transitional justice involves many fundamental rights that are under the protection of core international human rights treaties, such as the International Covenant on Civil and Political Rights and the Convention Against Torture, which guarantee rights such as freedom from torture; rights to compensation, truth, and judicial remedy are also crucial (UN Security Council 2004). Therefore, according to Article 2, Section 3 of the Organization Act of the Control Yuan National Human Rights Commission, the Commission should propose special reports on transitional justice, monitor and review the progress and implementation of existing mechanisms in an active and timely manner (Wei 2020, 125–26), to ensure that rights related to transitional justice remain protected and promptly remedied.

Moreover, civil society plays a crucial supervisory role in transitional justice implementation. As demonstrated by international examples, the active support and oversight of civil society are also necessary after the final reports of truth commissions and apart from reliance on official mechanisms to implement recommendations. Especially when official mechanisms fail to function, civil groups may establish corresponding organizations to replace official mechanisms. For example, in Guatemala, despite the final report of the Historical Clarification Commission recommending the establishment of a Foundation for Peace and Harmony, local civil groups and human rights workers formed a Multi-Institutional Authority for Peace and Harmony to implement the recommendations (Skaar, Wiebelhaus-Brahm and Gracia-Godos 2022).

As previously mentioned, the success or failure of mechanisms internationally indicates that they require substantial human and material resources to effectively integrate forces from civil groups, media, and other social organizations to achieve the goals of advocacy, supervision, and execution of final reports. In Taiwan, as transitional justice mechanisms move forward to a new stage, active participation and oversight of civil society in terms of monitoring the performance of related mechanisms are necessary.

c) Lack of Women's Presence

Burgeoning human rights and women's groups made significant strides in enhancing the conditions of women through legal and judicial means. For example, they initiated strategic constitutional litigation before the Constitutional Court of Taiwan, thus successfully influencing changes in laws and policies related to various gender issues. In addition, they have exerted effort to integrate gender considerations into broad reforms, and laws specifically designed to improve the economic and social status of women were enacted (Chang 2010, 142–44; Chang 2009, 221). The democratization process led to a constitutional recognition of formal equality and implemented quotas for women in electoral politics (Rubio-Marin and Chang 2012, 308), which increased female representation in local and national legislatures and enabled a number of female victims of the former authoritarian regime to participate in elections. Their political campaigns brought their past suffering to public attention, with a number of them becoming notable political figures and assuming significant official roles.

However, progress in gender equality was inadequately reflected in the design of transitional justice mechanisms because women's rights groups and activists mainly prioritized issues such as equal pay and family rights over gender-based violence within the frameworks of transitional justice. These mechanisms failed to capture the complex experiences of women during the authoritarian period and overlooked specific instances of women's victimization due to the lack of a gender perspective. This omission in transitional justice led to shortcomings in accountability, truth-finding, and social reconciliation. For instance, transitional justice policies that focused on compensation have insufficiently addressed the responsibility of perpetrators of human rights violations, which hindered female victims from seeking legal redress for the physical and mental harm they obtained. Without a clear framework for accountability, these women faced substantial challenges in identifying the entities responsible for their suffering. Moreover, the limited scope of truth investigation, which also lacked a gender perspective, failed to comprehensively document the historical experiences of women during the authoritarian regime. Furthermore, the narrowly defined categories of compensation laws only partially met the unique material and psychological needs of female victims. These shortcomings inevitably led to social division and hindered political reconciliation in Taiwan.

d) Lack of Social Dialogue

Despite this progress, new transitional justice mechanisms that were initiated since 2016 encountered severe political accusations and judicial challenges, even under the parliamentary majority of the DPP and the leadership of President Tsai. Political conflicts and societal divisions related to the implementation of these mechanisms inevitably mirrored the complex historical and political landscapes of Taiwan's authoritarian past. Transitional justice is not meant to serve as political vengeance at the convenience of partisan interests. Moreover, the pursuit of transitional justice cannot solely rely on short-term political victories or a simple electoral majority, as demonstrated by the experiences of the DPP government in the 2016 and 2020 elections. Without a broad social consensus, efforts to gain partisan advantage through transitional justice initiatives can lead to significant political repercussions.

A notable instance was the contentious appointment of the chief and vice-chief commissioners to the Transitional Justice Commission (Huang 2021, 221; Li 2018a; Li 2018b). Made by President Tsai and confirmed by the DPP's majority, both appointments drew intense criticism from DPP and KMT supporters. The selection of a chief commissioner with past ties to the KMT and who was perceived as moderate incited anger among civil society groups that supported the DPP. These groups felt that doing so betrayed the agenda of transitional justice. Conversely, KMT supporters accused the vice-chief commissioner of being overtly partisan, favoring the DPP, and using power to undermine an emerging KMT politician. Within months, the chief commissioner resigned (Hsu 2018a), while the vice-chief commissioner was forced to resign (Hsu 2018b) and was further impeached by the Control Yuan for the violation of political neutrality in civil service (Control Yuan 2019). This discord between the DPP government and civil society groups provides a stark illustration that the success of transitional justice cannot solely depend on an electoral majority but requires a wider consensus.

These examples underscore the formidable challenges that Taiwan faced in continuing its efforts toward transitional justice, which were constrained by its negotiated democratization and the dynamics of its context (Lee and Chang 2023, 699). Without a wide public engagement and social consensus, political conflicts and partisan division can easily stall the progress of transitional justice reforms. Thus, participating in trustful and open dialogues is crucial for all stakeholders. As further reforms are necessary, mechanisms must be grounded in constitutional and legal norms and built with high levels of political trust and social consensus through long-term, nonpartisan efforts that involve active citizen engagement and set against the background of evolving international human rights norms.

IV. Conclusion

Taiwan's transitional justice journey, from initial compensation to a comprehensive investigation of authoritarian abuses, illustrates its commitment to confronting historical wrongs. Challenges remain, however, including the need for a centralized coordinating body, clearer institutional roles for human rights commissions, and stronger civil society involvement.

Transitional justice also reflects the complexity of Taiwan's constitutional history under authoritarian rule, political conflict and social division are inevitable. To prevent transitional justice from becoming a tool for short-term partisan interests or electoral gains, the mechanisms that drive transitional justice projects must adhere to constitutional and legal norms and embrace principles of democracy, transparency, and openness. Sustained and nonpartisan efforts that align with international human rights norms and ongoing dialogue and cooperation with all sectors of society are essential for building increased political trust and social consensus, thus ensuring that the achievements of transitional justice reforms are long-lasting. This collaborative effort will make transitional justice in Taiwan more representative of all affected communities, fostering enduring reconciliation and reinforcing the rule of law. Taiwan's experience shows that effective transitional justice requires not only legal structures but also a deep societal commitment to dialogue and healing.

References

Act on Governing the Handling of Illegally Seized Assets by Political Parties and Their Affiliated Organisations. 2016. https://law.moj.gov.tw/ENG/LawClass/LawAll.aspx?pcode=A0030286.

Act on Political Archives. 2019. https://law.moj.gov.tw/ENG/LawClass/LawAll.aspx?pcode=A0030312.

Act on Promoting Transitional Justice. 2017. https://law.moj.gov.tw/ENG/LawClass/LawAll.aspx?pcode=A0030296.

Bowman, Daniel. 2012. "Righting the Wrongs of the Past? The Human Rights Policies of Chen Shui-bian and Ma Ying-jeou." In *Taiwan Since Martial Law: Society, Culture, Politics, Economy*, edited by David Blundell, 485–526. Taipei: Shung Ye Museum of Formosan Aborigines.

Caldwell, Ernest. 2018. "Transitional Justice Legislation in Taiwan Before and During the TSAI Administration." *Washington International Law Journal* 27 (2): 449–83.

Chang, W. C. 2009. "An Isolated Nation with Global-Minded Citizens: Bottom-up Transnational Constitutionalism in Taiwan." *NTU Law Review* 4 (3): 221–56.

Chang, W. C. 2010. "Public-Interest Litigation in Taiwan: Strategy for Law and Policy Reforms in Course of Democratization." In *Public Interest*

Litigation in Asia, edited by Po Jen Yap and Holning Lau, 142–44. London: Routledge.

Chang, W. C. 2019. "Taiwan's Human Rights Implementation Acts: A Model for Successful Incorporation?" In *Taiwan and International Human Rights: A Story of Transformation*, edited by Jerome A. Cohen, William P. Alford and Chang-fa Lo, 227–247, Springer.

Chang, W. C. 2021. "Opportunities and Challenges of Constitutional Transformation of Control Yuan." *Taiwan Law Review*, no. 318: 93–101.

Chang, W. C., and Y. L. Lee 2021. "Transitional Justice: Institutional Mechanisms and Contextual Dynamics." In *The Max Planck Encyclopedia of Public International Law.* Oxford: Oxford University Law Online. Accessed September 13, 2021. https://opil.ouplaw.com/view/10.1093/law:epil/9780199231690/law-9780199231690-e219.

Chang-Liao, N. C., and Y. J. Chen 2019. "Transitional Justice in Taiwan: Changes and Challenges." *Washington International Law Journal* 28 (3): 619–43.

Chen, Y. F. 2023. "The Urgency of Strengthening the Legal Framework for Transitional Justice." Paper presented at the 2023 Taiwan Forever Association Workshop, Taipei, September 16.

Chen, Z. H. 2023. "On the Eve of the February 28 Incident, President Tsai: Facing Our Mistakes Together, Moving Towards a United Future." *Radio Taiwan International*, February 27. https://www.rti.org.tw/news/view/id/2160444.

Constitutional Court of Taiwan. 1991. "Interpretation No. 272." January 18. http://www.judicial.gov.tw/constitutionalcourt/EN/p03_01.asp?expno=277.

Control Yuan. 2019. "The Vice-Chief Commissioner Was Impeached by the Control Yuan on the Ground of Violating Political Neutrality in Civil Service." October 1. https://www.cy.gov.tw/News_Content.aspx?n=124&s=14612.

Executive Yuan. 2023. "Chairing the Executive Yuan's Meeting on Promoting Transitional Justice, Premier Chen Stated: 'Collaboration Between Public and Private Sectors Is Essential to Advance Transitional Justice Education and Enhance Social Communication to Improve the Legal Operations of Transitional Justice.'" October 18. https://www.ey.gov.tw/Page/9277F759E41CCD91/166f23f2-3cf7-4013-ad22-6681e9a8a7f7.

Hansen, Thomas Obel. 2014. "The Vertical and Horizontal Expansion of Transitional Justice: Explanations and Implications for a Contested Field." In *Transitional Justice Theories*, edited by Susanne Buckley-Zistel, et al., 105–24. New York: Routledge.

Historical Research Commission of Taiwan Province. 1995. *Historical Archives on the 50's Political Events in Taiwan Area During the Period of Martial Law.* Vol. 1. Taipei: Historical Research Commission of Taiwan Province.

Hsu, Stacy. 2018a. "Transitional Justice Chairman Resigns." *Taipei Times*, October 7. https://www.taipeitimes.com/News/front/archives/2018/10/07/2003701885. Accessed August 3, 2022.

Hsu, Stacy. 2018b. "Deputy Chairman Resigns from Transitional Justice." *Taipei Times*, September 13. https://www.taipeitimes.com/News/front/archives/2018/09/13/2003700317. Accessed August 3, 2022.

Huang, C. Y. 2021. "A Noble Dream Undelivered: The Quest for Transitional Justice during Tsai Ing-wen's First Term." In *Taiwan during the First Administration of Tsai Ing-wen: Navigating in Stormy Waters*, edited by Gunter Schubert and Chun-yi Lee, 209–33. London: Routledge.

Huang, S. L., and Y. B. Huang 2021. "The First Year of National Human Rights Commission in Taiwan: The Dilemma of Dual Identity." *Taiwan Human Rights Journal* 6 (2): 108–14.

Ill-Gotten Party Assets Settlement Committee. 2016. Official website. https://www.cipas.gov.tw/. (In Chinese).

International Group of Independent Experts, *Review of the Initial Reports of the Government of Taiwan on the Implementation of the International Human Rights Covenants: Concluding Observations and Recommendations Adopted by the International Group of Independent Experts* (Taipei, 1 March 2013) para 3 <https://www.moj.gov.tw/dl-16948-b02cdbe343ef4f6daef3edf54f1b0f8f.html>

International Review Committee, *Review of the Second Reports of the Government of Taiwan on the Implementation of the International Human Rights Covenants: Concluding Observations and Recommendations Adopted by the International Review Committee* (Taipei, 20 January 2017) para 10 <https://www.humanrights.moj.gov.tw/media/12296/327200414160793f3e.pdf?mediaDL=true>

Kent, L., N. Kinsella, and N. R. Tchailoro. 2016. "Chega! Ten Years On: A Neglected National Resource—The Fate of the CAVR Final Report in Timor-Leste." Canberra: Australian National University. https://dpa.bellschool.anu.edu.au/experts-publications/publications/4155/chega-ten-years-neglected-national-resource.

Kritz, Neil J., ed. 1995. *Transitional Justice: How Emerging Democracies Reckon with Former Regimes.* 3 vols. Washington, DC: United States Institute for Peace Press.

Lai, P. Y. 2022. "Scholars Call for Extension of the Transitional Justice Commission's Term and Urge Its Transformation into a Permanent Research Body." *TARO News*, March 4. https://taronews.tw/2020/03/04/627116/.

Lee, C. L. 2022. "The Development and Transformation of Legal Institution of Transitional Justice." *Formosan Jurist*, no. 13: 180–82.

Lee, Y. L. 2016. *Mechanisms and Contexts of Transitional Justice: South Korea and Taiwan in Comparative Perspective*. Taipei: Angle Publishing.

Lee. Y. L. 2022. "The Incorporation of the International Covenant on Civil and Political Rights in Taiwan: Progress and Challenge". In *Reinvention by Necessity: Implementation of International Human Rights Treaties in Taiwan*, edited by Mab Huang & Vivianne Yen-Ching Weng, 9–34, Taipei: Taiwan Foundation for Democracy.

Lee. Y.L. and W. C. Chang. 2023. "A Contextual Analysis of the Evolution of Transitional Justice: the Story of Taiwan." *International Journal of Human Rights* 27 (4): 685–709. DOI: 10.1080/13642987.2022.2153120.

Li, B. F. 2022. "The Dissolution of the Transitional Justice Commission: Is the Unfinished State of Taiwan's Transitional Justice Due to the Commission's Lack of Credibility or a Lack of Social Consensus?" *The News Lens*, June 2. https://www.thenewslens.com/feature/transitionaljustice/166775.

Li, N. T. 2020. "Prospects for the Establishment of the National Human Rights Commission under the Control Yuan: The Perspective of the Paris Principles of the United Nations." *Taiwan Human Rights Journal* 5 (3): 114–20.

Li, Y. M. 2018a. "The Nomination to Chief Commissioner to Transitional Justice Commission Was Criticized by DPP Supporters." *CredereMedia*, March 30. https://www.cmmedia.com.tw/home/articles/9242. Accessed October 10, 2022. (In Chinese).

Li, Y. M. 2018b. "NGOs Criticised the Nomination to Commissioners of Transitional Justice Commission." *CredereMedia*, May 1. https://www.cmmedia.com.tw/home/articles/9688. Accessed October 10, 2022. (In Chinese).

Lin, C. H. 2023. "Criminal Prosecution, Amnesty, and Rehabilitation: System Design and Implementation in Taiwan." Paper presented at the 2023 Taiwan Forever Association Workshop, Taipei, September 16.

National Mobilization Law. 1942. https://law.moj.gov.tw/LawClass/LawAll.aspx?pcode=A0030024.

Office of the President Republic of China (ROC). 2016. "President Tsai Apologizes to Indigenous Peoples on Behalf of Government." August 1. https://english.president.gov.tw/NEWS/4950. Accessed November 29, 2019.

Pan, B. H. 2022. "The Future of Transitional Justice: Concerns Arise as the Transitional Justice Commission Fails to 'Hold Perpetrators Accountable' and the Ministry of Justice Takes Over." *The News Lens*, June 6. https://www.thenewslens.com/feature/transitionaljustice/167249. (In Chinese).

Presidential Office Indigenous Historical Justice and Transitional Justice Committee. n.d. Official website (English). https://indigenous-justice.president.gov.tw/EN.

Rowen, Ian, and Jamie Rowen. 2017. "Taiwan's Truth and Reconciliation Committee: The Geopolitics of Transitional Justice in a Contested State." I*nternational Journal of Transitional Justice* 11 (1): 92–112.

Rubio-Marin, Ruth, and W. C. Chang. 2012. "Sites of Constitutional Struggle for Women's Equality." In *Routledge Handbook of Constitutional Law,* edited by Mark Tushnet, Thomas Fleiner, and Cheryl Saunders, 308–20. London: Routledge.

Skaar, E., E. Wiebelhaus-Brahm, and J. Garcia-Godos. 2022. *Exploring Truth Commission Recommendations in a Comparative Perspective: Beyond Words.* Vol. 1. Cambridge: Intersentia.

Statute for the Eradication of Communist Espionage. 1950. https://law.moj.gov.tw/LawClass/LawAll.aspx?pcode=C0000012.

Statute for the Punishment of Treason. 1949. https://law.moj.gov.tw/LawClass/LawAll.aspx?pcode=C0000010.

Su, Y. T. 2019. "Transitional Justice and Political Compromise in Taiwan." Paper presented at the International Colloquium on Global Ethics of Compromise, CESPRA, EHESS, Paris, France, March.

Taipei High Administrative Court Judgement (104) Su Tzu No 1348 (2015). (In Chinese).

Teitel, Ruti G. 2002. *Transitional Justice.* Oxford: Oxford University Press.

Teitel, Ruti G. 2014. *Globalizing Transitional Justice: Contemporary Essays.* Oxford: Oxford University Press.

Transitional Justice Commission. 2018. Official website. https://www.tjc.gov.tw/. (In Chinese).

Transitional Justice Commission. 2022. *The Final Report.* June 20. https://gazette2.nat.gov.tw/EG_FileManager/eguploadpub/eg028098/ch01/type7/gov01/num2/Eg.htm.

Truth and Reconciliation Commission of South Korea (2021). *About the Commission.* Truth and Reconciliation Commission, Republic of Korea. https://www.jinsil.go.kr/en/bbm/bbs/selectBoardArticleView. do?nttId=23429.

United Nations Security Council. 2004. "The Rule of Law and Transitional Justice in Conflict and Post-Conflict Societies: Report of the Secretary-General." United Nations and the Rule of Law. https://www.un.org/

ruleoflaw/blog/document/the-rule-of-law-and-transitional-justice-in-conflict-and-post-conflict-societies-report-of-the-secretary-general/.

Wei, C. F. 2020. "A Short Discussion on the Structure and Operation of the Control Yuan National Human Rights Commission." *Taiwan Human Rights Journal* 5 (3): 119–28.

Wu, N. T. 2005. "Transitional Justice Without Justice or Justice Without History: Transitional Justice in Taiwan." *Taiwan Journal of Democracy* 1 (1): 77–102.

Yeh, J. R. 2016. *The Constitution of Taiwan: A Contextual Analysis*. Oxford: Hart Publishing.

J. From Representation to Resistance: Democratic Practices Under Authoritarian Rule in the EU Context

Bernadett Szél[1]

Abstract

The paper examines how traditional political representation often reinforces autocracy in authoritarian systems, stressing the need for alternative democratic strategies. Focusing on Hungary's autocratization since 2010, it moves beyond systemic decline to explore how democratic actors resist without strengthening authoritarianism. Using reflexive action research based on the author's parliamentary experience, it identifies strategies for resilience, including innovative parliamentary tactics, civil society activism, and media independence. Comparing Hungary to Russia's model, the study highlights authoritarian adaptation within the EU. The paper concludes by calling for a rethinking of democratic representation to challenge oppression and harness international support for democratic renewal, showing how international organizations, though unable to halt Hungary's autocratization, have shaped resistance strategies and enabled non-traditional engagement through normative frameworks supporting democratic action in constrained environments.

Keywords:

action research; autocratic backsliding, authoritarian regimes; democratic resilience; European Union (EU); Hungary; civil society; non-governmental organizations (NGOs); Putinism; Hybrid regimes

I. Introduction

What has taken place in Hungary since 2010 cannot be adequately described simply as the erosion of democracy and the rule of law, or as a case of state capture by a political elite. It reflects far deeper transformations:

---

1 Dr. Bernadett Szél, economist and sociologist, affiliated with the Central European University, member of the Public Body of the Hungarian Academy of Sciences, researches democratic resilience against autocratic pressures and Europe-Taiwan relations. A former Hungarian MP (2012–2022), she conducted 2024 fieldwork in Taiwan and holds the Taiwan Fellowship in 2025.

the authorities have targeted not only the political and social system but also the mindset and value system of society. This process has been documented by numerous Hungarian and international scholars (Scheppele 2018; Magyar 2016; Bozóki and Fleck 2024, 123–217), but there are still further implications of this ongoing procedure.

This research engages with the question of how democratic actors and institutions can maintain their democratic function and integrity in environments increasingly shaped by authoritarian tendencies. While building on a rich body of academic findings that offers critical insights into the mechanisms and trajectories of autocratization, this study contributes an innovative perspective by shifting the analytical focus from systemic description to strategic agency: it adopts a goal-oriented approach that seeks to identify actionable strategies for democratic resilience. In doing so, the research foregrounds the question of how democratic actors can operate meaningfully within autocratic settings, and how their practices might inform broader efforts to defend and revitalize democratic norms. More specifically, employing a reflexive, action research methodology, the study examines the author's own parliamentary practice as a site of inquiry, focusing on the challenges and strategies of operating as a democratic actor within an autocratizing regime. The analysis extends beyond the individual case to draw parallels with other critical arenas, such as civil society organizations, independent media, and the European Union's (EU) engagement with illiberal national governments.

In Chapter 1, a review of the relevant terminology of the process is provided. This is necessary because a diverse range of terminology is used to describe the processes of autocratization in Hungary, depending on which aspect of the process is being emphasized. A review of these definitions can, in itself, bring us closer to a deeper understanding of the process.

In Chapter 2, key steps of the post-2010 autocratization process in Hungary are discussed, with particular emphasis on their relationship to certain stages of autocratization in Russia. This comparison is relevant because Hungary's transformation represents an adaptation of the 'Putin recipe' to the EU's context—something that was once thought impossible within the Union's normative and institutional framework, and which now stands as a warning to other member states.

Chapter 3 focuses on strategic agency. Drawing on the author's personal experience as a Member of Parliament (MP), the study looks into her parliamentary practice as the subject of action research (AR), examining the dynamics of democratic erosion and exploring practical tools for agency in autocratizing environments. The firsthand experience in navigating a politically constrained and autocratic landscape provides a unique lens through which to investigate the broader question: What strategies should democratic opposition actors pursue under conditions of autocratization, and what societal responsibilities emerge in such a context? While autocratic regimes aim to shrink the space for democratic action, strategic footholds remain that can be leveraged to challenge—or even reconfigure—the boundaries imposed by the regime. The study highlights practical relevance in areas such as parliamentary practice, EU-Hungary relations, independent journalism, and civil society activism.[2]

Chapter 4, as conclusions, introduces that the process of autocratization has been accompanied by recommendations and expectations from international organizations, which attempted to keep the processes on the democratic path. While these could not stop the process, they were able to influence it and provided support for non-traditional forms of engagement at various points. In the concluding part of the study, we offer insight into how these international norms shape resistance strategies in the context of Hungary's autocratic backslide and the framework they provide for action in politically constrained environments.

II. Conceptual Framework and Methodology

A key practical concern guiding this research is how democratic actors and institutions can avoid, even inadvertently, reinforcing the consolidation of authoritarianism. Accordingly, this project is both analytical and normative: it aims not only to map the dynamics of autocratic backsliding but also to identify the conditions and strategies that can support democratic resilience in adverse political environments. For the current research, three key aspects should be emphasized. First, while a global wave of autocratization can be observed (Lührmann and Lindberg 2019), Hungary is unique in that it has undergone this process as a member of the European Union (Bozóki and Fleck 2024). Second, in comparison to other cases of autocratic backsliding, Hungary has pursued this path at a notably rapid pace (V-Dem Democracy Report 2022, 2025). Third, amid the broader global trend of dem-

2 The Action Research methodology is supported by extensive foundational literature, such as Greenwood and Levin's Introduction to Action Research (2007) and Jean McNiff's Action Research: Principles and Practice (2013), both of which provided significant inspiration throughout the course of the research.

ocratic backsliding, Hungary continues to erode its democratic characteristics (Enyedi and Mikola 2024), with the system's hardening becoming increasingly unpredictable.

The political and social reconfiguration of Hungary post-2010 marks a fundamental departure from liberal democratic norms (Krastev and Holmes 2019). This transformation was institutionalized through the adoption of the Fundamental Law in 2011, a process described by former constitutional judge Imre Vörös as a "constitutional coup": the new constitution of the country was initiated and voted on by one party, public consultation was missed out, and all legal norms typically required for such foundational legislation were broken (Vörös 2014). The legitimacy of this document has been widely questioned ever since (Bozóki and Fleck 2024). Hungarian economist János Kornai already sent early warnings about the nature of the system change in 2011, identifying the systematic erosion of democratic checks and balances (Kornai 2011). The Varieties of Democracy (V-Dem) dataset tracks Hungary's decline[3], a degradation from a liberal democracy to an electoral democracy first, and an electoral autocracy after 2018 (Papada et al. 2023).

Bálint Magyar has emphasized a different feature of the system, proposing that Hungary no longer fits within traditional ideological frameworks and is better understood as a mafia state, marked by centralized, personalized power and hierarchical patron-client relations. This system, he argues, resembles the pre-1989 party-state in many of its operational logics (Magyar 2016).

Although the regime has undergone a gradual process of degradation—and the terminology used to describe it may vary depending on which of its characteristics are emphasized—the Prime Minister (PM) himself left no doubt in 2014 that the fundamental features of Hungary's socio-economic and political order had been profoundly altered. In 2014, Viktor Orbán publicly acknowledged this ideological shift, stating: "The new state that we are building is an illiberal state, a non-liberal state" (Orbán 2014). However, the institutional foundations of this regime—its restructured constitution, captured media, and centralized executive—had already been laid by that point (Bozóki and Fleck 2024).

3 Based on the V-Dem Dataset (Coppedge et al. 2024), Enyedi and his co-authors produced a highly illustrative figure that traces Hungary's democratic trajectory from 2000 to 2023 (Enyedi and Mikola 2024). The data reveal a shift from liberal democracy to electoral democracy following the governmental changes after 2010, culminating in the crossing of a critical threshold after the 2018 elections, marking the emergence of electoral autocracy. For further insightful support of this process, see *The Global State of Democracy 2023* (Papada et al. 2023).

An important question is whether the EU posed a barrier to this transformation. Since the early 2010s, the EU has repeatedly attempted to counter the erosion of liberal democratic norms in Hungary. Despite early warnings and later infringement procedures, these efforts have largely proven insufficient in halting what many scholars characterized later as "competitive authoritarian consolidation" (Bozóki and Hegedűs 2018). Although the launch of Article 7 proceedings in 2018 marked a symbolic recognition of systemic threats to EU values, unanimity requirements in the European Council have rendered the mechanism politically ineffective. More recently, the introduction of the Rule of Law Conditionality Regulation (Regulation (EU, Euratom) 2020/2092) empowered the European Commission to suspend EU funds based on rule of law violations.[4] As of early 2025, over 1 billion euros of these funds have been permanently lost following the government's continued non-compliance (Financial Times 2025). Yet, the Hungarian government has often responded to EU pressure with superficial legal adjustments, while continuing to centralize power and undermine independent institutions. In parallel, strategic alliances with other illiberal governments, such as Poland's Law and Justice (PiS) party until 2023, enabled mutual shielding within the Council framework. As such, the EU's toolkit has proven reactive, often constrained by its intergovernmental structure and the reluctance of key member states to escalate confrontation.

Bozóki and Hegedűs concluded that the Orbán government used Hungary's EU and Western embeddedness not as a constraint, but as a shield for advancing autocratization. Contrary to liberal expectations, the high level of international linkage did not serve as an obstacle to authoritarian consolidation, but rather became a strategic tool in dismantling democratic institutions from within (Bozóki and Hegedűs 2018). From their research perspective, the authors refer to Hungary's political system as a hybrid regime and emphasize the EU's dual role in this degradation, where the European Union both limits and supports the Hungarian system.

Madlovics and Magyar also explain why the EU was first paralyzed as the autocratization in Hungary evolved, highlighting that the EU presumed all members would remain liberal democracies grounded in shared norms; hence, it did not develop adequate tools to deal with regime divergence (Madlovics and Magyar 2023). The authors also emphasize that the system

4 This instrument was invoked in 2022 under the rule-of-law conditionality mechanism, leading to the suspension of €6.3 billion in cohesion funds for Hungary due to systemic rule-of-law concerns (Council of the European Union 2022).

in Hungary, which they refer to as a patronal autocracy, is particularly dangerous for the EU, as it undermines the EU's political and economic foundations, being incompatible with Western liberal democracies and the EU's core values, such as the market economy and democratic norms.

As we see, while EU legal frameworks and institutions have the potential to limit authoritarian drift, the regime has simultaneously benefited both from EU membership and from the centrally allocated financial transfers, which have been largely captured and consumed by a highly corrupt governing circle, paradoxically reinforcing its power and legitimacy (Scheiring 2020). Hence, on the one hand, EU membership can safeguard democracy through the community's institutions and legal framework; however, what we practically see is that if the EU fails to implement effective sanctions, it indirectly legitimizes the regime. This line of reasoning is particularly significant for our paper, as the scope of the research is on how democratic engagement (like committed opposition representatives dedicated to safeguarding democracy and the rule of law), functioning under autocratic conditions, can operate in a way that does not legitimize the system, but instead calls for a democratic return. Just as the EU's role has been dual in Hungary, so too is the role of opposition representatives; just as the EU could not step up effectively for years while the Hungarian government used the union's financial resources to build its corruption networks, through which the autocracy was further developed, opposition representatives, if they fail to innovate, reinforce the belief among voters and external observers that democracy is fundamentally intact.

Building on this, the research is conceived as a unique form of Action Research, which aligns with the original concept of the method by being an action-oriented process. It echoes a key insight shared by the widow of Alexei Navalny—Putin's most prominent opposition figure, who died under unclear circumstances in a Russian prison—during her address to the European Parliament (EP): "He was the opposite of everything boring. (...) If you really want to defeat Putin, you have to become an innovator. You have to stop being boring" (European Parliament 2024). To fully appreciate the significance of this suggestion, it is useful to recall Anne Applebaum's assertion that the essence of autocracy lies in its hypocrisy (Applebaum 2019). As we see, autocratic regimes manipulate rules arbitrarily to serve their interests, demanding strict adherence to them from opposition actors while simultaneously obstructing meaningful political engagement. In response, we conceptualize AR as a means of exploring how democratic systems can avoid reinforcing autocratic behavior when interacting with them. The primary aim is to advance both academic and public discourse on this issue: how democratic systems, when confronted with autocratic regimes, can avoid inadvertently reinforcing autocratic practices.

This is explored through the lens of parliamentary work but can be applied to broader contexts, including the European Union's relationship with Hungary, the interaction between the independent press and authoritarian leaders, as well as the engagement of independent civil society organizations with autocratic political parties. This research is AR in nature because it is closely connected to practical application and direct social change, where the researcher—as a former active participant in the political process—played a critical role in attempting to resolve the tension between democratic and autocratic behaviors, and hereby does not assume a purely observational role but actively participates in addressing the issues at hand, contributing to democratic problem-solving efforts.

III. Copying Putin by Hungarian Standards

To understand Orbán's regime clearly, it is important to recognize that after coming to power in 2010, his government consciously turned towards Putin's Russia. As we will argue in the following, Orbán could rely on Putin's traditions and toolbox in shaping the system, while adapting it to fit within the EU framework, thereby transforming Hungary's democracy.

As Madlovics and Magyar argue, Orbán, breaking away from his previous ideological roots, intentionally restructured Hungary's relationship with Russia (Madlovics and Magyar 2023). According to the authors, the strategy to normalize relations with Russia and promote a positive view of the Kremlin involves three key elements: first, Orbán's government reinterprets anti-communism, using the term "communist" as a broad slur to delegitimize political opponents, including the opposition and the EU. Second, both public and private Hungarian media spread Russian propaganda, portraying Russia positively, often through narratives that contrast it with "decadent" Western values. Finally, high-profile meetings between Hungarian and Russian leaders, such as Orbán and Putin, contribute to the normalization of Eastern actors, boosting Putin's popularity, particularly among Fidesz voters (Madlovics and Magyar 2023). Therefore, it is crucial to understand that Orbán, in breaking with his previous political credo, placed Hungary's relationship with Russia on new foundations, adopting traditional autocratic elements within this context, in a situation where both the EU and domestic dissenting opinions are largely paralyzed.

1. System Opposition vs Anti-System (Real) Opposition

Putin's opposition consisted of radical nationalists and liberal, pro-Western forces, with the president's dominant party in the center, much like Orbán's system. Orbán learned how to preserve the appearance of elections while ensuring the ruling party's victory. Beyond altering the electoral system, the key idea is maintaining a harmless, systemic opposition made up of small or medium-sized parties that are fragmented and ideologically diverse. Meanwhile, the dangerous anti-system opposition actors were attacked by all means. In Russia, opposition leaders are barred from elections, imprisoned, or even killed, and election results are falsified to the extent that the regime can no longer be ousted through elections. Hungary is not at this stage yet, but its propaganda machinery—unprecedented in the EU—uses public funds for smear campaigns and perhaps even covert intelligence operations to target opponents. Recently, the system has tightened its grip: MPs were stripped of their mandates in show trials, and politically motivated lawsuits are ongoing against other politicians and public figures, including the author of these lines, which could end in exclusion from elections and a prison sentence, either suspended or custodial.

2. Dismantling of the Free Press

In Russia, the silencing of critical voices began in the 2000s, with state media coming under strict government control and the largest independent outlets taken over by loyal oligarchs. The 2012 foreign agent law labeled independent media as "foreign agents" or "undesirable organizations," threatening to ban their operations. The 2022 censorship laws during the Ukraine war made reliable reporting impossible; spreading "false information" about the war can lead to 15 years in prison and asset confiscation. From 2023, the last free media outlets were banned. The Hungarian media landscape shares many similarities: public media is also the government's propaganda channel, most of the media market is under government control, and the media authority acts as an extension of power. The Sovereignty Protection Office (SPO) threatens the remaining independent media with investigations. However, there are differences: independent outlets are constantly threatened but not yet banned, fined, or blocked, and journalists are not imprisoned. There are no censorship laws or social media restrictions. Nevertheless, the government predominantly controls the flow of information.

3. The Foreign Agent Label Against NGOs

The original Russian law dates back to 2012, with roots in a 2005 law introduced as a reaction to the Ukrainian and Georgian revolutions, tightening financial controls over internationally funded NGOs. The 2012 law, enacted after protests in Russia, labeled internationally funded NGOs as foreign agents working to overthrow the government. Over time, this law has been expanded to include media and individuals, and foreign funding is no longer necessary for someone to face repercussions. Hungary adopted its own version of this law in 2017, but it had to be repealed due to a European Court ruling. But this did not solve the problem—on the contrary, the next step was the creation of the Sovereignty Protection Office to regulate internationally funded NGOs and media. Hungary's "Lex NGO" was nearly a verbatim copy of Russian law, and the accompanying narrative mirrored Russia's. As early as 2014, Orbán stated in his infamous illiberal speech that "if we want to reorganize our national state instead of a liberal state, it must be made clear that we are not dealing with civil organizations but paid political activists representing foreign interests in Hungary" (Orbán 2014). He repurposed Putin's obsession: that critics of the regime (opposition, media, NGOs) are exclusively foreign agents, and without them, there would be no social discontent. Crackdowns on them are thus framed as a national interest. This law has also inspired other autocratic regimes (e.g., Georgia, Turkey, Kyrgyzstan, Bosnia-Herzegovina, Slovakia).

4. The 2013 Russian Anti-LGBTQ+ Law as a Model for Hungary

Russia's 2013 law banning the "promotion" of non-traditional sexual relationships to minors served as a template for Hungary's 2021 so-called "child protection law", which is fundamentally homophobic. While the Hungarian law is stricter in its text, prohibiting even the "depiction of homosexuality" and the "promotion of gender transition", in practice, Russia also treats any depiction as propaganda. In 2022, Russia further tightened its law, banning such content for adults in addition to minors across media, the internet, and film. In 2023, Russia escalated further by labeling the international LGBTQ+ movement "an extremist terrorist organization" and banning it outright. Both the Russian and Hungarian governments persecute sexual minorities under the guise of protecting traditional values and families. Russia frames LGBTQ+ activism as a Western attack on traditional Russian values, just as Hungary's government claims that "Brussels," as they refer to the EU, abuses its power to dictate how Hungarians should live. In both cases, anti-LGBTQ+

sentiment is intertwined with anti-Western rhetoric, rejecting both Western liberalism and the rights of sexual minorities.

5. Attacks on Academic Freedom and University Autonomy

In 2016, Russia revoked the operating license of the European University at St. Petersburg (EUSP), a liberal, Western-oriented institution supported by the Soros Foundation since 1994.

Hungary's government did the same to the Central European University (CEU) in 2017, forcing it to leave the country. In 2023, Russia's prosecutor general designated CEU as an undesirable organization, accusing it of discrediting Russia's leadership and military operations. This designation effectively bans the university and exposes those affiliated with it to criminal prosecution, including its Russian faculty and students.

These steps illustrate how Orbán followed Putin's playbook and triggered a democratic backlash in Hungary, a full-fledged EU member state. Just as the EU was unprepared for a member state drifting in this direction, Hungarian society and the political community were similarly caught off guard by this transformation. The Hungarian case also offers a crucial empirical instance of how elements of the Putin-style authoritarian governance model can be transplanted within certain structural constraints into the institutional fabric of an EU member state (Krekó and Juhász 2017; Magyar 2016). The third part of this study turns inward, analyzing domestic-level dynamics through the lens of action research. Drawing on the author's own experience as an MP, it explores how everyday political practice is reshaped within an illiberal context, particularly when democratic actors attempt to navigate—and resist—authoritarian encroachment.

IV. Making It Hard for the Rivals: Resisting Autocratic Forces

Since the 2011 electoral reform[5], the Hungarian opposition has faced progressively more challenging conditions. Notably, in 2010, the government, a soon later, firmly on an autocratic trajectory, won within a democratic system. However, it exploited its two-thirds mandate to establish an autocratic framework, reshaping political and legal structures to centralize

5 Hungary, Act CXXXI of 2011 on Electoral Law. 2011.

power. In this research, we frame AR as a tool to examine how democratic systems can avoid reinforcing autocratic behaviors when engaging with autocratic regimes. Building on this, a crucial question arises: What can a democracy-oriented opposition representative do in the face of autocratic backsliding? The following three features have widely emerged in Hungary while discussing efficient and ethical opposition behavior.[6]

1. Pretending and acting as if democracy still exists is profoundly detrimental. In a system shifting toward autocratization, if the opposition refrains from bold political action and avoids confronting those in power, it risks losing its relevance, resulting in serious consequences: the most significant is its failure to serve as an example to voters. When the opposition is passive, unresponsive, or repetitive, voters too become disengaged.
2. Given the manipulated electoral system and omnipresent state propaganda, the opposition faces slim prospects of success. The ruling party's two-thirds majority provides near-absolute power: it can amend the constitution unilaterally, alter electoral rules to serve its interests, and install loyalists in key state positions. Under these circumstances, in Hungary, debates have centered on whether it is still "worthwhile" for the opposition to participate in elections or even remain in parliament.
3. The terms "old opposition" and "new opposition" have emerged within the system. The first refers to parties that failed to innovate as the autocratic backsliding was strengthening, while the latter, though not universally defined, includes the new challenger party to Fidesz, formed in 2024, and politicians who refuse to accept the autocratic regime's rules. Through their political maneuvering, these figures consistently challenge the system and expose its true nature, something autocrats often seek to conceal.

Where a society's democratic resilience is weak, autocratic forces face resistance that they can easily dismantle. In such a case, public figures—especially politicians—need to focus on organizing new forms of resistance. In Hungary, after seeing two successive two-thirds majorities, it has become clear that social resistance can be fostered by innovative legislators prepared to take risks and operate outside the usual comfort zones associated with parliamentary work. Under autocratic circumstances, rather than allowing the government to control their work in parliament, legislators can work more authentically and many times more efficiently by

---

6 The conclusions drawn under this point are grounded in the researcher's active participation in public debates concerning opposition strategies.

engaging in fieldwork and actively using a representative toolkit there, or, when it is necessary to be present at the Parliament, they can step up in an innovative and inspiring way. Many believe that, in an autocracy, MPs must simultaneously act as opposition representatives, civil activists, and investigative journalists.

To provide an example, the autocratic regime's increasing control over Hungarian media heightened the importance of alternative channels, especially social media. Effectively stepping in for the degraded Hungarian public media, non-traditional MPs started to report to the Hungarian public through live broadcasts on Facebook regularly. The mobile phones emerged at the most unexpected moments, causing serious anxiety among the ruling party representatives who, accustomed to control and their own safe space, are not fond of surprises.[7] The very first high-impact live broadcast was made in 2018 at the public media building, when opposition representatives, demanding real news instead of propaganda, entered the building. Although the group of us did make it to the studios, the events were followed both domestically and internationally via the live broadcast (Rényi 2018).

Nevertheless, this did not render the innovative opposition immune to the inherent challenges of social media: navigating the presence of paid commenters, the unpredictable fluctuations in reach driven by opaque algorithmic mechanisms, and the underlying reality that meaningful engagement on these platforms ultimately requires financial resources. The government side invested substantially more in social media than any other actor, not only surpassing the opposition, but, relative to population size, exceeding all other European countries during the 2024 European Parliament elections (Lakmusz 2024). As a result, the playing field was far from level; yet, even so, this medium proved more accessible and effective than traditional television studios, which remain largely inaccessible to opposition voices. Through the lens of the action research framework, the following toolkit offers a context-specific overview of methods applied and reflected upon in practice by political actors facing similar constraints.

7 After the state secretary proved unavailable through formal parliamentary channels, the author, as an MP, resorted to an unconventional method: posing questions in a corridor of the Parliament and broadcasting the exchange live via mobile phone. This "alternative interpellation" reached a wide audience and effectively drew public attention to the issue of child protection (Szél 2019).

V. Nontraditional Representative Tasks[8]

In the Hungarian context, access to public interest data, particularly information that the government sought to conceal or deny, was frequently achieved through persistent legal action, often requiring multiple court proceedings. Over time, it became evident that, in the author's case, more time was spent in courtrooms than in Parliament itself, as the judiciary, at least at that point, exhibited a greater degree of independence than the legislature, which had already come under significant influence from the ruling party. This legal activism enabled the disclosure of data that would have otherwise remained inaccessible to the public.

Operating as an opposition MP in an autocratic system required stepping into roles more commonly associated with investigative journalism, though with the added benefit of institutional tools available to legislators. Efforts to counter government opacity involved uncovering hidden initiatives, such as the attempted closure of a children's home. Site visits to state-run institutions exposed unacceptable conditions, particularly in the child protection system. Instead of triggering structural reforms, these revelations resulted in a ban on further parliamentary inspections.

In other instances, government misinformation was systematically challenged. In the case of the Central European University, public statements were discredited by demonstrating that the government had willfully delayed the signing of a bilateral agreement enabling CEU's continued operation, under the pretense of awaiting the opinion of non-existent "educational experts" (Biró 2019). Similarly, the request for access to the so-called "Soros Plan" revealed its fictitious nature[9]—an entirely fabricated construct used for political mobilization.

Narratives concerning the defense of national sovereignty were also scrutinized through legal channels. In the context of the Budapest-Belgrade railway reconstruction project, court proceedings compelled the government to acknowledge that, due to the lack of consent from its contracting

8 In the context of this article, *nontraditional parliamentary tasks* refer to activities that go beyond the conventional understanding of parliamentary roles, such as legislation, interpellation, and committee work. Instead, these tasks respond to the specific characteristics of an authoritarian system and seek alternative means to exercise representation, ensure accountability, and maintain social oversight.

9 In response to a written parliamentary question regarding the content of the concept introduced by the government under the label of the "Soros Plan," I received the following official material. This response underscores the propagandistic essence of the so-called "plan." (Government of Hungary, 2019) ["Response to Szél Bernadett Regarding the Soros Plan."].

partner, it had withheld key information from the public, thereby violating fundamental transparency norms (Magyari 2022). Field visits to refugee transit zones further exposed the inhumane conditions under which asylum seekers, including minors (Szél 2018), were held, culminating in cases where individuals were denied food, thereby raising serious human rights concerns (Erdélyi 2019).

Petitions and formal complaints submitted to state institutions revealed the erosion of the rule of law, as once-independent oversight bodies increasingly functioned as executors of executive will. Their perfunctory dismissal of complaints underscored the extent of political capture. For example, government propaganda was reclassified as "public interest advertising," thereby legitimizing the unrestricted use of public funds for partisan messaging and precluding any investigation into potential misuse (Political Capital 2022).

In response to this constrained environment, alternative forms of political protest were developed, often in collaboration with like-minded MPs. These included the orchestration of symbolic actions such as the “sound the horn protests” during the COVID-19 pandemic (Magyari 2020a), the refusal to pay politically motivated fines (with penalized individuals instead opting for public service), and the occupation of the parliamentary podium using megaphones (Jámbor 2018). Parliamentary privileges were also strategically employed, including gaining access to state media headquarters in protest against the exclusion of opposition voices from public broadcasting.

To circumvent the heavily controlled media landscape, new channels of communication were established. These included livestreaming parliamentary and committee sessions and utilizing independent media platforms, many of which reached significantly broader audiences than state-controlled outlets. Direct, unscripted engagement—such as confronting government officials on camera—became an important tactic in amplifying accountability.

One illustrative case concerning legislative compliance involved the Prime Minister’s obligation to report to Parliament following European Council meetings—a legal requirement that had gone largely unobserved and unchallenged. Upon recognizing this oversight, the author, as an MP, formally petitioned the Speaker of the House, pointing out the violation. The issue carried symbolic and substantive weight, since the PM often conveyed divergent messages to domestic and international audiences, reinforcing a perception of unaccountability. Although the aim was to reinforce legislative oversight, the institutional response instead normalized non-compliance—echoing similar outcomes in cases such as the legal challenge to the PM's use of military aircraft, which led not to transparency, but to retroactive legal amendments permitting the practice.[10] Nevertheless, the use of these tools helps to highlight the increasingly industrialized scale of autocratic legal practices and hinders the autocrat's ability to emphasize the democratic character of the regime.

A defining feature of autocratic systems is the transformation of Parliament into a space dominated by the ruling leader and their apparatus. Nonetheless, as demonstrated above, certain opportunities for resistance remain, albeit in forms distinct from those available in democratic contexts. The strategies previously outlined illustrate methods of navigating this contradiction, while additional approaches aim to circumvent authoritarian constraints.

In the absence of viable parliamentary mechanisms, legal instruments and formal procedures offered alternative avenues for accessing information. These included public data requests, litigation, administrative procedures, and official complaints. Direct engagement with ministries and state institutions also facilitated transparency and accountability. The CEU case, for instance, exemplifies how on-the-field ministry visits revealed government misconduct (Farkas 2018).

On-the-ground presence emerged as another crucial tool. Nationwide tours and site visits enabled the assessment of public sector conditions, such as the employment terms of public workers and the treatment of children under state supervision. Collaborations with trade unions, environmental organizations, and social advocacy groups ensured that pressing social issues remained part of the public agenda.

Participation in mass protests and advocacy campaigns further supported democratic values, whether in defense of academic freedom, independent journalism, or LGBTQ+ rights. Protests against the exclusion of opposition voices from public media spotlighted systemic restrictions on public discourse.

Resistance should not diminish even under states of emergency, as autocrats frequently exploit such exceptional legal regimes to silence public dissent. Alternative protest methods were employed to circumvent official constraints, for example, honking demonstrations that complied with pandemic regulations or choosing community service over unjust fines.

---

10 The case was continuously covered by the Hungarian press, i.e., Kálmán 2019a, Kálmán 2019b.

Countering propaganda remains a cornerstone and enduring bastion of resistance within autocratizing regimes. Among various initiatives, the establishment of an independent signature-collection network in response to the so-called "National Consultation" stands out, as it successfully mobilized citizens nationwide, directly challenging the autocrats' system built on silencing dissent (Magyari 2020b). This initiative enhanced democratic participation, demonstrating that grassroots resistance can weaken authoritarian narratives and provide hope for systemic change.

VI. Conclusions: Oppositional Parliamentary Activities in an Autocratic System in Light of International Human Rights Standards

As noted in the Introduction, Yulia Navalnaya stated in the European Parliament that, following Navalny's death in prison, confronting Putin requires innovation, resourcefulness, and boldness (European Parliament 2024). This principle applies to all autocrats: if people, particularly politicians, adhere to the undemocratic rules set by the autocrat, the system survives. By staying within the boundaries established by the autocrat, the regime's legitimacy is reinforced through the illusion of functioning properly. Electoral autocracies are façades of democracy—featuring fake parliaments, a fake rule of law, and fake elections. In such systems, traditional, system-conforming opposition politics perpetuate the illusion of democracy. In reality, when the system is not genuinely democratic, every action taken by the opposition must aim at revealing its true nature. A strategy must be developed based on the understanding that nothing within the system is what it appears to be. The essence of resistance is to seek encounters with power that expose the system's oppressive nature, as the true face of a system is revealed by how it treats dissent.

The alternative forms of parliamentary work presented above—legal activism, fieldwork, symbolic actions, and the strategic use of social media—are all forms of democratic resistance that are not only relevant in a domestic context but are also closely linked to international human rights and rule-of-law norms, as well as proceedings initiated against their violations.

These strategies can be seen as responses that consciously break the rules of the autocracy in an attempt to keep democratic norms alive and visible. Therefore, they are not merely creative forms of resistance, but also responses to human rights and democratic expectations, especially when examined based on international standards.

The Venice Commission, the constitutional advisory body of the Council of Europe, has emphasized that the parliamentary opposition is not only a political actor but also a guardian of the constitutional order. In its 2010 report entitled *"The Role of the Opposition in a Democratic Parliament,"* the Venice Commission emphasizes that the effective protection of opposition rights is essential for the proper functioning of democratic parliaments (Venice Commission 2010). Without this protection, the system of checks and balances is undermined. It also outlines the principles by which the opposition should enjoy equality before the law (Venice Commission 2010).

Referring to Hungary's process of autocratization, it particularly stands out how the tools deemed essential by the Venice Commission have been hollowed out: during the autocratization process, it was observed that these guidelines have been emptied of meaning[11]. The quality of governmental responses in the parliament has gradually declined, with substantive information transfer becoming increasingly rare: a notorious example occurred when, in response to a parliamentary question concerning national security and corruption, the PM replied: *"Merry Christmas"* (hvg.hu 2017). In an autocracy, it is typical that although formal answers are given, they do not carry substantive information. Similarly, the ruling party does not attend extraordinary parliamentary sessions called by the opposition, thus preventing the discussion of poorly timed or politically unfavorable issues. A prime example of this was the extraordinary parliamentary session called by the opposition regarding Sweden's NATO membership, which Fidesz sabotaged (Szabad Európa 2023).

Focusing on the Hungarian autocratic backlash, since 2010, the Venice Commission has addressed the country on several occasions. Notable statements related to the new Fundamental Law adopted in 2011– according to the

11 For example:
"2.2.1. opposition members have the right to information; opposition members and members of the majority are entitled to receive the same information from the government.";
"2.2.2. opposition members have the right to ask written and oral questions, and to receive replies to these questions";
"2.2.3. opposition members shall be privileged during question time with the government [...]";
"2.2.4. opposition members have the right to interpellation [...] and the right to move a motion of no confidence";
"2.2.5. opposition members have the right to request the convening of a plenary sitting [...]".
In these points, the Commission tries to codify opposition rights under democratic frameworks, clearly instructing the government majority (Venice Commission 2010).

Commission, the constitutional process was opaque and did not ensure sufficient democratic participation (Venice Commission 2011). Later on, it also addressed issues with the electoral system's distortions, problematic media laws, restrictions on civil society, and the legal environment regarding the so-called "child protection" laws, which were anti-LGBTQ+. In some cases, such as the 2021 "child protection law" or the 2024 sovereignty protection law, the Commission expressed serious concerns regarding political pluralism, freedom of expression, and legal certainty (Venice Commission 2021 and 2024).

The Venice Commission's activities serve as a benchmark for international rule-of-law norms in Hungary: although its recommendations are not legally binding, they serve as an important reference for the international public and all European institutions when grounding EU actions, and the latter indeed have a more direct effect on governments following autocratic paths. The Hungarian government has primarily built a political narrative around the Commission's criticism, particularly when the report touched on sensitive issues (e.g., the electoral system, press freedom, civil society, LGBTQ+ rights). However, when other international institutions—especially those with sanctioning power—became involved, they were able to influence the process of autocratic backsliding.

Hungary's case illustrates how the rule of law can significantly erode in practice, even within a fully integrated member state of the EU. We also noted that the EU was fundamentally unprepared for autocratic backsliding and that the community is learning how to manage this process democratically through Hungary's example. Since 2010, the European Union has been increasingly active in addressing the rule-of-law violations in Hungary, expanding its legal and financial toolkit. The European Commission launched the first accelerated infringement proceedings in 2012. The most severe political mechanism, the Article 7 procedure, was triggered in 2018. In the CEU case, the European Court of Justice ruled in 2020 that Hungary violated academic freedom. Currently, proceedings are ongoing due to the 2021 anti-LGBTQ+ "child protection law", and the rule-of-law mechanism implemented since 2021 led to the suspension of 6.3 billion euros, and in January 2025, the country permanently lost over 1 billion euros. The European Court of Justice also imposed a fine of over 200 million euros for violations of refugee rules, with a daily fine of 1 million euros.

All in all, the speed of the autocratization is often striking, as it can rapidly reshape institutional frameworks and power structures while efforts to enforce legal norms, particularly those tied to international organizations, unfold gradually. This discrepancy between the pace of political change and the enforcement of legal norms creates an ongoing dialectic between the autocratic regime and international legal institutions tasked with ensuring compliance. This dynamic can be seen as a form of norm contestation, where autocratic governments selectively engage with or subvert international expectations to maintain legitimacy and control. Beyond these objective measures of enforcement, a critical component of this dialogue is the formation of political narratives within the country, which offers a rich avenue for further research.

Institutions and international norms are essential for maintaining democracy, yet—as the case of the EU and Hungary clearly illustrates—they are not, on their own, sufficient to prevent the emergence or escalation of authoritarian forces. Addressing such challenges requires a complex strategy that demands ingenuity and a shift in perspective from all actors involved. Actions and the supporting international framework together show that opposition politics in an autocratic context is not only about functioning within the system but also constitutes democratic resistance. The methods chosen—especially when linked to EU or global, for example, UN mechanisms—are not only legitimate but may also serve as exemplary models for other opposition actors in similar situations. Non-traditional representative tools serve as practical instruments to enforce democratic international norms, such as several articles of the EU Charter of Fundamental Rights, too. These tools especially implement Article 41 (the right to good administration), Article 42 (the right of access to documents), and Article 11 (the freedom to express opinions and access information) (European Union, Consolidated Version of the Treaty on European Union 2012). Specific cases, such as the CEU case or the dismantling of the "Soros Plan" narrative, highlight that these tools not only shape national public opinion but also contribute to democratic accountability at the EU level, for example, by facilitating the Article 7 procedure.

The key conclusion is that the conscious violation of autocratic rules, if done in the spirit of transparency, public visibility, and rule-of-law principles, is not subverting the system, but rather fulfilling a democratic responsibility. This research, by turning a former parliamentary experience into the subject of action research, aims to offer insight into this necessary rethinking. The essence of autocracies is that they do not play by the rules while expecting everyone else to follow the ones they set. Breaking out of this game requires committed, values-based cooperation—an alliance whose benefits can be felt globally. This is a cause that merits pursuit.

References

Applebaum, Anne. 2019. "It's Not Xenophobia That Links the New Populists. It's Hypocrisy." *The Washington Post*, February 11. https://www.washingtonpost.com/opinions/2019/02/11/its-not-xenophobia-that-links-new-populists-its-hypocrisy/.

Biró, Marianna. 2019. "A CEU-t Senki Nem Kereste, Pedig Az Oktatási Hivatal Állítja: Ütemterv Szerint Vizsgálódik" [No One Sought Out the CEU, But the Educational Authority Claims It Is Investigating According to a Set Schedule]. *Index.hu*, January 31. https://index.hu/belfold/2019/01/31/kutya_nem_kereste_a_ceu-t_de_az_oktatasi_hivatal_allitja_utemterv_szerint_vizsgalodik/?token=61ebd88b2d057b7296f2f098c3a384ec.

Bozóki, András, and Zoltán Fleck. 2024. Embedded Autocracy: Hungary in the European Union. *Rowman and Littlefield.*

Bozóki, András, and Dániel Hegedűs. 2018. "An Externally Constrained Hybrid Regime: Hungary in the European Union." *Democratization* 25(7): 1173–1189.

Coppedge, Michael, John Gerring, Carl Henrik Knutsen, Staffan I. Lindberg, Jan Teorell, David Altman, et al. 2024. *V-Dem [Country-Year/Country-Date] Dataset v14.* Gothenburg: Varieties of Democracy (V-Dem) Project.

Council of the European Union. 2022. "Rule of Law Conditionality Mechanism: Council Decides to Suspend €6.3 Billion Given Only Partial Remedial Action by Hungary." Press release, December 12. https://www.consilium.europa.eu/en/press/press-releases/2022/12/12/rule-of-law-conditionality-mechanism/.

Enyedi, Zsolt, and Bálint Mikola. 2024. "Legislative Capture in Hungary: Well-Managed Autocratization." *The ANNALS of the American Academy of Political and Social Science.* https://doi.org/10.1177/00027162241307778.

Erdélyi, Péter. 2019. "Annyi Embert Éheztettek Már a Tranzitzónában, Hogy Az Emberi Jogi Bíróságnak Formalevele Van, Amiben Kötelezik a Magyar Hatóságokat, Hogy Azonnal Adjanak Enni a Külföldieknek" [So Many People Have Been Starved in the Transit Zone That the European Court of Human Rights Has a Formal Letter Requiring Hungarian Authorities to Immediately Provide Food to Foreigners]. *444.hu*, August 7. https://444.hu/2019/08/07/annyi-embert-eheztettek-mar-a-tranzitzonaban-hogy-az-emberi-jogi-birosagnak-formalevele-van-amiben-kotelezik-a-magyar-hatosagokat-hogy-azonnal-adjanak-enni-a-kulfoldieknek.

European Parliament. 2024. *Verbatim Report of Proceedings – Formal Sitting: Address by Yulia Navalnaya.* Strasbourg, February 28. https://www.europarl.europa.eu/doceo/document/CRE-9-2024-02-28-ITM-006_EN.html.

European Union. 2012. *Consolidated Version of the Treaty on European Union (TEU). Official Journal of the European Union*, C 326, December 26. https://eur-lex.europa.eu/legal-content/HU/TXT/HTML/?uri=CELEX:12012P/TXT&from=HU#d1e237-393-1.

Farkas, György. 2018. "Szél Bernadett: CEU-ügyben kamuzik a kormány" [Szél Bernadett: The Government Lies in the CEU Case.]. *24.hu*, 2018. október 30. https://24.hu/belfold/2018/10/30/szel-bernadett-ceu-ugyben-kamuzik-a-kormany/.

Financial Times. 2025. "Hungary Loses EU Funds as Economic Slump Deepens." *Financial Times*, January 15. https://www.ft.com/content/fe893219-7ac3-4ff4-a01f-5cfc3e99be7c.

Government of Hungary. 2019. "Válasz Szél Bernadettnek a Soros-tervvel Kapcsolatban" [Response to Szél Bernadett Regarding the Soros Plan]. Government of Hungary. https://2015-2019.kormany.hu/download/7/9a/31000/V%C3%A1lasz%20Sz%C3%A9l%20Bernadettnek%20a%20Soros-tervvel%20kapcsolatban.pdf#!DocumentBrowse.

Greenwood, Davydd J., and Morten Levin. 2007. *Introduction to Action Research: Social Research for Social Change.* 2nd ed. Thousand Oaks, CA: SAGE.

Hungary. *Act CXXXI of 2011 on Electoral Law.* 2011.

HVG.hu. 2017. "Orbánt nemzetbiztonsági kockázatról kérdezték, azt válaszolta: Boldog karácsonyt" [Orbán was asked about a national security risk, he replied: Merry Christmas]. *HVG.hu*, December 11. https://hvg.hu/itthon/20171211_Orbant_nemzetbiztonsagi_kockazatrol_kerdeztek_azt_valaszolta_boldog_karacsonyt.

Jámbor, András. 2018. "Így kell tiltakozni egy rabszolgatorvény ellen" [This Is How to Protest Against a Slave Law]. *Mérce*, December 10. https://merce.hu/2018/12/10/igy-kell-tiltakozni-egy-rabszolgatorveny-ellen/.

Kálmán, Attila. 2019a. "Orbán Viktor felszólítása elmulasztott beszámolójának pótlására" [Viktor Orbán Called Upon to Provide a Missing Report]. *24.hu*, June 28. https://24.hu/belfold/2019/06/28/orban-viktor-szel-bernadett-europai-tanacs-veto-beszamolo-klima/.

Kálmán, Attila. 2019b. "Kövér elismerte, hogy Orbán törvényt szegett, majd Orbánra bízta a megoldást" [Kövér Acknowledged That Orbán Broke the Law, Then Left the Solution to Orbán]. *24.hu*, July 18. https://24.hu/belfold/2019/07/18/kover-laszlo-orban-viktor-szel-bernadett/.

Kornai, János. 2011. "Számvetés" [Assessment]. *Népszabadság*, October 6.

Krastev, Ivan, and Stephen Holmes. 2019. *The Light That Failed: Why the West Is Losing the Fight for Democracy.* London: Penguin.

Krekó, Péter, and Juhász, Attila. 2017. *The Hungarian Far Right: Social Demand, Political Supply, and International Context.* Stuttgart: Ibidem Press.

Lakmusz. 2024. "A lakosságszámhoz viszonyítva toronymagasan nálunk költik a legtöbbet Facebook-hirdetésekre az EP-választás előtt" [In Relation to Population Size, We Spend by Far the Most on Facebook Advertisements Before the EP Elections]. *Lakmusz*, 2024. https://www.lakmusz.hu/a-lakossagszamhoz-viszonyitva-toronymagasan-nalunk-koltik-a-legtobbet-facebook-hirdetesekre-az-ep-valasztas-elott/.

Lührmann, Anna, and Staffan I. Lindberg. 2019. "A Third Wave of Autocratization Is Here: What Is New About It?" *Democratization* 26(7): 1095–1113.

Madlovics, Bálint, and Bálint Magyar. 2023. *Hungary's Dubious Loyalty: Orbán's Regime Strategy in the Russia-Ukraine War.* CEU Democracy Institute Working Papers No. 7.

Magyar, Bálint. 2016. *Post-Communist Mafia State: The Case of Hungary.* Budapest–New York: Central European University Press.

Magyari, Péter. 2020a. "Aki felvételről dudál, azt nem állították le a rendőrök a kormányellenes tüntetésen" [Those Who Honked from a Recording Were Not Stopped by the Police at the Anti-Government Protest]. *444.hu*, May 4. https://444.hu/2020/05/04/aki-felvetelrol-dudal-azt-nem-allitottak-le-a-rendorok-a-kormanyellenes-tuntetesen.

Magyari, Péter. 2020b. "Szél és Hadházy kéri a konzultációs íveket" [Szél and Hadházy Request the National Consultation Forms]. *444.hu*, June 10. https://444.hu/2020/06/10/szel-es-hadhazy-keri-a-konzultacios-iveket.

Magyari, Péter. 2022. "Kína Óhajára Titkosította Szijjártó Péter a Budapest–Belgrád Vasút Hitelszerződését" [At China's Request, Péter Szijjártó Classified the Budapest–Belgrade Railway Loan Agreement]. *444.hu*, September 5. https://444.hu/2022/09/05/kina-ohajara-titkositotta-szijjarto-peter-a-budapestbelgrad-vasut-hitelszerzodeset.

McNiff, Jean. 2013. *Action Research: Principles and Practice.* 3rd ed. London: Routledge.

Nord, Marina, David Altman, Fabio Angiolillo, Tiago Fernandes, Ana Good God, and Staffan I. Lindberg. 2025. *Democracy Report 2025: 25 Years of Autocratization – Democracy Trumped?* Göteborg: V-Dem Institute. https://www.v-dem.net/documents/60/V-dem-dr__2025_lowres.pdf.

Orbán, Viktor. 2014. "Prime Minister Viktor Orbán's Speech at the 25th Bálványos Summer Free University and Student Camp." Tusnádfürdő, July 26. https://2010-2015.miniszterelnok.hu/in-english/prime-minister-viktor-orbans-speech-at-the-25th-balvanyos-summer-free-university-and-student-camp/.

Papada, Evie, Richard Youngs, Ken Godfrey, and Staffan I. Lindberg. 2023. *The Global State of Democracy 2023: The New Checks and Balances.* Göteborg: V-Dem Institute.

Political Capital. 2022. "Pro-government Political Advertisements Are in Record Heights in Hungary, Promoting Hostile Narratives Against the West." *Political Capital.* https://politicalcapital.hu/news.php?article_id=3364&article_read=1.

Regulation (EU, Euratom) 2020/2092 of the European Parliament and of the Council of 16 December 2020 on a General Regime of Conditionality for the Protection of the Union Budget. 2022. *Official Journal of the European Union,* December 22. https://eur-lex.europa.eu/eli/reg/2020/2092/oj/eng.

Rényi, Pál Dániel. 2018. "Szél Bernadett Facebook-közvetítése megközelítette az M1 híradó nézettségét" [Szél Bernadett's Facebook Broadcast Reached the Viewership of the M1 News]. *444.hu,* December 17. https://444.hu/2018/12/17/szel-bernadett-facebook-kozvetitese-megkozelitette-az-m1-hirado-nezettseget.

Scheiring, Gábor. 2020. *The Retreat of Liberal Democracy: Authoritarian Capitalism and the Accumulative State in Hungary.* London: Palgrave Macmillan.

Scheppele, Kim Lane. 2018. "Autocratic Legalism." University of Chicago Law Review 85(2): 545–583. https://sociology.princeton.edu/sites/g/files/toruqf1236/files/people-cv/scheppele_cv_july2020.pdf.

Szabad Európa [Radio Free Europe]. 2023. "Svéd NATO-csatlakozás: hétfőn rendkívüli ülés, a Fidesz–KDNP kihagyja" [Swedish NATO Accession: Extraordinary Session on Monday, Fidesz–KDNP to Skip It]. *Szabad Európa,* August. https://www.szabadeuropa.hu/a/sved-nato-csatlakozas-hetfon-rendkivuli-ules-a-fidesz-kdnp-kihagyja/32802990.html.

Szél, Bernadett. 2018. "Gyermekként a Tranzitzónában – Szél Bernadett a Magyar-Szerb Határnál Járt" [As a Child in the Transit Zone – Bernadett Szél Visited the Hungarian-Serbian Border]. *Mérce,* September 9. https://merce.hu/2018/09/09/gyermekkent-a-tranzitzonaban-szel-bernadett-a-magyar-szerb-hatarnal-jart/.

Szél, Bernadett. 2019. Facebook post, December 13. https://www.facebook.com/szelbernadett/posts/2015093725270226/?comment_id=2015221045257494.

V-Dem Institute. 2022. "Parliamentary Elections in Hungary and Its Autocratization." https://v-dem.net/weekly_graph/parliamentary-elections-in-hungary-and-its-autocra?

Venice Commission. 2010. *Report on the Role of the Opposition in a Democratic Parliament.* CDL-AD(2010)025. Strasbourg: Council of Europe. https://www.venice.coe.int/webforms/documents/default.aspx?pdffile=CDL-AD(2010)025-e.

Venice Commission. 2011. *Opinion on the New Constitution of Hungary.* CDL-AD(2011)016. Strasbourg: Council of Europe. https://www.coe.int/en/web/venice-commission/-/CDL-AD(2011)016-e.

Venice Commission. 2021. *Opinion on the Compatibility with International Human Rights Standards of Act LXXIX Amending Certain Acts for the Protection of Children.* CDL-AD(2021)050. Strasbourg: Council of Europe. https://www.coe.int/en/web/venice-commission/-/CDL-AD(2021)050-e.

Venice Commission. 2024. *Opinion on Act LXXXVIII of 2023 on the Protection of National Sovereignty.* CDL-AD(2024)001. Strasbourg: Council of Europe. https://www.coe.int/en/web/venice-commission/-/CDL-AD(2024)001-e.

Vörös, Imre. 2014. "Alkotmányos puccs" [Constitutional Coup]. *Élet és Irodalom* 58 (6).

K. Concluding remarks

Professor Jau-hwa Chen as Director of the Chang Fo-Chuan Center for the Study of Human Rights at Soochow University in Taipei included in this book contributions of her Research Center and also contributions by lecturers at the Center on several human rights issues which were then elaborated in article form. As *Jau-hwa Chen* outlined in the Introduction, some key concerns of human rights practice needing further research were assembled and then coordinated with *Eibe Riedel* at University of Mannheim (Germany). The inter-disciplinary context to each contribution opened up new and novel approaches that inspired the researchers. *Mary Robinson*, former President of Ireland and former UN High Commissioner for Human Rights set the trail for the book, as *Jau-hwa Chen* stated.

Mary Robinson in her contribution following the winning of the Tang Prize concentrated her remarks on the current challenges facing Human Rights and Global Justice, highlighting also the pushbacks on economic, social and cultural rights (ESC-rights) and especially the backsliding of diversity and inclusion (DEI), as well as on women's rights generally.

Dagmar Yu's contribution strengthens the general points raised by *Mary Robinson* in her article and provides telling examples of developments in Taiwan. She succinctly discusses the evolution of the women's movement in Taiwan showing how women and NGOs successfully advanced awareness and need for change in Taiwanese society at all levels, illustrating this by the (in)famous *Wanru Case* of 1996. A new law relating to gender equality later was adopted. Women's groups felt that legislation contained flaws and therefore strongly propagated adopting CEDAW in national law. As Taiwan was stopped from remaining in the UN since 1971, the Women's NGOs strongly propagated adopting CEDAW in national law. Taiwan then decided to set-up an independent committee of UN experts on those issues. In 2016, after the Democratic Progressive Party had won majorities in the Executive and Legislative Yuans, and the first woman President Tsai Ing-wen had endorsed same-sex marriage, finally legalized in 2019, further steps of equalization of same-sex marriage have been established in law by 2024, always with strong participation of civil society women's rights organizations. *Dagmar Yu* concludes that presently cyber-bullying incidents, and anti-women speech, corporal examinations violating privacy and fake information abound. By showing the flaws of the existing statute needing persistent opposition by civil society organizations *Yu* convincingly focusses on the vitally important role that civil society plays.

The key focus of this book is on the interaction of human rights norms at international, regional, national and local levels, and portraying reactions to political action by human rights professionals, civil society organizations, but also media reactions and activism. The role of women in society at all levels represents a prominent focus in all human rights protection efforts in Taiwan, Germany and Europe, and in all other parts of the world. Taiwanese efforts in this human rights area can serve as a model for many Asian but also other States.

Writing and debating at the international and academic levels achieves stronger focus on marginalized and disadvantaged individuals and groups, and particularly on women, in Taiwan, ensuring that fundamental human rights concerns are not forgotten or belittled. The focus of several contributions concentrates on everyday life experiences, illustrating deficiencies and suffering elementary experiences of injustice at all levels of society, particularly in Taiwan, Germany and Europe.

Nearly all contributions highlight "*best practices*", because of the growing recognition that discussion of advances of protection may start in other countries but then seep into Taiwan's and Germany's national-level reflections, discussion, parliamentary, judicial and administrative practice, where previously these issues had been neglected, by-passed or left unattended. Unfortunately, human rights recognition and affirmation at the international level does not always initiate automatic reflection but instead may produce ups and downs of protection. Court judgments with human rights relevance often trigger off developments at the national level, quickly serving as precedents or becoming leading cases in legal discussion, political or ethical debate, and help to entrench the human rights vision in constitutional and international fora.

Realization grows that local level realization of rights is most important. National and international level discussion often produces debates of the human rights issues at a high level of abstraction, frequently leaving aside the concrete effects of measures at the individual or local level. To pick out just one good example discussed in this book, presented by *Yi-Chun Chou* on the Atayal Tribe in Taiwan, the concentration on the local level apart from regional and national levels is a good case in point.

Moreover, as *Jau-hwa Chen* cogently points out, differences in legal frameworks, political will and ability to implement the human rights standards play a big part in most countries and cultural settings. Lack of resources used as a defence by human rights critics does not stand the test of the UN Covenants and other major human rights treaties in national implementation and actual application. Suffering individuals or people devoid of human rights protection frequently do not even know about practical effects of legal measures but also about lacking legal provisions.

Taiwan, for wrong reasons, is not a member of the UN and of the human rights mechanisms. Although, because of continuing and remarkable efforts by civil society experts and persistent pleadings by academics and private institutions, interaction with the UN mechanisms of human rights protection in practice does take place. This led Taiwan becoming one of the few Asian States that place great emphasis on human rights protection measures and especially the implementation of the Geneva processes at national level. Setting up its own *National Human Rights Commission (NHRC)* was a logical conclusion.

The following specific remarks only present some of the conclusions reached by the contributors in this book.

The discussion of LGBT same-sex marriage and family relations in my contribution addresses the initially slow development, acceptance and propagation of LGBT people rights, and shows that initially largely non-binding but eminently important principles like the Yogyakarta Principles in effect can play a crucial role in advancing knowledge, acceptance, and taking account of important social changes, and even changing cultural traditions, in order to enhance the situation of marginalized and disadvantaged LGBT people, their possibilities for formation of families, and their general and widespread suffering from gross human rights violations. The article draws a picture of mixed success and failures in the field of protecting LGBT families. Legislative and administrative new approaches to previously challenged positions can be found in Germany and Taiwan and may even serve as "best practices" for reticent other states. As far as Transgender people are concerned, in this area rights protection remains highly disputed in the countries discussed. Debates on that issue may produce negative effects on the realization of other LGBT rights, but civil society keeps on propagating necessary changes of law, awareness raising, and mindset of society.

Pei-Chun Lin meticulously presents the contents of a famous ruling by the Taiwanese Constitutional Court (CC) in its Interpretation No. 748, which has interpreted a much-discussed equality rights problem in relation to the legalization of same-sex marriages. *Lin* carefully outlines the contents and reach of that ruling. The decision had declared that the Taiwanese Civil Code that previously prohibited non-binary people from forming a permanent and exclusive union for living together was unconstitutional, violating the freedom of marriage and equality for all citizens. The article, however, emphasizes that not all problems of discriminatory treatment, as far as policies and practices are concerned, including adoption rights, gender-affirming surgeries and workplace equality, not all problems were yet covered. *Lin* convincingly argues that "sexual orientation is not a characteristic that can justify unequal treatment" and critically concludes that the CC seems to follow a course that focuses more on "comparing LGBTIQ+ individuals to a binary norm, without fully addressing the distinct and diverse needs of these communities". The proposed general non-discrimination act so far does not include sexual orientation as a protected characteristic. *Lin* strengthens the view that court decisions and activism by civil society actors can be most effective in the long run.

Chong-Min Su and *Po-Han Lee* concentrate on disabled women's sexual and reproductive health, placing particular emphasis on 'intersectionality' in the human rights reporting context, by carefully drawing on health reports, NGO submissions, and review committee documents from 2009 until 2022. The contribution draws attention to the Taiwanese CEDAW and CRPD Review Committee findings, maintaining that intersectionality importantly addresses several discriminatory practices in better integrated approaches and fuller appreciation of the conjoined issues. Equality and non-discrimination situations are discussed in an integrated manner and are addressed at the same time. That approach leads to a fuller appreciation of multiple discrimination, a major problem in all countries. The authors throughout provide very interesting statistics on the sexual and reproductive rights situation in Taiwan and on particularly important issues, such as on accessibility of the medical environment and services. The authors argue that the institutional recognition of intersectionality "opens possibilities for applying the concept across the policy areas." They plead for addressing the multilayered realities of discrimination that particularly shape the lives of marginalized groups, avoiding too limited standards of review. All these efforts stress that women's role in human rights protection must remain a priority concern.

In her study *Yi-Chun Chou* then focuses on issues that have not received as much attention as they deserve: persons with disabilities among Indigenous Peoples in Taiwan. Internationally, the Western notions of "social disability" as structuring the CRPD are carefully contrasted with "social suffering". *Chou* opines that the CRPD prioritizes individual rights and self-determination, while Indigenous self-determination emphasizes collective cultural rights. "Indigenous societies operate on communal decision-making rather than individual autonomy." The study then presents several well-argued positions on particular Indigenous problems, such as how to deal with long-term care (LTC) in Indigenous Peoples, and concludes that Taiwan's LTC policies largely fail to achieve their goals. Very persuasive statistical analysis follows. In the research findings *Chou* criticizes the CRPD-inspired community services in the Atayal tribe and concludes that the interviews conducted with 14 members of the Atayal persons revealed that interviewees with acquired disabilities suffered mainly from insufficient health access, limited transportation, poverty, and fragile social support systems, often caused by long-term social marginalization, and health disparities rather than by social discrimination. *Chou* maintains with good arguments based on relevant factual situations that challenges of Indigenous persons with disabilities demand comprehensive healthcare access, employment security, and culturally appropriate support services. At the end of the day the Atayal "require as priorities family care and financial aid" instead of "Western community service models ...". The article shows how concentration on local situations and cultural settings run counter to CRPD-guided larger framework solutions, particularly affecting "social suffering" of Indigenous persons with disabilities. The current Human Rights Council's work on the right to solidarity clearly supports *Yi-Chun Chou's* analysis.

Lukas Romberg provides a comprehensive overview of the legal implications of the human right to housing laid down in article 11 (1) ICESCR. He rightly points out that the right to housing in UN practice is one of the most discussed human rights problems, and in particular the issue of forced evictions, and how the CESCR should deal with that problem, bearing in mind that article 11 ICESCR does not contain details on that. The latest developments of social change are also addressed by discussion of the right to land as a human right which states and large parts of literature still disagree with. The Optional Protocol (OP ICESCR) has now been in force since 2013, and *Romberg* carefully analyses the first ten years of its existence. The Communications decided so far under the OP ICESCR almost entirely deal with the right to housing and specifically forms of forced eviction. The existence of the OP ICESCR clearly has enhanced the relevance of all human rights provisions in the two covenants. *Romberg's* discussion of the principle of proportionality deserves special mention by raising very interesting points of comparative law, bridging '*proportionality*' criteria developed in European Union and Council of Europe states with '*reasonableness*' criteria mirroring the court practices in common law countries. The reasonableness standard following the common law judicial tradition in effect is narrower in scope than proportionality. *Romberg* carefully describes the CESCR five criteria that must be scanned in each communication received when the right to housing under article 11 ICESCR in conjunction with article 8 (4) OP ICESCR are at issue. The novel discussion on General Comment No. 26 on Land and ESC Rights of 2022 raises interesting new dimensions of the right to housing, hitherto less discussed by UN bodies.

Jau-hwa Chen then discusses the Concluding Report of Taiwan's Transitional Justice Commission, arguing persuasively that in general a holistic approach to transitional justice ought to be followed. Otherwise, affected victims of the authoritarian settings in the decades prior to 2000 would not be properly protected, and the goals of transitional justice – to assess and recompense the victims of authoritarian and illegal practice, but also to establish truth-finding and preparing the way for a learning process to redress past wrongs and to prepare the way for real reconciliation – could not be met. *Chen* succinctly summarizes this by pointing out: "If Taiwan then is to empower victims to restore their dignity, to overcome psychological trauma, and then to build up genuine reconciliation, transitional justice measures taken by the Government must go beyond compensation". *Chen* convincingly concludes that a full list of additional measures ought to be applied, without which no real transitional justice would ensue. Thus, to bring in the views of all sides only promises success if a requisite institutional framework is agreed to. The article concludes with a critique of the Justice Commission's refusal to investigate fully the alleged offences committed by perpetrators. As many other transitional justice efforts so far have tried that, the more holistic approach should be continued and broadened.

Yi-Li Lee in the next article describes achievements and challenges of the Taiwanese Transitional Justice Commission and similar to Chen comes to the conclusion that the Transitional Justice Commission did not achieve all goals promised to be fulfilled at the outset and comes to the result that this could only have been successful, if the NHRC had been tasked accordingly by the Control Yuan, to bring in the human rights dimensions of protection to redress violations of those rights suffered by victims. *Lee* maintains with good arguments that the NHRC plays a crucial role, stating that when existing mechanisms underperform, the NHRC by monitoring the transitional Justice Commission's reporting, the NHRC should step up to protect and uphold human rights, so that "rights related to transitional justice are protected and promptly remedied". Considering the complexities of Taiwan's constitutional history under authoritarian rule, all efforts should be undertaken to "Uphold[...] the principles of democracy, transparency, and openness essential to ensure legitimacy and public trust". The reader can only agree with that conclusion of the article cogently presented by *Lee*.

The book concludes with an insightful presentation of the problems posed by the move away from parliamentary representation under Hungary's present authoritarian rule, decrying crucial democratic values and practices. As outlined in the introduction, *Bernadett Szél*, a former Member of Parliament, describes the gradual transition from governance according to rule of law parameters to following closely the authoritarian stances that the Russian Putin régime has established. Using Russia's anti-LGBT positions and homophobic legislation and administrative and judicial practice as a standard that Prime Minister Victor Orbán now openly follows but equally applies to the rule of law. *Szél* meticulously traces that process of political change step by step, hollowing out rule of law principles that apply across the European Union. At the international and regional levels, unfortunately too little is achieved by unveiling the undemocratic, non-representative and increasingly authoritarian practice of her country. The reader can only admire the courageous discussion of legitimate opposition available in such a system. The article portrays clearly the remaining opposition tactics and strategies that opponents of the regime can have resort to. One can only hope that the opposition inside and outside Parliament will eventually bring Hungary back into the fold of democracy and rule of law (*"Rechtsstaat", "état de droit"*), that took so long to be fully accepted in the 20th century by most of Europe. Truly novel steps suggested in *Szél's* article are thoughtfully discussed and open the way for further in-depth studies of action research, showing how former parliamentary action had to be transformed, listing and discussing the modalities of opposition to authoritarianism in all its forms, but also the price to be paid for that.

As stated in the introduction and followed through by all contributors of this book, the human rights standards ranging from recognizing human rights as such, confirming them in national and regional law, and affirming them legally and politically in each national context, represent the key focus throughout. A second red thread throughout the book is the still largely under-reported and largely unchanged violation of women's rights in all countries, and together with intersectional dimensions of their rights played a key role, just as in all ten Human Rights Committees at UN level. This dimension of human rights protection is one of the most serious fields of violations encountered by marginalized and disadvantaged persons. Social changes always play an important role, and may be reflected in new interpretations, but local activism which can advance the protection levels can also lead to reducing the level of human rights protection, as unfortunately presently happens in large parts of the world. Human rights activists have no choice but to carry on regardless.

Eibe Riedel